# Essays on Form
# and Interpretation

# STUDIES IN LINGUISTIC ANALYSIS

*Editors*
Noam Chomsky, Joan W. Bresnan,
and Michael K. Brame

CONJECTURES AND REFUTATIONS
IN SYNTAX AND SEMANTICS
Michael K. Brame

ESSAYS ON FORM AND INTERPRETATION
Noam Chomsky

# Essays
# on Form
# and Interpretation

## Noam Chomsky

**NORTH-HOLLAND**
NEW YORK • AMSTERDAM • OXFORD

Elsevier North Holland, Inc.
52 Vanderbilt Avenue, New York, New York 10017

North-Holland Publishing Company
P.O. Box 211
Amsterdam, The Netherlands

© 1977 by Noam Chomsky
Second printing, 1979.

**Library of Congress Cataloging in Publication Data**

Chomsky, Noam.
  Essays on form and interpretation.
  (Studies in linguistic analysis)
  Includes bibliographical references and index.
  1.  Grammar, Comparative and general—Addresses,
essays, lectures.  2.  Generative grammar—Addresses,
essays, lectures.  I.  Title.
P151.C47     415     77-4001
ISBN 0-7204-8615-7
ISBN 0-444-00229-4

*Manufactured in the United States of America*

# Contents

# Introduction

The essays that follow fall within the framework of the so-called "extended standard theory" (EST).[1] More generally, the framework of assumptions, methodological and substantive, is essentially as presented in my *Aspects of the Theory of Syntax*[2] and related work. A more recent discussion of background issues, including an informal account of some of the work presented here and consideration of some of the controversy that has arisen concerning this approach to the study of language, appears in my *Reflections on Language*.[3]

The first essay appeared in *Linguistic Analysis*, Vol. 1, No. 1, 1975. It was a paper delivered to the Linguistic Society of America on the occasion of its Golden Anniversary Symposium in June, 1974, at the University of Massachusetts in Amherst, Massachusetts, and appears also in the Proceedings of this symposium (Robert Austerlitz, ed., Peter de Ridder Press, 1975). The second essay was delivered at a conference sponsored by the New York Academy of Sciences in September, 1975, and appears in Stevan R. Harnad, Horst D. Steklis and Jane Lancaster, eds., *Origins and Evolution of Language and Speech*, Annals of the New York Academy of Sciences, Volume 280 (1976). The third essay was circulated by the Indiana University Linguistics Club in October, 1971, and appears in Steven Anderson and Paul Kiparsky, eds., *A Festschrift for Morris Halle*, Holt, Rinehart and Winston, 1973. The fourth essay appeared in *Linguistic Analysis*, Vol. 2, No. 4, 1976. It is based on lectures presented at the

---

[1] See Ray S. Jackendoff, *Semantic Interpretation in Generative Grammar*, MIT Press, 1972; and my *Studies on Semantics in Generative Grammar*, Mouton, 1972.
[2] *Aspects of the Theory of Syntax*, MIT Press, 1965.
[3] *Reflections on Language*, Pantheon, 1975.

1

summer session of the Linguistic Society of America at the University of South Florida, June, 1975, and is also to appear in a volume of essays based on that series of lectures (Roger Cole, ed., *Current Issues in Linguistic Theory*, Indiana University Press). Minor revisions have been introduced for clarification and consistency.

These essays represent ongoing work. Alternative analyses are presented at a number of points and explored, at times inconclusively, and later essays introduce modifications and criticisms of those that preceded. A subsequent paper, "On *Wh*-movement,"[4] extends this work further and discusses a number of the criticisms that have been raised concerning it. I hope to present a more comprehensive account in a monograph now in preparation.

The following remarks outline the general point of view adopted and developed in these essays, with some further modifications.

The class of possible human languages is, I assume, specified by a genetically determined property, apparently species-specific in important respects. Any proposed linguistic theory — in particular, EST — may be regarded as an attempt to capture this property, at least in part. Thus a linguistic theory may be understood as a theory of the biological endowment that underlies the acquisition and use of language; in other terms, as a theory of universal grammar (UG), where we take the goal of UG to be the expression of those properties of human language that are biologically necessary. So understood, UG is the theory of the human faculty of language. Any particular grammar conforms to the principles of UG, but is further articulated; it presents as well accidental facts that distinguish the particular language in question.

One may imagine an inquiry still more general than UG in this sense, namely, an attempt to characterize the notion "language" itself as distinct from other systems, with human language as a subspecies, determined by UG. This broader enterprise would be essentially conceptual rather than empirical in nature, granting, of course, that the distinction is hardly clear-cut. Suppose it to be accomplished. We would then have a characterization of language. This broader theory, whatever interest it might have, would identify and elaborate what we might call "logically necessary" or "conceptually necessary" properties of language. The empirical enterprise of UG would then specify those properties of human language that are

---

[4] "On *Wh*-movement," to appear in *Formal Syntax*, Adrian Akmajian, Peter Culicover, and Thomas Wasow, eds., Academic Press, forthcoming.

2

neither accidental nor logically necessary, in this sense. Some ways to study this innate system are discussed in the second essay.

Beginning in a biologically given "initial cognitive state" specified in part by UG, the mind that is acquiring a language passes through a series of cognitive states, ultimately reaching a "steady state" that is then modified only in marginal ways, as far as knowledge of language is concerned. Knowledge of language is represented in this steady state (and perhaps in intermediate states as well) in the form of a system of rules and principles conforming to UG, namely, a grammar of a particular language. The grammar assigns to each possible linguistic expression (this, a notion of UG) a structural description, which consists of a representation of this expression on each level of linguistic description. Expressions conforming to all of the principles of the grammar are the well-formed expressions of the language. Among these are the fully grammatical sentences of the language, identified by their structural descriptions as sentences (this, again, a notion of UG). Other expressions deviate in one or another respect.

A person who knows a language normally knows how to use it to achieve certain human ends. We may say that he attains a system of "pragmatic competence" interacting with his grammatical competence, characterized by the grammar. Thus we distinguish grammatical and pragmatic competence as two components of the attained cognitive state. Grammar, it seems, is language-specific in two senses: (a) the system of basic principles, UG, appears to be unique in significant measure to this faculty of mind; (b) within the framework of UG, grammars differ from language to language. Whether pragmatic competence is language-specific in either sense, and if so, in what respects, is far from clear.

Knowledge of language falls within a richer complex of belief and knowledge. A full account of the initial cognitive state will present the principles that make possible the attainment of this full system. From this point of view, the theory of grammar is simply one part of cognitive psychology, concerned with a particular mental faculty, its mature state and the innate principles that provide the basis for its development.

Use of language involves cognitive systems beyond grammatical and pragmatic competence. The theory of performance, then, will attempt to develop models incorporating grammar and other cognitive structures, as well as an account of the physical and social conditions of language use that are ignored in the abstraction to grammar.

The conceptual distinction between competence and perform-

3

ance — between what a person knows and what he does — and the concepts themselves are reasonably clear pretheoretically, as much so as any notions concerning human thought and action. Further clarification of these notions is not, I believe, primarily a problem for conceptual analysis but rather for constructive work, the development and empirical evaluation of specific theories of competence and performance.

A system of concepts, however clear, may prove inappropriate to the task at hand, in this case, the study of language. Any serious inquiry will involve abstraction and idealization, but the particular framework adopted must be evaluated in terms of the consequences to which it leads: does it lay the basis for a successful and insightful account of relevant phenomena, with significant explanatory principles of some depth and scope? Idealization is a necessary element of rational inquiry; the legitimacy of particular idealizations is ultimately an empirical matter, though the issues are joined at a rather abstract level.

The phenomena presented to us do not, of course, come provided with a system of appropriate categories or explanatory principles. It is only in the light of a particular theory that we can draw conclusions as to how some phenomenon is to be interpreted. For example, we may make an intuitive judgment that some linguistic expression is odd or deviant. But we cannot in general know, pretheoretically, whether this deviance is a matter of syntax, semantics, pragmatics, belief, memory limitation, style, etc., or even whether these are appropriate categories for the interpretation of the judgment in question. It is an obvious and uncontroversial fact that informant judgments and other data do not fall neatly into clear categories: syntactic, semantic, etc. From the fact that data are confused, complex, often uncertain, etc., we can conclude nothing with regard to the nature of the systems that yield these data. It may be that the rules of grammar themselves essentially involve a complex of factors at every point (or many points), or it may be that there are separate cognitive structures, each with its specific properties, interacting to produce or interpret the flow of speech, or to provide the flux of judgments, reactions, etc. that constitute the linguist's primary data. My working hypothesis is that the latter assumption is basically correct, as shown by its relative success in providing insight into what Hume describes as that "vast variety of springs and principles, which are hid, by reason of their minuteness or remoteness," and which we expect to find contained "almost in every part of nature." The system of grammatical competence is one of these interacting structures. This system itself consists of several subcomponents with their specific properties and mode of interaction specified by UG.

Thus I am assuming that the apparent complexity and heterogeneity of the presented phenomena can be factored into the contribution of interacting systems, each based on simple principles, each subject to a certain range of permissible variation, yielding the variety of possible languages. Questions of legitimate abstraction and idealization, in particular, with reference to syntax and semantics, are discussed in the first essay in this book, and specific proposals are developed further in the other essays.

Assuming the approach just sketched to be generally on the right track, let us consider further the system of grammar. A grammar, again, assigns to each sentence (in particular) a structural description consisting of a representation on each of a set of linguistic levels; specifically, on the level of phonetics, phonology, words, morphemes, higher level syntax, and what I will call here "logical form" (LF). I use the latter term to refer to those aspects of semantic representation that are strictly determined by grammar, abstracted from other cognitive systems.[5]

The essays that follow are concerned primarily with higher level syntax and LF. Adopting a version of EST, I assume that the grammar consists of rules of various categories: base, transformational, phonological, and semantic interpretive rules. The base consists of a categorial component and a lexicon. The categorial component is a system of context-free rules with categories provided by some version of the so-called "$X$-bar system."[6] The lexicon provides specific properties of lexical entries and general principles concerning these. The "lexicalist hypothesis" (see references of note 1) is assumed without further discussion. The base-generated structure that underlies a sentence we may call its "deep structure" or "initial phrase-marker."[7] Transformational and interpretive rules map deep structures ultimately onto representations in LF. These essays are primarily concerned with transformational derivation and mapping to LF.

I assume that cyclic transformational rules apply to embedded

---

[5] See my *Reflections on Language* for further discussion. The approach here assumed is developed (however, in a somewhat different way) in my *Logical Structure of Linguistic Theory*, 1955; Plenum, 1975.

[6] For some recent discussion of this system see the references cited below, and also several papers in Akmajian, Culicover, and Wasow, *op. cit.*

[7] Cf. *Reflections on Language* for discussion of some terminological issues and misunderstandings.

phrases in accordance with the principle of the strict cycle,[8] and that root transformations, with somewhat different properties, apply to root sentences in Emonds' sense.[9] The result is a class of near-surface structures — call them "shallow structures" (in one sense of this term, due to Postal), to which rules of a different category (scrambling, etc.) may apply to give the actual form of sentences. Interpretive rules relate shallow structures to LF.[10] Among the cyclic rules I will be concerned primarily with rules of NP-movement and *wh*-movement; among the interpretive rules, primarily with "rules of construal" in roughly the sense suggested by Kenneth Hale; in particular, rules relating anaphoric expressions (pronouns and reciprocals) to others within the same sentence. These movement and construal rules constitute a kind of "core grammar" for English, with properties explored below. I try to show that they observe certain quite general conditions and can be formulated with a strict economy of theoretical apparatus. These matters are discussed informally in the second essay and in more detail in the third and fourth essays.

These essays also introduce and develop the trace theory of movement rules; cf. references cited for other relevant work. We might understand this theory as follows, along lines explained in more detail in "On *Wh*-movement." Let us assume that each occurrence of a category in deep structure is assigned a numerical index by some general procedure. I assume that thematic relations[11] are determined, perhaps completely, by deep structure configurations that may be modified by transformations. But the rules of (semantic) interpretation are assumed to apply to shallow structures. Therefore, the indices must be carried over in some fashion under transformational rules.

To make the discussion concrete, let us consider one possible analysis of English passive constructions. Suppose that the deep structure underlying *Bill was hit by John* is essentially (1), where the NP's are indexed:

---

[8] For a recent clarification and sharpening of the principle of the strict cycle, see Juan Mascaró, *Catalan Phonology and the Phonological Cycle*, Doctoral dissertation, MIT, 1976.

[9] Joseph E. Emonds, *A Transformational Approach to English Syntax*, Academic Press, 1976.

[10] On the relation of syntactic structures to phonetic representation, I assume here, without discussion, the general approach developed in N. Chomsky and M. Halle, *Sound Pattern of English*, Harper and Row, 1967, as modified by Joan Bresnan in "Sentence stress and syntactic transformations," *Language*, Vol. 47, No. 2, 1971.

[11] In the sense of Jeffrey Gruber and Ray Jackendoff; more or less the semantic relations of Jerrold Katz and the case relations of Charles Fillmore. See references cited for details.

6

(1)

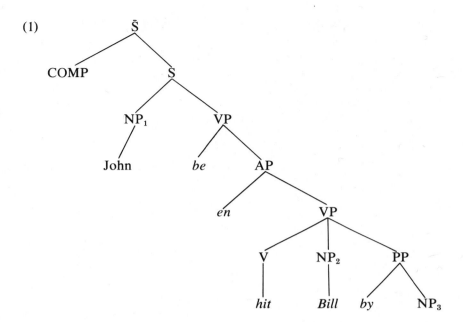

(2)

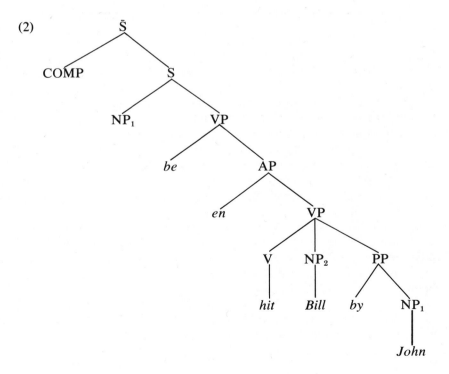

7

(3)

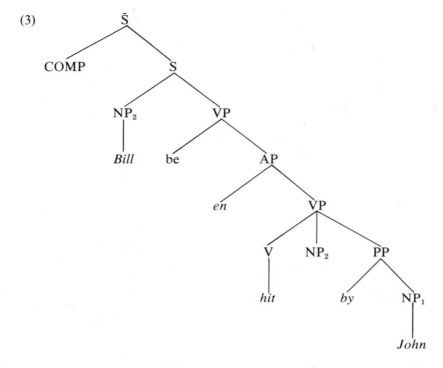

Suppose that a rule of NP-postposing moves *John* to the unfilled position $NP_3$, and that a later rule of NP-preposing places *Bill* in the position of the original $NP_1$, giving the form directly underlying *Bill was hit by John*. Consider in more detail the conventions involved in forming the intermediate and final structures.

In accordance with Emonds' structure-preserving hypothesis (cf. note 9), we assume that each application of the movement rule places the NP moved in an NP position. To permit NP-preposing, then, we must assume that movement of *John* to the position of $NP_3$ by NP-postposing "leaves behind" the unfilled NP position formerly occupied by *John*; the result of the NP-postposing rule is not an S exclusively dominating a VP (*be en hit Bill by John*) but rather an S dominating an NP VP construction, with an unfilled NP. The latter position is then filled by the structure-preserving rule of NP-preposing, which moves the NP *Bill* to the subject position, again leaving behind an unfilled NP position.

A question then arises about the indexing of the NP's, under NP-movement. We adopt the quite natural convention that a moved phrase retains its index, which thus replaces that of the NP to which

8

it moves. In accordance with this convention, NP-postposing applied to (1) gives (2), and NP-preposing applied to (2) gives finally (3):

Let us now refer to the unfilled category $NP_1$ of (2) as the "trace" of [$_{NP_1}$ *John*], i.e., of the occurrence of *John* as $NP_1$ in (2) in the position of the former $NP_3$ of (1). Similarly, the unfilled $NP_2$ of (3) is the trace of [$_{NP_2}$ *Bill*] in (3). NP-preposing, giving (3) from (2), "erases" the trace of *John* in (2). A trace, then, is just an indexed category with no lexical content, a phonetically null category — in this case, an NP.

In (3), the fact that *Bill* bears the underlying grammatical relation of direct object to the verb *hit* (or, in another terminology, to the VP) is indicated by means of the trace relation. We may assume that in (2) and (3) the grammatical function of *John* is indicated directly by the structure itself, specifically, by the *by*-phrase. Following a suggestion of John Goldsmith, we adopt the convention that erasure of a trace is permitted only when the grammatical function of its antecedent is indicated in the phrase-marker independently of the trace. It follows, then, that insofar as thematic relations are determined by interaction of deep structure grammatical relations and lexical properties, they are also determined by the shallow structure, through the medium of traces.

The relation of an NP to its trace is naturally construed as, in effect, a relation of bound anaphora, analogous to the relation between *John* and *his* in (4) or *John* and *him* (which, following Michael Helke, we take to be a morphological variant here of *his*) in (5):

(4)   John lost his way
(5)   John hurt him-self

Adopting these conventions for transformations, we may assume that interpretive rules yielding representations in LF apply to shallow structures; just that property of deep structures that enters into the determination of meaning is carried over to shallow structure under these conventions, while other properties may be "lost." It seems that apart from thematic relations, all properties of LF are determined by shallow structures. Thus we can develop a unified theory of semantic interpretive rules. These rules apply directly to shallow structure, giving representations in LF. We thus have a single extended derivation from the base-generated deep structure to shallow structure to LF. Strictly speaking, we might say that the rules mapping shallow structure to LF are not "semantic rules" but rather rules concerned with the syntax of LF, that is, rules that give the representations that are directly interpreted through the theories of meaning, reference, and language use, in interaction with other cognitive structures beyond the grammar that specifies grammatical competence.

We might distinguish "formal grammar" from semantic aspects of grammar, along the following lines. Formal grammar consists of the rules giving shallow structures (by base rules and transformations) and phonetic representations. If Bresnan's theory (cf. note 10) is correct, as assumed below, then the rules of phonology apply cyclically within the transformational cycle, so that a shallow structure already contains a phonetic representation. The rules of semantic interpretation associate these phonetically represented shallow structures with representations in LF. Formal grammar, then, is concerned with all levels of linguistic representation apart from LF. The relation of formal grammar, so construed, to semantic representation is discussed in a general way in the first essay here, and in more technical terms, in the third and fourth essays.

By taking the relation of NP to trace to be that of bound anaphora, we exclude at once a large class of possible rules and sequences of rules on the grounds that they yield shallow structures violating the general conditions of "command" for anaphora. Specifically, it follows that for NP's, there will be "raising" rules but not "lowering" rules (unless there is subsequent trace erasure, as in NP-postposing in (1)–(3) or in *there*-insertion), rules moving object to subject but not conversely, etc. These conclusions follow from general conditions on anaphora that are independently motivated, and therefore need not be stipulated but are explained in terms of trace theory. Sequences of rule applications that give unwanted structures are eliminated, in certain cases, making possible a simpler formulation of transformational rules with a much more restricted theoretical apparatus.[12]

Assuming categorial rules of the base to be optional, base-generated structures may have categories that are not filled by lexical items (as NP$_3$, in (1)). By general convention, shallow structures containing such nodes are excluded, although we have now departed from this convention in the specific case of traces. In the case of NP, a trace is

---

[12] For further discussion of these points, see *Reflections on Language* and references cited there, particularly, the work of Robert Fiengo (*Semantic Conditions on Surface Structure,* Doctoral dissertation, MIT, 1974); also my *Amherst Lectures,* mimeographed, Université de Paris VII, Département de Recherches Linguistiques, 1974.

analogous to a bound variable, and an NP node with no lexical representation and not bound by the trace relation might be thought of as analogous to a free variable. To say that an NP must be either bound, by the trace relation, or lexically specified, is in effect to say that open sentences are not sentences.

Pursuing this line of thinking a bit further, recall that in the base, NP's may be either (a) developed by categorial rules to the specific forms of NP, with ultimate lexical substitution, or (b) left as is, subject to no base rule at all. In case (b), we stipulate that NP is assigned a variable index. Thus consider the deep structure (6):

(6)

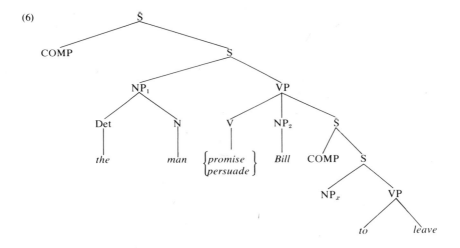

In this structure, the subject of the embedded sentential complement to the main verb is not accessible to base rules and therefore remains as $NP_x$, but all other NP's must be further analyzed, ultimately into terminal symbols, if the structure is to be well-formed. Rules of *control* apply in the familiar way to fix the variable $x$ as 1 or 2, depending on the choice of main verb (*promise* or *persuade*); cf. Jackendoff, *op. cit.*. Once the variable is fixed as 1 or 2, the category resulting from $NP_x$ is indistinguishable from trace and is therefore subject to the same rules as trace and under the same conditions. The rules giving LF will take an $NP_i$ with no lexical content to be, in effect, a variable controlled by the occurrence of $NP_i$ with lexical content.

The element $NP_x$ is what is designated PRO in the following essays, and commonly elsewhere. We therefore in effect identify trace and

PRO. They differ only in how control is assigned: in one case by a movement rule, in the other, by a rule of interpretation.

Though PRO, once assigned a numerical index by a rule of control, is indistinguishable from trace, nevertheless there are a number of differences between NP–PRO and NP–trace relations, by virtue of the rules that assign these relations. To cite only the most obvious difference, NP's that are not freely generated (e.g., idiom chunks, *there*) may appear as "antecedents" removed from the determining context in NP-trace pairs formed by a movement rule, but not in NP–PRO pairs, since they are not introduced into the antecedent position in the latter case. Thus we have (7) but not (8) ($t$ = trace of the moved surface subject):

(7) a1. there is certain [$t$ to be a reward]
    a2. there is believed [$t$ to be a reward]
    b. the ice was finally broken $t$

(8) a1. there promised Bill [$t$ to be a reward]
    a2. we persuaded there [$t$ to be a reward]
    b. the ice is easy to break $t$

Sentences (7a) are derived by NP-preposing of *there*, leaving trace. But there is no comparable analysis of (8a). The embedded subject in these cases must be PRO, controlled by the matrix subject in (a1) and the matrix object in (a2). Thus the sentences are not formed by NP-preposing, but must have PRO in place of trace $t$. Since they cannot be formed directly by the rules that give *there*-constructions, they cannot be generated at all. Sentence (7b) can be understood in the idiomatic sense, but not (8b). The reason is that (7b) is derived by NP-preposing from a deep structure containing the idiom *break the ice,* but the subject *the ice* is base-generated as matrix subject in (8b), and although there is a trace in the shallow structure, it is not the trace of NP-preposing but of *wh*-movement, I believe (cf. "On *Wh*-movement" for an analysis of these structures). Thus PRO cannot appear in the position of $t$ and the idiomatic interpretation is unavailable. The situation is similar to what we find typically in such examples as (9):

(9) a. John was taught $t$ to swim
    b. John was untaught $t$ to swim
    c. John was untaught.

In case (a), NP-preposing generates the sentence with $t$ = trace of

*John*. But by the lexicalist hypothesis, *untaught*—a derived form—must be lexically entered as an adjective, and NP X is not a possible adjective complement structure. Therefore (9b) cannot be generated though (c) is a possible form, with a meaning that is not strictly determined compositionally from its elements *un–teach–en*, as is commonly the case with lexically entered forms.

Furthermore, rules assigning control are subject to conditions inapplicable to movement rules (and conversely). For example, rules of control typically involve the main verb of a verb phrase, its subject or object, and the subject of a clause embedded in the verb phrase. The rule of control for *promise* assigns $x$ of (6) the value 1 (of the subject), while the rule for *persuade* assigns $x$ the value 2 (of the object). But suppose that the sentences appear in the corresponding passive forms, with the structure (10), analogous to (3):

(10)

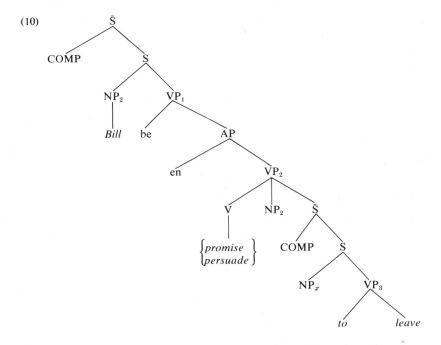

The rule of control for *persuade* applies within $VP_2$, assigning to $x$ of $NP_x$ the value 2, as before, *persuade* being the main verb of $VP_2$ with $NP_2$ as its object. But the rule of control for *promise* is inapplicable since *promise* in (10) is not the main verb of $VP_1$ with the surface subject *Bill*; compare in contrast (6), where *promise* was the main verb of the VP sister to the matrix subject. Therefore (10) is grammatical with *persuade* but not *promise*; we have (11) but not (12):

(11)    Bill was persuaded to leave.
(12)    *Bill was promised to leave[13]

More generally, it follows that a verb with subject control (*promise, strike,* etc.) cannot appear in the passive.[14] There is no comparable condition on movement rules; compare (7a2), which has approximately the structure of (12) but is grammatical.

In these and a number of other ways, trace and PRO differ, but they are alike in their behavior under subsequent rules. For such rules, both trace and PRO act as noun phrases, despite their null phonetic representation, a matter that is illustrated and discussed in essays 2–4 of this book. A number of other distinctions between interpretive and movement rules are also discussed. For some general comments on the clustering of rule types, see the final pages of essay 4.

Trace theory, so understood, resolves an ambiguity in the formulation of earlier versions of transformational grammar in a particular way. The ambiguity had to do with a question of derived constituent structure: when a phrase moves, is its former position deleted, or does it remain, with null lexical content? As noted, the latter assumption is in accord with the structure-preserving hypothesis, and is adopted here. The alternative assumption is neither more nor less preferable from a methodological point of view. Rather, it just leads to different empirical consequences in a class of interesting cases. There are several intertwined empirical questions. Does a position vacated by an NP-movement rule behave with respect to further rules as if it were present or absent? If the former, how does this position

---

[13] The NP object of *promise* can be preposed when control is irrelevant, as expected: thus we have *Bill was promised a job*. Note that the NP object of *promise*, for many speakers, resists *wh*-movement, as in *whom did you promise* t *a job, whom did you promise* t *to offer Mary a job*. The phenomenon seems independent of (12), relating probably to a similar resistance to *wh*-movement in indirect object structures quite generally: e.g., *whom did you give a book*, etc.

[14] This resolves a problem noted in *Aspects of the Theory of Syntax*, p. 229. On the analysis of passive constructions, see *Reflections on Language*, Chapter 3. There remain a few as yet unexplained exceptions.

14

relate to PRO? The analysis that follows indicates that the position vacated remains in the abstract representation and influences subsequent rules just as an NP with lexical content does. The rules of mental computation that form derivations apply blindly, unaware of the fact that some NP's will ultimately be phonetically null. As for the relation between trace and PRO, it appears to be as indicated in the preceding remarks.

Slightly different conventions and assumptions with regard to these matters will lead to markedly different empirical consequences within the framework of the theory developed below, a matter that is discussed in some detail in essays 2–4. The conventions and assumptions just sketched are entirely natural within the framework of transformational generative grammar, but they are by no means necessary. They are surely not logically necessary properties of language. It would not be very plausible to maintain that they are, if correct, accidental properties of particular languages; it is hardly likely that they are learned, since the empirical consequences that differentiate alternative assumptions and conventions appear only in unusual constructions that are difficult to contrive and are surely rare or nonexistent in normal speech. Furthermore, crucial evidence is often negative, i.e., having to do with ungrammatical structures. The question then arises why these are not ruled grammatical by "analogy" or "induction" or "generalization." It cannot reasonably be supposed that people who are able to make the relevant judgments in a uniform and consistent way have invariably (or, for that matter, ever) been specifically instructed or even presented with information bearing on the issues. Thus these conventions and assumptions seem plausible candidates for UG. If they are correct for English, we would expect them to be universal, or to be specific realizations of more abstract universal principles that we do not yet understand. See the second essay for some general discussion of these matters, and the third and fourth essays for more detailed analysis.

In my personal opinion, it is questions and issues such as these that make the study of language intellectually interesting. That is, at a sufficient level of depth and abstractness of theory, we can expect to discover that small modifications in theoretical assumptions will have varied and complex effects on predicted phenomena. If the predictions are verified, and furthermore, if it cannot plausibly be maintained that the principles have been learned, we can reasonably conclude that we are obtaining some insight into the general principles of UG that govern the mental computations underlying the use of language. Thus we gain some understanding of the innate factors that

15

endow the human language faculty with its remarkable properties. The more abstract are the principles, the more deeply embedded in a particular theoretical structure and remote from presented phenomena, the more interesting and significant is the study of language.

I stress again that the issues discussed in the preceding remarks and in more detail in the essays that follow are strictly empirical ones. There are no methodological considerations that select among the alternative hypotheses with regard to movement rules or the status of trace and PRO. It is a question of the correct explanation of certain facts. See my *Reflections on Language*, pp. 117–18, for discussion of some misunderstandings that have arisen in this connection.

Consider now the application of the trace theory to the rule of *wh*-movement. Applying this rule to (13) we derive (14):

(13) a. you saw who
     b. you saw whose book

(14) a. who did you see *t*
     b. whose book did you see *t*

Interpretive rules now apply to (14). The *wh*-elements function, in effect, as quantifiers, controlling variables. We may assume that the rule of *wh*-interpretation assigns to (14) representations more or less along the lines of (15):

(15) a. for which person $x$, you saw $x$
     b. for which person $x$, you saw $x$'s book

We may think of this interpretive rule as introducing the variable $x$ — a terminal symbol of LF — in the position indicated by the trace of the *wh*-phrase, along with other relevant material from the *wh*-phrase, as in (b). Thus while the trace is null, the string following application of the rule of *wh*-interpretation contains a nonnull terminal symbol in the position of trace. Considering only such examples as (14a), we may in effect regard the trace itself as the variable, as is done in the fourth essay below. But a more careful account would follow the lines just sketched. Furthermore, the natural rule of *wh*-interpretation will introduce the variable only in the position from which the *wh*-phrase moved to COMP from within the S sister to COMP; the rule thus introduces the variable in just a single position. These matters, not developed at all in these essays, are discussed in "On *Wh*-movement." The general idea as to how to proceed should be clear enough, however.

Noting the rule of interpretation for *wh*-phrases, we might propose as well a rule of *wh*-interpretation in place of *wh*-movement, as suggested in the last footnote of essay 3. However, the phenomena we discover in studying *wh*-phrases appear to share the properties of movement transformations rather than those of interpretive rules, a matter discussed below and in more detail in "On *Wh*-movement." Thus if we reconstruct the rule as interpretive — i.e., as mapping shallow structure to LF with the *wh*-phrase base-generated in its shallow structure position — we will in effect be establishing a new class of interpretive rules, distinct in crucial properties from others and sharing crucial properties of movement rules. On the significance of the choice among these alternatives, see the concluding remarks of essay 4.

The structures resulting from *wh*-movement and interpretation have variables governed by a kind of quantifier, and are analogous in form to expressions with variables and quantifiers resulting from the interpretation of such phrases as *everyone, every book,* etc., if we assume a standard logical analysis of the latter. In essay 4 some of the ramifications of this analogy are developed. If the mapping from shallow structure to LF were a "one-step" operation, then it would be difficult if at all possible to distinguish two theories of LF, equivalent in expressive power, on empirical grounds. But if shallow structure is converted to LF by a derivation, analogous to the derivations that yield phonetic representation, then it may be possible to adduce empirical considerations to choose among theories of LF and intermediate representations that are equivalent in expressive power, just as we do in the case of competing theories of phonetic representation, say, two distinctive feature theories. One theory may permit the formulation of certain generalizations that are excluded by the other, for example; this may even be the case if the two theories are intertranslatable. It is argued in essay 4 that such considerations favor standard logical representations, with quantifiers and variables, over variable-free representations. That is, it appears that the standard representation permits certain significant generalizations in the rules of interpretation and are also directly derivable by straightforward rules from the shallow structures, eliminating any empirical motivation for "intermediate" variable-free representations.

Questions of this general nature are taken up in the third and fourth essays, and more informally, in essay 2. The approach just sketched, developed further in "On *Wh*-movement," I believe offers an improvement over the formulations discussed in the following essays, but the main points carry over to this improved version.

It is noted in essay 4 that if the theory of *wh*-movement suggested there is correct, it should apply to a considerable range of constructions, including relatives (finite and infinitival), questions (direct or indirect), comparatives, topicalization, clefts and a variety of adjectival complement and degree complement constructions. In "On *Wh*-movement" I attempt to show that in fact all of these constructions do involve the rule of *wh*-movement, and that many of their properties can be explained on this assumption. In contrast, we find a different cluster of properties in the case of NP-movement and still a different cluster for rules of construal. Other phenomena — e.g., rules of control (see above) or interpretation of quantifiers (cf. essay 1) — exhibit quite different properties, for principled reasons, I believe.

The fundamental problem in the study of language, it seems to me, is to explain how it is possible for a person to attain knowledge of a language, knowledge that is certainly far underdetermined by experience. Somehow, from the disordered flux of ordinary linguistic experience, a rich and highly articulated system of grammatical competence develops in the mind in a specific way, fairly uniformly in a given speech community despite considerable variety in care and exposure, much as the visual system or other bodily organs develop under conditions set by experience in a largely predetermined manner, given appropriate triggering experience. To account for this normal human accomplishment, it seems that we must assume that UG provides an elaborate and highly restrictive schematism to which grammars must conform; the matter seems to me no different, though less well understood, in the case of other cognitive structures. Cf. *Reflections on Language* for discussion.

On the assumptions of EST, the class of accessible grammars can be constrained by UG at several points: in particular, by conditions on the base, the transformational component, the system of interpretive rules, the shallow structures that are produced by transformational derivations, and the system LF. The $X$-bar theory, for example, is an attempt to constrain the class of possible base systems in a principled way. In the essays that follow I explore the possibility that the range of possible transformational and interpretive rules, at least for a significant core grammar, can also be narrowly constrained. A theory of quite limited expressive power is proposed for investigation and its consequences explored. It seems to me reasonable to set as a goal the construction of a theory of formal grammar with autonomous and interacting components, each of a special but rather simple

18

structure. As for the transformational rules and the rules of construal of the core grammar, it may be that these are optional, unordered, without distinctions as to boundedness, limited to a few elementary operations (substitution, adjunction), with only restricted use of constants and no recourse to quantifiers or truth functions in the structural description of rules.[15] Deletion can perhaps be restricted, within sentence grammar, to a marginal class of rules that delete specific grammatical morphemes of limited distribution. If this goal can be attained or approximated, the expressive power of rules is considerably restricted and correspondingly, the class of accessible grammars sharply reduced.[16]

As the expressive power of rules is restricted, they will naturally tend to overgenerate — or more generally, to misgenerate — since specific conditions on their application can no longer be built into the rules themselves. In these essays, I explore the possibility that some quite general conditions on rule application suffice to compensate for the lack of expressive power of the rules. In the earliest work on transformational grammar, it was assumed that the peculiar restrictions on applicability of rules would have to be built into the rules themselves; cf., for example the discussion of restrictions on applicability of *wh*-movement in *Logical Structure of Linguistic Theory,* Chapter X, §95.3. Correspondingly, the theory of transformations developed was very rich in expressive power and the class of transformational grammars possible in principle was very large. Later work attempted to formulate general principles that would constrain the application of rules. Cf. the several versions of my *Current Issues in Linguistic Theory* (Mouton, 1964) and particularly, Ross's comprehensive though still unpublished MIT Ph.D. dissertation *Constraints on Variables in Syntax,* 1967. In essays 2–4 I approach these questions from a somewhat different point of view, attempting to construct a unified theory of conditions on rule application that will incorporate a number of "island phenomena" (in Ross's sense) as

---

[15] For a careful presentation of a theory of basically the sort I have in mind here, see Howard Lasnik and Joseph Kupin, "A Restrictive Theory of Transformational Grammar," forthcoming.

[16] Stanley Peters and Robert Ritchie have shown how transformational grammars with cyclic rules can be restricted to generation of recursive languages, in some quite natural ways. If deletion can be restricted as assumed here, it should be possible to apply their results to demonstrate that the generated languages are recursive. For some discussion, see "On *Wh*-movement," and for some remarks on the significance of the issue, see the concluding comments of Chapter 1 of *Aspects of the Theory of Syntax.* Note that the crucial issue is not the recursiveness of generable languages but restriction of the class of accessible grammars. See references cited for discussion.

special cases. These conditions permit the rules themselves to be of quite a simple sort, since many of their detailed properties are, in effect, "factored out." The conditions also imply a certain clustering of properties of rules. In these essays and again in "On *Wh*-movement" I attempt to show that the predicted clustering is in fact what we find.

The conditions that play the essential role in this discussion are the subjacency condition, the specified subject condition (SSC), and the tensed-S condition. Subjacency may be regarded as a property of cyclic rules: in effect, part of the definition of the transformational cycle. The condition stipulates in essence that at a given stage of the cycle, rules are restricted to elements that appear at this or the immediately preceding stage. Thus the subjacency condition imposes a kind of "memory limitation" on the depth of processing that can be carried out by cyclic transformational rules. SSC stipulates that in an embedded cyclic category (noun phrase or sentence), there is a "most prominent" element that is alone accessible to rules' if present. The tensed-S condition immunizes certain full propositional structures from rule application. These two conditions apply to transformational as well as interpretive rules. In fact, we might assume that they apply only to interpretive rules of construal, under the trace theory, continuing to pursue the idea that the NP-trace relation is in effect a case of bound anaphora. Thus a condition applying to the NP-trace relation constrains the application of a movement rule by imposing anaphora conditions on its output. Each condition imposes certain limitations on the principles of mental computation that form representations in LF and phonetics, i.e., the principles that determine sound–meaning relations through the derivations of formal grammar and interpretive rules. The limitations, I think, are rather natural ones. In these essays and in "On *Wh*-movement" I explore their empirical consequences in a variety of cases.

Note again that a crucial contribution of a theory of conditions on rules is that if successful, it makes it unnecessary for individual rules to be richly articulated. While conditions on rule application do not in themselves restrict the class of accessible grammars, they contribute significantly to this end in an indirect manner, by permitting the class of possible rules to be sharply restricted. In this way a theory of conditions on rules can contribute to a solution of the fundamental problem of accounting for the growth of language, what is called (with misleading connotations, I believe) "language learning."

Note also that on this approach, it is possible for a grammar to contain rules that go beyond the general conditions, by explicit

20

stipulation. Such rules will be "highly marked," under the theory, and can be expected to be unstable, variable across dialects and styles, and late learned. This matter is pursued further in "On *Wh*-movement." It is also worth stressing that a condition on rules can neither be confirmed nor refuted directly by presented phenomena. Particular observations may be used to test postulated rules, but only rules, not observations, serve as confirming or refuting instances for conditions on rules. This is a simple point of logic, often overlooked. To support or refute a proposed condition, it does not suffice to cite examples of grammatical or ungrammatical constructions from some language, or other informant judgments or observed phenomena. The empirical facts do indeed bear on the correctness of a theory of conditions on rules, but only indirectly, through the medium of proposed rule systems that do or do not conform to the conditions. Conditions on rules are neither immune from refutation nor impossible to verify. But to evaluate them, it is necessary to proceed to a certain level of depth of analysis, at least to the postulation of a system of rules governing the phenomena in question. Given unanalyzed and unexplained phenomena, we have no way of knowing what bearing (if any) they have on conditions on rules or on any general principle of grammar. The atomistic approach of much linguistic work, citing phenomena and generalizations from a variety of languages but not proposing partial rule systems that conform to some proposed theory of UG, whatever its value, is simply not very helpful in the present context.

In the study of language as in any other nontrivial inquiry, the phenomena are often dazzling in their apparent complexity and variety. Our glimmerings of understanding can only be expected to illuminate some narrow range. If we hope to proceed beyond taxonomy, it is necessary to select and discard, to concentrate on facts that seem to have some bearing on such explanatory principles as we can devise, ignoring much else in the hope that it will ultimately be explained by deeper theories or perhaps on quite different grounds. This is no more than the lesson of rationality, and in particular, the clear lesson of the sciences that have achieved substantial intellectual content. But it is occasionally forgotten in the pursuit of emerging disciplines, much to their detriment.

# Questions of
# Form and Interpretation

# Questions of Form and Interpretation*

The goal of this Golden Anniversary Symposium is to determine "where we are at" in the several domains of linguistic inquiry. I think it may be useful to begin by asking "where we were" 50 years ago with regard to the problems that I would like to survey briefly this evening.

In the year of the founding of the Linguistic Society of America, Otto Jespersen published an original and provocative investigation of these problems.[1] His point of departure was a version of the Aristotelian dictum that speech is sound production "accompanied by an act of imagination, for voice is a sound *with a meaning.*"[2] For Jespersen, "the essence of language is human activity — activity on the part of one individual to make himself understood by another, and activity on the part of that other to understand what was in the mind of the first." Each linguistic phenomenon "may be regarded...either from the outward form or from the inner meaning." Phonetics describes "the world of sounds," outward form; "the world of ideas" is the domain of a "sound psychology," which "should assist us in understanding what is going on in the mind of speakers," and a "sane logic," which deals with the "notional categories" that may in principle receive linguistic expression. The grammar is concerned with the "connecting links" between these two worlds.

The central concern of the grammarian is free creation, and at a deeper level, the problem of how the structures of grammar "come into existence in the mind of a speaker" who is not taught grammatical rules "and yet, without any grammatical instruction, from innumerable sentences heard and understood...will abstract some notion of their structure which is

---

\* This paper was delivered to the Linguistic Society of America on the occasion of its Golden Anniversary Symposium in June, 1974, and appeared in *Linguistic Analysis*, Vol. 1, No. 1 (1975).

[1] Otto Jespersen, *The Philosophy of Grammar*, George Allen & Unwin, London, 1924. For perceptive discussion of this and related work of Jespersen's, in a context relevant to the present discussion, see Audrey L. Reynolds, "What *did* Otto Jespersen say?" *Papers of the Chicago Linguistic Society*, 1971.

[2] *De Anima*, 420[b]; *The Basic Works of Aristotle*, Richard McKeon, ed., Random House, 1941.

definite enough to guide him in framing sentences of his own..."[3] This "notion of structure" is to be captured in the linguist's grammar and dictionary, the former dealing with "the general facts of language" and the latter, with "special facts."[4] Given the concern for "free expressions," the central domain of grammar is syntax, which deals with grammatical categories and their "rôle and employment in speech." It is "the grammarian's task in each case to investigate the relation between the notional and the syntactic categories," to determine the notional categories "in so far as they find grammatical expression, and to investigate the mutual relation of these two 'worlds' in various languages." "Syntactic categories thus, Janus-like, face both ways, towards form, and towards notion."

The principle of investigation that Jespersen advocates is that "we should recognize in the syntax of any language only such categories as have found in that language formal expression," taking *formal expression* in a very wide sense, including form-words and word-position. I assume that he would have felt comfortable with "covert categories," in Whorf's sense. But "in thus making form the supreme criterion," we must "look at the language as a whole" and not be misled by departures from general patterns. The method is to proceed from "notion or inner meaning," then "examining how each of the fundamental ideas common to all mankind is expressed in various languages, thus proceeding through . . . function . . . to . . . form."

Jespersen is concerned with categories of particular languages and their use, but also with the further question:

> ...are these categories purely logical categories, or are they merely linguistic categories? If the former, then it is evident that they are universal...if the latter, then they, or at any rate some of them, are peculiar to one or more languages as distinct from the rest.

He considers the view of John Stuart Mill that grammar is simply "the

[3] For Jespersen, it is an unconscious "notion of structure" that "guides" the speaker. Others have taken exception to this view. Quine argues that it is an "enigmatic doctrine," perhaps pure "folly," and that we may speak of "guiding" only when rules are consciously applied to "cause" behavior. Otherwise, we may speak only of behavior as fitting one or another system of weakly equivalent grammars, that is, grammars that generate the same set of sentences. See his "Methodological reflections on current linguistic theory," in Donald Davidson and Gilbert Harman, eds., *Semantics of Natural Language,* Reidel, 1972. Others have taken a similar position. For a discussion, and a defense of Jespersen's notion, see my "Problems and mysteries in the study of human language," in A. Kasher, ed., *Language in Focus; Essays in Memory of Yehoshua Bar-Hillel,* Reidel, 1976; it appears in a somewhat extended form as chapter 4 of my *Reflections on Language,* Pantheon, 1975.

[4] In addition to grammar and dictionary, the linguist will be concerned with still another domain, "the theory of the significations of words," but Jespersen asks to be "excused if I leave [this domain] out of consideration in this volume."

most elementary part of Logic" and that its principles and rules "are the means by which the forms of language are made to correspond with the universal forms of thought" so that "the structure of every sentence is a lesson in logic" (Mill, 1867). He notes that such ideas are generally rejected by philologists and linguists, who tend to the opinion that "grammatical categories have nothing to do with the real relations of things in themselves."

Jespersen asks: "Can there be such a thing as a universal (or general) grammar?" He points out that "no one ever dreamed of a universal morphology," because the specific features of particular languages were too obvious.

> It is only with regard to syntax that people have been inclined to think that there must be something in common to all human speech, something immediately based on the nature of human thought, in other words on logic, and therefore exalted above the accidental forms of expression found in this or that particular language.

It is our ignorance of syntax that makes plausible the belief that grammar is nothing but applied logic. Jespersen seems to be suggesting that if we investigate syntax more deeply we will find structures that are independent of the nature of human thought (though related to it, in that they give it expression) and that vary among languages (while observing important general principles).

Jespersen's own view of the matter is subtle and complex, and I think, generally persuasive. In investigating the "two 'worlds' " of thought and expression, we find systematic links between them, though "often enough we shall find that grammatical categories are at best symptoms, foreshadowings of notional categories, and sometimes the 'notion' behind a grammatical phenomenon is as elusive as Kant's *ding an sich*." "The correspondence between external and grammatical categories is...never complete, and we find the most curious and unexpected overlappings and intersections everywhere." Thus the English preterit has various forms and its "logical purport" may range over such notions as past time, unreality in present time, future time, shifted present, and all times. We may discover a systematic theory of the forms and of the notions, and significant relations between the two theories, but the system of forms will not be simply a projection of the system of notions, and languages will vary in their categories of expression. Similarly, many languages have a subjunctive mood, but "it would be perfectly impossible to give a definition...as would at the same time cover its employment in all the languages mentioned."[5] Again, the system of forms will have its independent structure, related to "the world of ideas" though not simply a projection of it, and we will also expect to find (and do find) variety among languages in the expression of this "notion," within the limits of universal grammar.

Universal grammar is, therefore, possible. It will study such concepts as "preterit," "irrealis," "subjunctive," and so on, but will not succeed in providing us with language-independent definitions of the categories of syntax solely in these terms. "On the whole we must not expect to arrive at a 'universal grammar' in the sense of the old philosophical grammarians," who took the system of grammatical categories to be simply a reflection of immutable notional categories.[6] Rather, "what we obtain is the nearest approach to [universal grammar] that modern linguistic science will allow." The specific concern of the grammarian is to determine the nature of the abstract "connecting link between the world of sounds and the world of ideas," keeping to the "actual linguistic facts...recognized by the speech-instinct of [each] community or nation." He must determine how a particular language solves the problem of connecting the worlds of sound and thought, and at a deeper level of analysis, he must seek to establish the general principles that govern these abstract systems. He must attempt to unearth "the great principles underlying the grammars of all languages." Jespersen hopes that his "preliminary sketch" will assist his successors in "gaining a deeper insight into the innermost nature of human language and of human thought."

Ideas of this sort were not characteristic of the American linguistics of the period, but they were not entirely unfamiliar. Sapir had argued that an examination of a range of languages would convince us that

> The 'part of speech' reflects not so much our intuitive analysis of reality as our ability to compose that reality into a variety of formal patterns. A part of speech outside of the limitations of syntactic form is but a will o' the wisp. For this reason no logical scheme of the parts of speech — their number, nature,

[5] Jespersen also holds that it is "impossible to give such a definition of the subjunctive in any of these languages as would assist us in deciding where to use it and where to use the indicative." I do not understand exactly what he means by this, or why he holds this view. The arguments he gives do not relate to it, so far as I can see. His discussion of the subjunctive and its expression seems to presuppose that there is a general notion of "subjunctive" relating to "the world of ideas," and if a grammar tells us how this notion is expressed in some language, then it would seem that we do have a "definition" that "would assist us in deciding where to use it."

[6] This does not seem to me an entirely fair rendition of traditional universal grammar. Consider, for example, the discussion of the "rule of Vaugelas" in the Port-Royal Grammar and the subsequent tradition, which was concerned with aspects of form specific to French. For some discussion, see my *Cartesian Linguistics*, Harper and Row, 1966.

and necessary confines — is of the slightest interest to the linguist. Each language has its own scheme. Everything depends on the formal demarcations which it recognizes.[7]

Nevertheless, Sapir added, "we must not be too destructive." Such basic notions as "something to talk about" and "something...said about this subject of discourse" are of such "fundamental importance" that we expect to find formal counterparts in the vast majority of languages. But Sapir was not willing to commit himself to the enterprise of universal grammar much beyond this.

Jespersen's observations on the relation of the system of grammar to notional categories can be illustrated with examples more central to logic than those he chose. Consider the various means for expressing something like universal quantification in English.[8] The means are quite varied, as in Jespersen's examples. Among them are the various quantifier words *(all, each, every, any)*, each with its special semantic and syntactic peculiarities[9]; the definite determiner ("the lights are out"), "bare" plurality ("books have covers"). Furthermore, a single formal device may have multiple interpretations, again as in Jespersen's examples. In saying "beavers are mammals," we are speaking of all beavers, but not when we say "beavers built this dam." The sentence "the citizens of England are demoralized by the economic crisis," taken literally, means that each is demoralized, though we may use it properly when we take the assertion to be only generally true.[10] But in the sentence "the citizens of England constitute a remarkedly cohesive social group," the same phrase, "the citizens of England," attributes no property to particular members of the class denoted. When we say "the citizens of England voted to join the Common

[7] Edward Sapir, *Language,* Harcourt, Brace, 1921; Harvest, 1949, p. 118–119.

[8] On the extraordinary richness of the system of quantification in natural language, see Jaakko Hintikka, "Quantifiers vs. Quantification Theory," *Linguistic Inquiry,* Spring 1974; Dov M. Gabbay and J.M.E. Moravcsik, "Branching quantifiers, English, and Montague-grammar," *Theoretical Linguistics,* 1 (1/2), 1974. The latter paper notes that there may be "an interesting asymmetry between the semantic and syntactic components, namely the set of valid sentences is not r.e. [recursively enumerable] while the set of well-formed sentences is recursive." Hintikka notes that the significant sets and relations (analytic sentences, synonymous pairs) in a system of branching quantifiers are not recursive, and concludes that "the methodology on which much recent work [in natural language semantics] has been based is bound to be inadequate in principle," for this reason. The conclusion seems to me stronger than the argument warrants. It is not obvious that an approach such as that of Jerrold Katz, which Hintikka cites, requires that the sets in question be recursive.

[9] These are partially uncorrelated. Thus "each" and "every" differ markedly in their syntactic behavior, but do not seem semantically different. For discussion, citing the contrary view of Vendler, see A. Kroch, *The Semantics of Scope in English*, Ph.D. dissertation, M.I.T., 1974.

[10] In contrast, such sentences as "the lights are out" require that each light is out (in the understood set).

Market," we do not imply that each citizen voted to do so; nor do we mean that only some did. Rather, a majority of some subclass so voted. Similar problems arise in the case of indefinite generics. The sentence "beavers build dams" does not imply that each beaver built a dam, or even that many do (perhaps most beavers are in zoos). But there is a universal quantifier over the subject lurking somewhere in the interpretation (under normal intonation), as we can see by comparing "beavers build dams" with "dams are built by beavers." The former states that all beavers are dam-builders, whether they exercise this capacity or not. The latter says nothing about all beavers, and the former says nothing about all dams. "Beavers build dams" is true, even if most never have, but "dams are built by beavers," under its natural interpretation, is false, since some are not.[11]

Matters are still more complex when we attend to the use of plural noun phrases in predicates. Thus *to have living parents* and *to have a living parent* are quite different properties. If John has living parents, both are alive, but not necessarily if he has a living parent. It is true of each unicycle that it has a wheel, but not that it has wheels.[12] But the expressions "have living parents," "have wheels," may have the sense of the corresponding singulars or their "inherent sense," depending on the means by which the

[11] The same examples show the relevance of surface structure to meaning. Thus "beavers build dams," with normal intonation, is not a statement about all dams. The situation is more complex. Consider: "beavers, on occasion, build dams"; "dams, on occasion, are built by beavers." Actual interpretation in performance also involves extra-grammatical factors. See below, p. 37. For some comments on related matters, see John Lawler, "Generic to a fault," *Papers of the Chicago Linguistic Society*, 1972; "Tracking the generic toad," *ibid*, 1973.

[12] Nor is it "simply false," Consider the truth values of "a unicycle has wheels," "a unicycle doesn't have wheels." Problems of truth for natural language can be complicated. See Austin's discussion of such sentences as "Belfast is north of London," "the galaxy is the shape of a fried egg," etc., in his "Truth," *Proceedings of the Aristotelian Society*, Supplementary Volume XXIV (1950), reprinted in J.O. Urmson and G. J. Warnock, eds., *J.L. Austin: Philosophical Papers*, Oxford, 1961. Consider the conditions under which the statement that New York is 200 miles from Boston (another Austinian example) would be true or false. Or, to take a case that has been recently discussed, consider "the temperature is falling." The notion "temperature" seems best analyzed as a function on times, places, and things. Thus "the temperature is 90°" does not mean "temperature = 90°," where "temperature" refers to some entity, but rather something like: "temperature (now, here) = 90°." Then "the temperature is falling" means that temperature is a decreasing function through some interval. What interval? Compare "the temperature is falling; a new ice age is on its way" and "the temperature is falling; evening is approaching." For truth, it suffices for the function to be generally decreasing, in some sense, through the relevant interval. If I mean that a new ice age is on the way, my statement that the temperature is falling may be true even if the temperature is, at the moment, rising. It is an interesting and useful idea to regard some aspect of meaning as a function from index sets onto truth and entities referred to; See David Lewis, "General semantics," in Davidson and Harman, *op. cit.* But to approach adequacy, the "index sets" will have to be far more intricate and complex than any that have so far been contemplated, though even the more limited inquiry has led to intriguing results.

subject noun phrase expresses quantification. Compare "the boys have living parents," "unicycles have wheels," "each boy has living parents," "each unicycle has wheels." In the first two cases, plurality is, in a sense, a semantic property of the sentence rather than the individual noun phrases in which it is formally expressed. "Unicycles have wheels" means that each unicycle has a wheel, and is thus true, though "each unicycle has wheels" is false.[13]

In these relatively simple examples, it seems possible to give an organized and systematic account of the syntax of the relevant expressions in terms of reasonably well-motivated principles of grammar, and the same may be true of the set of "readings" or correlates in some logic. But it seems plain that the syntactic structures are not a projection of the semantics, and that the relation between "the world of ideas" and the syntactic system is fairly intricate. As the "plural sentences" show, even a principle of compositionality is suspect. Global properties of the sentence, which may be quite involved,[14] seem to play a role. We cannot simply assign a meaning to the subject and a meaning to the predicate (or to a sentence form with a variable standing for the subject), and then combine the two. Rather, the meaning assigned to each phrase depends on the form of the phrase with which it is paired. The examples of set-reference versus multiple denotation[15] illustrate the same, quite general point. Examples of this sort lend plausibility to Jespersen's conception of the relation of expression to content.

I think that the program that Jespersen outlined for linguistic theory in 1924 has a great deal of merit, though it was, perhaps, premature. In any event, it found little resonance during roughly the first half of the history of the Linguistic Society of America. Linguists were concerned more with the "actual linguistic facts...recognized by the speech-instinct of [each] community or nation" and sometimes went so far as to deny the possibility in principle of a more general investigation of universal grammar, reflecting the skepticism that Sapir expressed in 1921. But the work of this period, both in linguistics and in logic, did lay the groundwork for a return to Jespersen's program, and his problems have become a major topic of investigation in the second half of this history.

Suppose that we recast Jespersen's project in the following terms. A "linguistic theory" is a system of concepts drawn from all of Jespersen's domains: the concepts of phonetics, from the domain of "outward form"; such notions as "subjunctive," "irrealis," "implies," "synonymous,"

[13] See Kroch, *op. cit.* for an interesting discussion of such cases.
[14] Compare "unicycles are believed to have wheels," "unicycles are believed to have been believed to have wheels," "conveyances have wheels in certain primitive societies," etc.
[15] In the sense of R. M. Martin, *Truth and Denotation*, Routledge and Kegan Paul, London, 1958.

"meaningful," and other notions pertaining to the "world of thought" and the "broader-minded logic" that must be constructed (Jespersen suggested) to describe accurately the world of thought as expressed in the forms of language, and also concepts that suffice for the "theory of the significations of words," which Jespersen omitted from his inquiry (see footnote 4); and finally, those theoretical concepts in terms of which we characterize the "notion of structure" that serves as a "connecting link" and the processes and properties peculiar to it, such concepts as "subject," "verb," "phonological unit," "grammatical transformation," and the like.

The goal of linguistic theory is to interrelate these concepts as densely as possible by general principles of "universal grammar." In the best case, some of these concepts can be taken as primitive and others defined in terms of them, with other principles serving as axioms of the theory. Each primitive notion should ideally be assigned a set of tests and criteria for applying it to data. Taking seriously the task of explaining how the structures of grammar "come into existence in the mind of a speaker," we can add further conditions on the choice of primitives. A particular choice of primitives can be considered an empirical hypothesis as to the preliminary analysis of data that serves for acquisition of language. Thus we assume (under appropriate idealization) that the learner analyzes utterances and the situations and events in which they are embedded in terms of these primitive notions, and "abstracts some notion of [the] structure" of linguistic expressions by applying the explicit and implicit definitions that constitute linguistic theory, the latter now being taken as a theory of a certain "faculty of mind." The primitive notions of the theory, so construed, provide the analysis of data in terms of which knowledge of language is acquired and verified. Let us assume that some theory of phonetic representation, at least, is fully provided by the primitive set.[16]

A person who knows a language can create and understand Jespersen's "free expressions." Thus he has acquired a system of rules and principles that characterize such expressions in terms of their phonetic, semantic, and other "abstract" properties. Call such a characterization the "structure" of the expression. Then among the concepts defined in linguistic theory there must be a sufficiently rich notion of "structure" for phonetically represented expressions. Furthermore, there must be a notion "grammar for D," where D is a class of data analyzed in terms of primitives, and the grammar generates an infinite class of expressions with their structures. The grammar is an account of Jespersen's "notion of structure" abstracted from data by the language learner that "guides him in framing sentences" and understanding what he hears.

---

[16] We may also assume that as much mathematical apparatus is available as needed for construction of theoretical notions.

The structure of an expression must be sufficiently articulated to mark its manner and degree of "deviance" from grammatical rule (if any). Thus some notion of "departure from rule" must be defined within linguistic theory. We may take the "language generated by the grammar for D" to be the set of expressions assigned structures with zero deviance, among them, a refinement of D.[17]

Regarding linguistics now as in effect a branch of theoretical psychology, concerned with one of the faculties of mind, we face the further problem of constructing performance models dealing with the ways in which knowledge of language is put to use. Given such models, we could bring new data to bear on the choice of grammars, hence indirectly, linguistic theory. A grammar, then, purports to be a true theory of one of the cognitive structures attained by a particular language-user, and linguistic theory may be regarded as a theory of one aspect of the "initial state of the organism," a species-specific property common to all normal humans.[18]

To return now to the problem of developing a linguistic theory along these lines, suppose that we construct a system of "levels," each constituting an integrated system of representation in terms of elements with well-defined properties and related to other levels in ways specified by the general theory. We might consider, for example, such levels of representation as the following: phonetics, phonology, word, morphology, word categories, surface structure, deep structure, semantic structure. On each level L, we define "L-markers" as objects assigned to expressions by rule, each L-marker specifying completely the properties of the assigned expression in terms of elements of the level L. We may, then, take the structure of an expression to be the set of its L-markers, one for each level L. The grammar must generate an infinite set of such structures.[19]

Proceeding in this way, we can try to construct a linguistic theory in which the central notions "grammar," "structure," and "language" are defined. Various approaches are possible. To mention two, consider a "procedural" or "taxonomic" conception of linguistic theory, which assumes levels to be arranged in a linear hierarchy and provides constructive procedures to determine the elements of a given level in terms

[17] A "refinement," in that a significant theory of language learning will have to deal with the fact that some of the data may be dismissed or assigned a special deviant status, in some instances, on the basis of the acquired grammar.
[18] The legitimacy of this formulation has been much discussed. For some recent discussion, see my "Problems and mysteries," (see footnote 3) and the references cited there. For another view of the matter, see J. A. Fodor, T. G. Bever and M. F. Garrett, *The Psychology of Language,* McGraw-Hill, 1974.
[19] A theory of this general sort, but with a different level structure, is outlined in my *Logical Structure of Linguistic Theory,* mimeographed, 1955–56; Plenum, 1975.

of the arrangement of elements on lower levels.[20] The grammar, then, will be a "grammar of lists" in the sense of Harris's *Methods of Structural Linguistics,* the most fully developed theory of this general sort.[21] An alternative approach might be to specify the class of possible grammars and the structures generated by grammars in purely formal terms, along with a notion of "optimality." The grammar for D, then, will be the optimal grammar of predetermined form generating D.[22] The elements of the various levels will be those that appear in the structures generated by this grammar; there need be no direct procedure for determining the elements from data, independently of the choice of grammar. I have argued elsewhere that these distinct approaches can plausibly be regarded as expressing leading ideas of empiricist and rationalist speculation, respectively, concerning the acquisition of knowledge.

Suppose that we have constructed a linguistic theory defining "grammar," "structure" and "language" in a general way. We can then ask how this theory helps set the "grammarian's task," as Jespersen saw it: "to investigate the relation between the notional and the syntactic categories." To investigate, say, the relation between the notion "subjunctive" and various forms of expression, we must have some understanding of both the notional and syntactic categories that enter into this relation (see footnote 5). More generally, if we are to study language as "sound with a meaning," we must give some account of sound and some account of meaning, or at least, some conditions on characterization of sound and meaning of expressions.

A phonetic theory, taken as a linguistic level in the sense just indicated, provides a universal mode for the representation of sound. The hypothesis that linguistic theory contains such a level of representation has rarely been questioned, but it is, of course, an empirical hypothesis. One might, without contradiction, propose a theory of language that related surface structure to, say, neural instructions, with no "intermediate level" of any systematic sort. Postulation of a level of phonetic representation requires justification. This might take several forms: demonstration that its elements have systematic properties and observe certain general principles, that they relate to other levels of linguistic structure by rules of

---

[20] Perhaps, with procedures of "reanalysis" of lower levels in terms of certain properties of higher levels, as in the theories of Harris and (in a more limited way) Pike.

[21] Z. S. Harris, *Methods of Structural Linguistics,* Chicago, 1951.

[22] But see footnote 17. D might be more complex. Suppose that "word" and "deviant" (i.e., corrected by the linguistic community) are primitives. Then the grammar for D must directly generate the phonetically represented sentences and assign the correct type of deviance to the deviant sentences, and must generate only strings analyzable into successive words. The richer the preliminary analysis of data in terms of primitive notions, the stronger the conditions to be satisfied by the grammar for D.

some generality and interest, that phonetic representations play a significant role in performance models.

Similar questions arise with regard to a postulated level of semantic representation. Is there a system of language-independent representation in terms of which we can characterize speech-act potential, role in inference, and so on, and which is related in some interesting way to other structures of language? Is there a "broader-minded logic" of the sort to which Jespersen alluded that enters into linguistic theory as a level of representation, playing a significant role in the use of expressions in thought and communication; or, alternatively, should a theory of speech-acts, inference, or truth be developed directly in terms of the categories of syntax themselves? Jespersen seems to have taken the former view, or he would not have spoken of "the mutual relation of these two 'worlds' in various languages." And the hypothesis seems to have considerable initial plausibility.[23] Consider just the "theory of the significations of words," which forms the basis for any semantics. The relations between "murder" and "assassinate," or "uncle" and "male," or "cheerful" and "unhappy," ought to be expressible in terms that are not drawn from the theory of syntactic forms and categories or the world of fact and belief. There are no possible worlds in which someone was assassinated but not murdered, an uncle but not male, cheerful but unhappy.[24] The necessary falsehood of "I found a female uncle" is not a matter of syntax or fact or belief. Considerations of modality do not suffice to make the relevant distinctions. "I found a proof of the parallel postulate" and "I found a Euclidean triangle with angles adding up to 200°" have the same truth value in all possible worlds, but are utterly different in meaning and correspondingly make different contributions to the truth value of sentences in which they are embedded (e.g., "John believes that..."). Furthermore, it seems reasonable to suppose that the factors that enter into determining the necessary falsehood of these expressions are different in kind from those that assign the same property to "I found a female uncle." While there is not much firm ground in this region, it seems plausible to hope that advances in semantic theory will clarify and explain these distinctions.

Consideration of further topics in semantics (e.g., the properties of quantificational structures briefly noted earlier) also lends plausibility to

---

[23] For varying views on these matters, see J. J. Katz, *Semantic Theory*, Harper and Row, 1972, and "Logic and language: an examination of recent criticisms of intensionalism" in K. Gunderson, ed., *Language, Mind, and Knowledge, Minnesota Studies in the Philosophy of Science*, v.VII, Univ. of Minnesota Press, 1975; Hilary Putnam, The meaning of 'meaning', *ibid.;* and many other sources.

[24] Note that "possible worlds semantics" presupposes that analytic connections among terms are fixed, as Quine pointed out years ago. See W.V.O. Quine, "Two dogmas of empiricism," in his *From a Logical Point of View*, Harvard, 1953.

the hypothesis that a level of semantic representation can be constructed within linguistic theory. If so, we can think of the levels of phonetic and semantic representation as providing the means for describing Jespersen's "outward form" and "inner meaning," the other levels constituting the "Janus-like" system that encounters these two worlds.

Knowledge of language does not, of course, exhaust the contents of mind. A grammar is a cognitive structure interacting with other systems of knowledge and belief. The nature of the interaction is far from a settled matter; in fact, it has often been contended that it makes no sense to postulate independent systems, each with its own structure, that interact in some manner. Idealization and abstraction are unavoidable in serious inquiry, but particular idealizations may be questioned, and must be justified on empirical grounds. It seems to me that the idealization of grammar as a cognitive structure with certain properties and principles, interacting with other structures, is a reasonable working hypothesis, justified by the success in discovering explanatory principles specific to grammar.

It is possible to accept the legitimacy of this idealization of grammar as a system with its own structure and properties, and at the same time to accept the view that the actual system of grammar for a particular language cannot be determined in strict isolation from questions of fact and belief. We might construct a theory of grammar with certain "parameters" determined by broader considerations. If the intrusion of questions of fact and belief is localized, this may be a feasible prospect. Study of language is part of a more general enterprise: to map out in detail the structure of mind. On the assumption just noted, we might continue to regard a grammar as a separable component of this more general system and proceed to investigate its specific properties.

A review of the arguments for inseparability of knowledge of language from belief and fact supports this line of reasoning, I believe. These arguments relate, or can be reduced to the "theory of significations of words," and thus, if correct, show only that that part of grammar that Jespersen called "the dictionary," which deals with "special facts," involves considerations of fact and belief. The conclusion, then, would be that a full dictionary cannot be distinguished in a principled way from an encyclopedia, while a grammar can be distinguished as a separate idealized structure, with certain aspects of dictionary entries as parameters. We might accept the legitimacy of the parametrized idealization, while agreeing with Hilary Putnam, for example, that "natural kinds" terms such as "lemon," "water," "run," and so on, cannot be provided with "dictionary entries" that ignore matters of fact and belief.[25] Then as

---

[25] Putnam, *op. cit.*

Quine has argued, analyticity will not always be distinguished from shared belief. Similarly, such an approach could incorporate, for example, David Kaplan's theory of "vivid names" and their role in inference,[26] while still adopting the idealization.

But consider the rules that determine the truth conditions for sentences and other aspects of their meaning in terms of the signification of words and the structure of the sentence at various linguistic levels; for example, the rules that enable us to assign the correct interpretations to such expressions as "beavers build dams," "dams are built by beavers," "beavers built this dam," etc. Suppose that these rules are independent of factual considerations in the manner in which they function and in the manner in which they are determined on the basis of preliminary analysis of data in terms of primitive notions of linguistic theory. Suppose further that these primitive notions provide basic elements for representing the significations of words, and suffice to represent certain analytic connections among words, e.g., between "uncle" and "male," "try" and "succeed," "persuade" and "intend," etc. Suppose also that they serve to delimit the class of possible concepts.[27] Then a rich theory of semantics with far-reaching explanatory principles might constitute a significant part of an independent theory of grammar, even though the grammar that "comes into existence in the mind of the speaker" will be intimately interwoven, at specific points, with other cognitive structures. The idealization to "grammar" will thus be entirely legitimate, but the theory of grammar will be in part "open": It will be an abstraction, leaving unspecified certain elements that are fixed in a broader theory. These seem to me to be reasonable assumptions on which to proceed.

Our elaboration of Jespersen's program poses problems at three levels of abstraction: We want to determine (1) the structure of particular sentences, (2) the grammar that characterizes all such structures for a particular language, and (3) the explanatory principles of universal grammar that characterize the class of possible grammars and in this way contribute to an account of how knowledge of language can be acquired. Furthermore, we have the problem of determining how this cognitive structure, grammar, interacts with others.

When we speak of "possible grammars" we are, of course, concerned with biological, not logical possibility. Such conditions as the structure-dependence of rules are not logically necessary, and are interesting, if

---

[26] David Kaplan, "Quantifying in," in D. Davidson and J. Hintikka, eds., *Words and Objections: Essays on the Work of W. V. Quine,* Reidel, 1969.

[27] For example, they may provide the means for expressing the conditions on "possible objects for reference" in terms of spatio-temporal contiguity, Gestalt properties, the relation to human will and action, and so forth. For some discussion of the complexity of these matters, see my *Problems of Knowledge and Freedom*, Pantheon, 1971.

correct, precisely for this reason. There are no logical grounds for determining that the expression "John seems to his friends to hate one another" deviates from grammatical rule. The rules of English grammar do not assign it the perfectly sensible meaning "it seems to each of John's friends that he hates the others," by analogy to similar sentences, though a different linguistic theory, specifying the initial state of another possible organism, might provide exactly this conclusion. The grammarian's task is to discover the explanatory principles that account for such phenomena.[28] For the moment, there is no reason to doubt that these principles of universal grammar are specific to the "language faculty".[29] If this is correct, then Jespersen's program can be extended to a significant and reasonably well-defined domain of theoretical psychology.

Notice that the thesis of independence of grammar, in the sense just outlined, does not imply what is in fact false, that the interpretation of sentences by hearers is independent of questions of fact and belief. What is implied is that the contribution of grammar to sentence interpretation is very different in kind from the contribution of fact or belief. Consider, for example, the sentence "John's friends seem to their wives to like their work." It may mean that to each wife, it seems that John's friends like their work; or it may be understood as the plural of "John's friend seems to his wife to like his work," that is, with a 1–1 relation between friends and wives.[30] Consider the closely analogous sentence "John's friends seem to their wives to like one another." Again, it may mean to each wife, it seems that John's friends like one another. What of the second interpretation, which in this case would be that each friend seems to his wife to like the other friends? This seems to me dubious; the relation of "John's friends" to "one another" requires that we take "John's friends" to be a true plural, multiply denoting independently of its context, while its relation to "their wives" precludes this reading, on this interpretation. Consider finally "John's friends asked their wives to visit one another." Again, it may mean that the friends ask that the wives mutually visit — analogous to the first interpretation above — or perhaps, that each friend asked his wife to visit the other wives.[31] It cannot mean that the wives were asked to visit the

[28] The explanation, I think, lies in the trace theory of movement rules and the specified subject condition, outlined in my "Conditions on transformations," in S. Anderson and P. Kiparsky, eds., *A Festschrift for Morris Halle,* Holt, Rinehart and Winston, 1973. [The third essay in this book.]

[29] For discussion of this question, and of opposing views, see my "Problems and mysteries."

[30] There are other interpretations, with "they" taken as nonanaphoric. I disregard these.

[31] Judgments are hazy, but it seems to me that this interpretation is considerably more accessible in this case than in "John's friends seem to their wives to like one another." Correspondingly, "each of John's friends seems to his wife to like one another" is ungrammatical (in the broad sense) but "each of John's friends asked his wife that she visit the other wives" is all right. The paraphrases suggest an explanation in terms of the associated abstract syntactic structures, but I will not pursue the matter here.

other friends. The correct interpretation of such examples raises many questions, but it seems fair to conclude that they are internal to grammar. However, there is another interpretation for the last example, namely, that each friend asked *his wives* to visit *his* other wives; this would be the natural interpretation if we replace "wives" by "children." We don't select the latter interpretation because of factual assumptions about monogamy. But such considerations, which surely enter into sentence-interpretation in performance, are easily separable (in this case at least) from grammatical considerations. It would merely be a kind of obscurantism to refuse to make the relevant distinctions in this case, arguing rather that the examples show that grammatical processes are inextricably intertwined with matters of fact and belief.

To mention a less clear case, consider again the generics "beavers build dams" and "dams are built by beavers." As noted earlier, the noun phrases in the predicates are not taken to be universally quantified, though the subject noun phrases are so understood, or at least may be.[32] This much seems to be a matter of grammar. But there is, I think, a further distinction. "Beavers build dams" is true, but does not imply that all beavers build dams, only that beavers are dam-builders: dam-building is a characteristic of the species. But "dams are built by beavers" is, I think, naturally understood to imply that all dams are built by beavers, and is thus false. These judgments (if correct) cannot be traced to the structure: compare "poems are written by fools like me," which I take to be a statement about all poems; "mountains are climbed by fools like me," which may be true even if some mountains are unscaled; and "mountains are formed by erosion," i.e., all mountains. The variation in judgment relates to the meaning of the verb. We might say that the sentences receive a uniform interpretation: poems are written only by fools, mountains are climbed only by fools, dams are built only by beavers, mountains are formed only by erosion. In each case, we are saying something about all poems, mountains, dams. When the passive verb is "creative," we understand further that the entities are formed in no other way, though there is no logical necessity for this, and in fact a different interpretation will be imposed by constrastive stress: "dams are BUILT only by beavers (but formed NATURALLY when trees fall)". In a world in which mountains are created by the act of climbing, we might correspondingly give the

---

[32] Recall that plural indefinites can be understood as expressing either universal or existential quantification (or set-denotation, rather than multiple denotation), depending on context, in subject position. Compare "beavers built this dam," "beavers have been known to climb trees," "beavers are indigenous to Australia," none of which attribute a property to all beavers. The last says nothing about individual beavers, and is perhaps most appropriately understood as a statement about the class of beavers, rather than about (members of) some subset of it.

"creative" interpretation to "mountains are climbed (only) by fools." It seems that there is an interaction of "structural meaning," grammatically determined; "connotation" of certain types of verbs; and certain factual judgments. Whatever the explanation for the full range of facts, it is clearly not the case that each datum comes marked, on its face, with an indication of the considerations that determine its status and range of interpretation. Rather, we would naturally expect that only a theory of grammar (in the broadest sense), a theory of belief, and a theory of their interaction, will settle individual cases.

The range of possibilities for interpretation of factual and grammatical considerations is immense. Consider the fact that today is Thursday. Suppose I have a friend who, I know, teaches a class on Monday and plays tennis on Thursday. Suppose he says to me "today was a disaster." If it is Thursday, I understand him to be saying that he played an awful game of tennis, and if it is Monday, that he taught a terrible class. But these factors in sentence-interpretation are easily separable from those that determine the literal, intrinsic meaning of the sentence, and it is surely proper to conclude that quite independent systems are interacting to provide the interpretation. There are innumerable less clear cases, but none, I believe, that seriously threaten the legitimacy of the standard idealization to a system of grammar — though, as noted, this system may be "open" at certain points.

In all such cases, we hope to discover language-specific rules that account for the literal, inherent form–meaning correlation; and, at a deeper level, we seek to determine the general theory of possible grammars that leads to the selection of particular rules operating under fixed general conditions. Similarly, we want this general theory to explain why the rules of grammar mark as deviant such sentences as "John seemed to his friends to hate one another" and require that the pronoun them not refer to the friends in "John's friends seem to their wives to like them," but rather to the wives (if anaphoric at all). And so on for numerous other related cases. It is hard to believe that people are taught these facts or the principles that determine them, and there is no concept of "learning from experience" that seems even remotely applicable. It seems that we must look to universal grammar for an explanation. To specify the possible rules, their organization, the conditions on their application, is the grammarian's task, while linguistic theory as a whole will be concerned as well with the integration of grammar in other cognitive systems.

Assuming the legitimacy of the idealization to grammar, let us turn to the specific question that concerned Jespersen, namely, the nature of the connection between the structures of syntax and the world of ideas; or in our present terms, the relations between the level of semantic representation and other levels of linguistic structure specified by a grammar. Let us consider the general relations that hold between these systems. I have already noted Jespersen's contention that syntactic structures do not simply reflect semantic properties and Sapir's far stronger affirmation of this position, and have indicated briefly why I think it has merit. But on these assumptions it still remains to discover the principles that govern the relations between these domains.

We might pursue the question at several levels of generality. Thus we might ask how some specific theory of language structure specifies these relations; it is here that the most important and interesting questions lie, in my opinion. Or we might inquire, more broadly, into the general nature of the relation that any theory must somehow capture. Let us first consider the latter, somewhat vague question.

Suppose our linguistic theory to be of the nonprocedural variety. Suppose that among the primitive notions of linguistic theory[33] we can distinguish some that are "semantic," and others that are "formal." Thus we might take such notions as "synonymous," "significant," "denotes," "satisfies," "refers to concrete objects," to be core notions of semantics, let us say, primitive in our linguistic theory; while the primitives of phonetic theory, or "is an utterance of a corpus" (possibly idealized), or those of footnotes 16 and 22, may be taken to be formal notions. Given a bifurcation of the primitive notions into "formal" and "semantic, " we can ask, for each defined concept, whether terms of one or the other category appear in its definition. There are, then, purely formal concepts, purely semantic ones, and mixed ones. Consider the purely formal concepts. We may refer to the theory concerning just these as "the theory of linguistic form." We might discover that this theory — which excludes the core notions of semantics — is virtually null, or quite uninteresting. Or, at the other extreme, we might find that it includes an interesting concept of "grammar" and "structure," perhaps all linguistic levels apart from semantic representation.[34]

The latter thesis — call it the thesis of "absolute autonomy of formal grammar"[35] — would not imply that there are no systematic connections

[33] Recall that the choice of primitives is an empirical matter, as formulated above. That is, not every logically adequate set is "epistemically primitive," on empirical grounds.

[34] Recall that grammars, in a nonprocedural theory, are purely formal objects. Suppose we take $D_F$ to be the data as analyzed in terms of formal primitives. Then the hypothesis in question asserts that "grammar for $D_F$" will be the same as "grammar for D," apart from the level of semantic representation, undetermined in the former.

[35] Terminology is inadequate here. I have been using "grammar" to refer to the system of rules that generates all levels of representation, including semantic representation. The term "syntax" is used generally either in a broad sense, as contrasted with semantics, or a narrow sense, as contrasted with phonology and morphology within the scope of syntax in the broad sense. I will continue to use "syntax" in the narrow sense, and will use "formal grammar" in place of "syntax" in the broad sense.

between form and meaning. No one, I am sure, has ever doubted that there are highly systematic connections and that a major problem of linguistic theory is to determine them. In particular, this has been a guiding assumption in all work in transformational generative grammar, since its origins.[36] Rather, the absolute autonomy thesis implies that the formal conditions on "possible grammars" and a formal property of "optimality" are so narrow and restrictive that a formal grammar can in principle be selected (and its structures generated) on the basis of a preliminary analysis of data in terms of formal primitives excluding the core notions of semantics, and that the systematic connections between formal grammar and semantics are determined on the basis of this independently selected system and the analysis of data in terms of the full range of semantic primitives. This thesis thus constitutes an empirical hypothesis about the organization of language, leaving ample scope for systematic form–meaning connections while excluding many imaginable possibilities.

One might formulate a "thesis of autonomy of formal grammar" of varying degrees of strength. As in the case of the question of independence of grammar, discussed a moment ago, we might construct a linguistic theory in which formal grammar is independent in its structure but "open" at certain designated points with respect to the full range of semantic primitives. The problem, then, will be to determine the specific ways in which semantic information enters into the determination of a formal grammar. If a fairly strong thesis of autonomy in this sense proves correct, we will proceed to supplement it with a theory of the interconnection of semantic and formal grammatical structures, much as in the case of the study of grammar in relation to fact and belief. The theory of linguistic form may still be a theory with significant internal structure, but it will be constructed with "semantic parameters." The actual choice of formal grammar will be determined by fixing these parameters. Suppose that the parametrized theory includes parts of the dictionary, and suppose further that the semantic parameters can be localized to the dictionary. Then questions of fact and belief may also enter into the choice of grammar at this point, consistent with the parametrized autonomy thesis. Note that the significant question with regard to the autonomy thesis may not be a question of "yes" or "no," but rather of "more" or "less," or more correctly, "where" and "how much."

We can distinguish, then, two versions of an autonomy thesis: an absolute thesis, which holds that the theory of linguistic form, including the concept, "formal grammar" and all levels apart from semantic representation, can be fully defined in terms of formal primitives, and a

[36] See my *Syntactic Structures*, Mouton, 1957, chapters 8 and 9, particularly 9.3–4.

weaker version, which holds that this is true only conditionally, with certain parameters, perhaps localized in the dictionary.

To clarify the issues, consider first the absolute thesis of autonomy, which was in fact tentatively put forth as a working hypothesis[37] in the earliest work on transformational generative grammar. To show that this thesis is incorrect in some respect and that a weaker thesis (or no interesting thesis) must be advanced, it is necessary to show that certain concepts of formal grammar must be, or should be defined in terms of a selection of primitives rich enough to provide definitions for (or to include) the core notions of semantics. Note that the question cannot sensibly be raised unless we assume an initial bifurcation of primitive notions into semantic and formal in some way. Note further that the question is imprecise, in that the precise scope of formal grammar is not clearly determined in presystematic terms.[38]

In accordance with the absolute thesis, considerations involving the core notions of semantics do not enter essentially into the selection of a formal grammar that generates the various levels of syntax, morphology, and phonology. But, of course, such semantic considerations do enter into the choice of the theory of linguistic form. That is, this general theory must be devised in such a way that the optimal grammar of predetermined form, selected on the basis of a preliminary analysis of data by formal primitives, will generate a structure for each sentence that provides the basis for semantic interpretation within a fixed semantic theory. Thus the theory of linguistic form must be constructed in such a way that the grammar selected for English provides a structure for such sentences as "the police were ordered to stop drinking" or "his suggestion was to become famous" (to take some of the earliest examples considered in this context) which will permit a presupposed theory of semantic interpretation to operate, applying its general principles and perhaps some language-specific ones to the levels assigned in the generated structure.

In the earliest work on transformational generative grammar, a kind of "use theory of meaning" was implicit, though never carefully formulated. Later, it was proposed that "projection rules" assign a representation to

[37] In the light of later misunderstandings, it is important to emphasize the character of this proposal. It was stressed that the systematic connections between the theory of linguistic form and the theory of the use of language must be studied in a broader theory of which each is a part, and that the study of reference and meaning must, obviously, be undertaken as part of this broader theory of language. It was further stressed that there is no point issuing manifestos about these matters; rather, there are empirical problems to be solved.

[38] On the problems of demarcation, see my *Aspects of the Theory of Syntax*, M.I.T., 1965, pp. 153–60; *Current Issues in Linguistic Theory*, Mouton, 1964, p. 51. Since that time, there has been much illuminating discussion of the issue, but I think that the questions noted there, and others like them, remain unresolved.

the sentence on a new level of semantic representation, and there have been various inquiries into just how this level is related to other levels of linguistic structure. It has invariably been a crucial assumption that the theory of linguistic form must be embedded in a broader "semiotic theory" that would be concerned with the meaning, reference, and conditions on use of expressions with assigned structures. The actual range of meaning or use-conditions on expressions thus plays a central role in determining the adequacy of the theory of linguistic form, and any advances in understanding of the overarching semiotic theory will, therefore, influence the theory of linguistic form, under the thesis of absolute autonomy.

To show this strong thesis to be false, it will not suffice, then, to show that there are systematic relations between semantic and syntactic notions. This assumption is not and has never been in question; on the contrary, it was formulated explicitly in conjunction with the thesis of absolute autonomy. It would be surprising indeed to find important formal elements that are devoid of semantic import. This contention is no part of Jespersen's thesis on the "indefinability" of syntactic notions in semantic terms, or Sapir's far stronger thesis, or the thesis of autonomy as developed in early work on generative grammar. Rather, the crucial question is whether these systematic relations involving the full range of semantic concepts enter into the determination (and perhaps the function) of the categories and rules of formal grammar, or whether they simply set conditions on the construction of a theory of linguistic form.

There have been some sweeping claims in this regard. Thus it has been argued that the concepts of phonology must be based on the notion "synonymous",[39] that syntax depends essentially on the notion "significant" or "meaningful expression," that transformations must be defined in terms of the relation "logical consequence", and so on.[40] Such claims — in fact, any specific claims as to how concepts must (or should, or can) be defined — must be supported by argument. The burden of proof always rests on one who advances the claim. In these cases, I think that the argument is defective, and that these contentions, so far as we know, are without foundation.[41]

[39] Or "difference of meaning," in the more usual formulation. It is surprising that this contention has sometimes been advanced by linguists who deny the existence of synonymous expressions. Thus their position must be that synonymy holds of tokens, not types. It is difficult to make much sense of this view, in my opinion.

[40] See, e.g., W.V.O. Quine, "Meaning in linguistics," in *From a Logical Point of View*; Yehoshua Bar-Hillel, "Logical syntax and semantics," *Language* 30, 230–37, 1954.

[41] For some discussion, see my *Syntactic Structures*, "Semantic considerations in grammar," *Monograph no. 8*, Institute of Languages and Linguistics, Georgetown University, 1955, and "Logical syntax and semantics: their linguistic relevance," *Language* 31, 36–45, 1955. In the light of more recent work, I think, in retrospect, that some of the broader assertions in the last article were themselves too sweeping, though the specific arguments seem to me correct.

Consider, then, some narrower and perhaps more defensible proposals. It might be argued that those parts of phonology that deal with such matters as English vowel shift rely essentially on a semantic notion "related word," involving some notion of "similarity of meaning." Thus, we must know that "declare"–"declarative," "compare"–"comparative" are properly related in meaning before we can proceed to investigate the regular phonological alternations among them. The proposal is that the semantic notion "related word" serves as a primitive notion that gives an analysis of raw data in theory-independent terms, and that once data are characterized in this way, phonological investigation proceeds. But is this proposal a reasonable one? Can the linguist or the language-learner determine, independently of grammar, that the relation of "declare" to "declarative" and "compare" to "comparative" is different in kind, on semantic grounds, from the relations among such sets as "travel," "trail," "train", "truck," etc.? This seems to me dubious; surely, there is no convincing argument to this effect in the literature.[42] The "related words" are no doubt semantically related, but these relations seem rather idiosyncratic. Given the relation, we can find associated semantic properties, possibly interesting ones. This we expect to be true in general of formal notions, under the absolute autonomy thesis. Some notion of "related word" may be crucial for phonology, but more must be shown to demonstrate that it can plausibly be taken as a semantic primitive — unless we simply use the term "semantic" to refer to any poorly understood aspect of language, thus depriving "semantics" of any real interest.

One might put forth a weaker and more tenable thesis. Perhaps the relevant notion "related word" depends in part on systematic features of grammar, in particular, on the possibility of formulating rules of a fixed type, constrained by general conditions, to express the phonological alternations in question; and in part on the requirement that the relation among related words be characterizable in terms of the semantic primitives — the more readily, the higher the value of the grammar in terms of an evaluation measure. The idea is not implausible, and can perhaps be given substance. If this proves to be the correct approach, we will have a "parametrized" autonomy thesis. For the moment, the question remains quite obscure.

It seems more promising to search for failures of the absolute autonomy thesis in the domain of sentence structure. Several interesting proposals have been made in this regard. Stanley Peters has suggested that perhaps "information about sense must appear in the basic data" (that is, the data as analyzed in terms of the primitives of linguistic theory). In particular,

[42] For possible steps towards such an argument see Joseph H. Greenberg, *Essays in Linguistics*, Chicago, 1957, chapter II. I know of nothing that improves substantially on Greenberg's proposals since. But the problems in this approach seem fairly serious. Cf. my review of Greenberg's book in *Word*, April, 1959.

"apparently, some information about meaning is crucial" in determining the interpretation of restrictive and nonrestrictive relative clauses and the differences of meaning associated with rising and falling intonation in questions, perhaps only information about truth value.[43] Insofar as his argument is that "some semantic information [is] needed for language learning" — that is, that semantic information is needed to determine the correct interpretation of these structures — it does not bear on the absolute autonomy thesis (nor does he suggest otherwise), since the latter would also insist on this point. Within the broader semiotic theory, interpretations of sentences are determined on the basis of semantic analysis of what Peters calls the "basic data."

But perhaps more can be claimed. Consider the various syntactic properties distinguishing restrictive from nonrestrictive relatives, for example, the intonational differences and the option of deleting complementizers and "*wh*-forms" plus "be" in restrictives. Must we — or can we — rely on semantically analyzed basic data for establishing these distinctions? The first question to ask is whether the combinations of properties associated with restrictives and nonrestrictives, respectively, are idiosyncratic and variable across languages, or whether these complexes are determined by properties of universal grammar. Would we expect to find, in the next language, that comma intonation and deletability of initial strings are associated in one type of relative, while noncomma intonation and nondeletability are associated in a different type? If not, then the matter is irrelevant to the absolute autonomy thesis, since a property of universal grammar is involved; there are no choices to be made, in this regard, in selecting particular grammars.

Consider the further question of how these clusters of formal properties are associated with semantic interpretations. Thus nonrestrictives, with their specific formal properties, are "asserted," while restrictives are generally not. Is this a matter of "choice of grammar," or is the association a general one? I suspect that the latter is true. That is, I do not think that we would expect to find the opposite correlation in the next language investigated. But in either case, the question has no bearing on the absolute autonomy thesis, which also insists that the theory of linguistic form is in part determined by the ways in which this theory fits into a broader semiotic theory concerned with the association of clusters of formal properties with particular kinds of interpretations.

On the matter of relative clauses, Barbara Partee has argued that "semantic arguments" can settle the much debated question as to the constituent structure of such expressions as "the book we ordered" in "the

---

[43] Stanley Peters, "The projection problem: how is a grammar to be selected?", in S. Peters, ed., *Goals of Linguistic Theory*, Prentice-Hall, 1972.

book we ordered arrived".[44] This example, she suggests, "shows that the requirement that semantic interpretation rules correspond structurally to the syntactic rules can put very strong constraints on possible syntactic analyses." The context is a contrast between the "logical tradition," which abides by "the principle of a one–one correspondence between syntactic and semantic rules," and linguistic approaches that depart radically from the principle: various approaches within generative grammar, and, we might add, Jespersen's discussion, outlined above. She suggests that the principle that "the syntactic and semantic rules are to correspond in compositional structure, which is a fundamental assumption in Montague's approach" (which she is elaborating), solves a problem of analysis of relative clauses that is left open by earlier "syntactic arguments." She interprets the fundamental principle in question as imposing a constraint on grammar so strong "that I think it is a serious open question whether natural languages can be so described." Thus, her example is of considerable general interest.

Partee's discussion of the problem proceeds from the familiar logical analysis of definite descriptions. She suggests that "the simplest way to give a semantically uniform treatment of definite descriptions is by referring to the property expressed by the whole common noun phrase," so that the expression should be analyzed with the major constituent break between "the" and "book we ordered".[45] This syntactic analysis "can provide a direct basis for the semantic interpretation in a way that [the alternatives] cannot." Namely, we can combine the two "class-denoting phrases" *book* and *we ordered x,* denoting the class of books and the class of things we ordered, respectively, "to form a complex class-denoting phrase, which can be interpreted as denoting the intersection of the two classes," the class of books and the class of things that we ordered; "combining *the* with the result leads to the correct assertion that it is that class that has one and only one member." The assumption is that there is a uniform interpretation of *the*, and that "A part of the analysis of any definite description is the proposition that one and only one object has the property designated by the common noun phrase to which *the* is attached".[46]

How does this argument bear on the absolute autonomy thesis? Again, we ask whether the principles on which the analysis is based are taken to

[44] Barbara Partee, *Montague Grammar and Transformational Grammar*, mimeographed, pp. 43f. This has since appeared in *Linguistic Inquiry*, VI, 2, Spring 1975. Also her paper "some transformational extensions of Montague grammar," in R. Rodman, ed., *Papers in Montague Grammar*, Occasional Papers in Linguistics, No. 2, U.C.L.A., Sept. 1972.

[45] Though nonrestrictive relatives, as she notes, might well have a different analysis, with "the book" as a constituent in "the book, which we ordered, arrived."

[46] *Montague Grammar and Transformational Grammar*, p. 44.

be universal or specific to English. It is reasonable to take them to be universal; that is, insofar as a language has relative clauses of the kind that we find in English,[47] we expect the same conclusions to hold. If so, Partee's argument tends to support the absolute autonomy thesis. That is, we can interpret the argument (as she does) as providing one of the "constraints on possible syntactic analyses," on semantic grounds, just as early work in transformational generative grammar argued, also on semantic grounds in part, that phrase structure and transformational rules should be so constrained as to rule out, for example, a structure for "they are eating sandwiches" as NP-be-NP, analogous to "they are friends of mine."

Keeping in mind the context of Partee's discussion of relative clauses, it is interesting to consider these structures in a bit more detail. Note first that the principles cited are true only of *singular* definite descriptions; the logical tradition that suggested Partee's analysis is concerned only with this special case. The analysis does not generalize to plurals, such as "the books we ordered arrived." We cannot proceed as before, taking the complex class-denoting phrase to denote the intersection of the two classes denoted by "books" and "we ordered $x$," then applying the principle that "one and only one object has the property designated by" this common noun phrase, for this procedure will give us the same interpretation as derived for "the book we ordered," an incorrect conclusion. We can easily modify the principles to accommodate all of these cases. Take the semantically relevant items to be the common noun "book," the expression "we ordered $x$," the definite article, and *plural*. We take "book" to denote the class of books, and "we ordered $x$" to denote the class of things we ordered. Then "book we ordered" denotes the intersection of these classes. Take *plural* to mean that the cardinality of the set denoted is greater than or equal to 2, and *nonplural* to mean that the cardinality is 1. Taking B, O, A to be (respectively) the class of books, things we ordered, and things that arrived, and taking $c[X]$ to be the cardinality of $X$, we can represent the meanings of the sentences (for present purposes) as follows:

(1)   the books we ordered arrived:   $B \cap O \subset A$; $c[B \cap O] \geq 2$

(2)   the book we ordered arrived:   $B \cap O \subset A$; $c[B \cap O] = 1$

[47] There are, however, systems of rather different types. Cf. Kenneth Hale, "Gaps in grammar and culture," mimeographed, 1971; "The adjoined relative clause in Australian," mimeographed, 1973; Ellavina Perkins, "Extraposition of relative clauses in Navajo," mimeographed, 1974. Thus in Navajo there are relative clauses which have, essentially, the interpretation: the dog is chasing the cat, which were fighting. These require a rather different analysis. It has been argued that English has adjoined relatives in underlying structure, and such examples as "the girl left and the boy arrived who met in Chicago" have been offered (analogous, in part, to the regular Navajo construction). To me, these examples seem at best quite marginal, and I would question whether anything can be based on them.

48

What is the function of the definite article in this analysis? To determine this, compare the sentences cited with their indefinite counterparts, "some books we ordered arrived",[48] "a book we ordered arrived." A natural analysis is as follows:

(3)  some books we ordered arrived:   $\exists K \subset B \cap O, K \subset A: c[K] \geq 2$

(4)  a book we ordered arrived:   $\exists K \subset B \cap O, K \subset A: c[K] = 1$

We now have the following notions: relative clause construction, which corresponds to set intersection as Partee suggests[49]; predication, corresponding to set inclusion; [± plural], which determines cardinality; [± definite], which determines the set that is the subject of predication, i.e., either the full set denoted or a subset of it. In this way, we arrive at a very simple semantic description, based on elements of the syntactic structure.

Consider now the consequences of this broader theory for the syntax. The simplest structure that provides the basis for "compositional" semantic interpretation is:

(5)

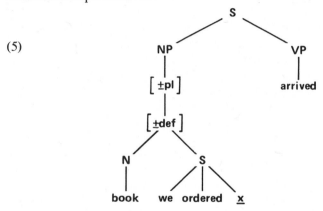

The structure [N S] determines the base set $B \cap O$; [± def] determines whether we are talking about the whole set or a subset; [± pl] determines the cardinality of the set we are talking about; and the structure [$_S$NP VP] determines predication. But the surface structure of the sentence "the books we ordered arrived" will be something like (5'):

[48]  A more careful analysis would consider also such sentences as "some of the books we ordered arrived."

[49]  We might take the corresponding syntactic operation to be a raising rule that gives [$_{\bar{N}}$ *book* [$_S$ *we ordered t*]] from [$_{\bar{N}}$ N [$_S$ *we ordered wh-book*]], where $\bar{N}$ is in the context [$_{\bar{N}}$ Det _____] and *t* is the trace left by *wh*-movement. For details of an analysis of this sort, with discussion of the semantics more or less along the lines indicated here, see Jean-Roger Vergnaud, *French Relative Clauses*, Ph.D. dissertation, M.I.T., 1974. See Kroch, *op. cit.*, for an illuminating discussion of a variety of structures of this sort.

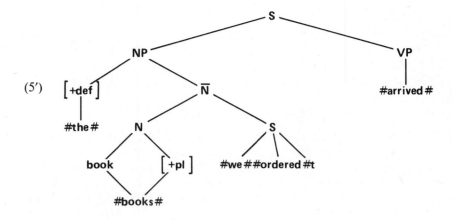

(5')

The element [+pl] appears within the word *books* in surface structure, and is thus "inferior" in the surface structure both to *the* and to the node dominating N and S, whatever the analysis. There is no point-by-point relation between the surface syntax and the semantic structures, and no consequences of the suggested sort for syntactic analysis.

The initial analysis, restricted to singular definite descriptions, leads to conclusions expected on the absolute autonomy thesis. The fuller and more adequate analysis considering other related structures as well suggests a still stronger thesis of autonomy. There is, in this case, a simple analysis of the semantics and also, I believe, of the syntax. The two are independent, though there is a natural, and no doubt quite general way to relate the two. But the syntax is not a reflection of the semantic structure, exactly as in the examples discussed by Jespersen, and others mentioned earlier. The examples thus support Jespersen's general thesis, and even Sapir's stronger thesis, regarding the connection between the "world of ideas" and the forms of syntax. They conflict with the principle that syntactic and semantic rules correspond in compositional structure, at least if we interpret this principle, as Partee suggests, as implying a strong constraint on syntactic analysis. (Cf. p. 45.)

It is illuminating, I think, to press the analysis of these cases a few steps further. The fact that the cardinality, in all the cases cited, is greater than or equal to 1 can be taken to be a general property of noun phrases in such contexts. Compare "beavers build dams," "all ravens are black," "most kids like baseball," etc. If so, then the sole meaning of the definite article can be taken to be "universality." In the sentence "the book we ordered arrived," the definite article determines that all members of a unit class arrived, and in "the books we ordered arrived," it determines that all members of a class of cardinality greater than or equal to 2 arrived. Thus [± def] corresponds here to universal-versus-existential quantification. The meaning of "the," then, is not that one and only one object has the property designated by the common noun phrase to which it is attached; rather, it is universal quantification. The definite article, in this usage, serves as one of the several universal quantifier words in English. As noted earlier, these differ in quite interesting ways in their semantic and syntactic properties.

It was also noted earlier that indefinite plural noun phrases can have either an existential or universal interpretation of a rather complex sort, depending on context, and that in some cases plurality is not really a semantic property of the noun phrase in which it appears at all. One context that obviously requires an existential interpretation is the context: *there is —.* If I say "there are beavers in that pond," I am not referring to all beavers. Another well-known constraint on these "existential structures" is that they do not permit definite noun phrases in the position following "there is".[50] Gary Milsark has observed that, given the interpretation of the definite article as a kind of universal quantifier, we can unify these observations. Thus the constraint on the rule of *there*-insertion is that the resulting structure does not tolerate universally quantified noun phrases: definite noun phrases, or indefinite ones with universal interpretation.[51] Milsark relates this observation to more general grammatical properties of predication.[52] If this line of argument is correct, it follows that the syntactic rule of *there*-insertion pays no attention to the definiteness or indefiniteness of the subject noun phrase in the structure to which it applies. It forms such structures as "there are beavers in the pond" and "there was the man hurt in the accident." The grammatical deviance of the latter is a consequence of the same rule of semantic interpretation that requires the existential reading of the former (but see footnote 50). The relevant property is the interpretation of the transformationally formed phrase "there is." The latter has existential import, as we can see, for example, by comparing "there is a unicorn believed to be in the garden", which is true

---

[50] This is not quite accurate. As is well-known, these can appear with a different intonational pattern and a rather different interpretation, as in the statement "well, there is the book that John wrote," in response to the question: "What books deal with dam-building?"

[51] Larry Horn points out that when the subject contains *any*, the rule of *there*-insertion can apply just in case *any* is interpreted not as the universal quantifier but rather as the polarity-pair of *some*. Thus we cannot have "there is anybody (everybody) who can win"; but "there wasn't anybody...," "was there anybody...," "there was somebody..." are grammatical. We need not impose this as a condition on the transformation (which would, in fact, be unstateable under a suitably restricted theory of transformations); rather, it is a consequence of the surface rule of interpretation. See Larry Horn, *On the Semantic Properties of Logical Operators in English*, Ph.D. dissertation, U.C.L.A., 1972, p. 146.

[52] See Gary Milsark, *Existential Sentences in English*, Ph.D. dissertation, M.I.T., 1974.

only if a unicorn exists, and the corresponding sentence that has not undergone *there*-insertion, "a unicorn is believed to be in the garden," which may be true even if there are no unicorns. Sentences of the form "there is definite NP. . ." are violations of the surface rules of semantic interpretation rather than syntactic rules, it appears.[53]

The conclusion is interesting in several respects. First, it indicates that we need not abandon certain natural and quite powerful constraints on the formulation of transformational rules, as would be necessary if the structural conditions of transformations had to refer to noun phrases with one or another determiner.[54] Furthermore, the example shows once again that well-motivated rules of formal grammar can operate quite independently, embedded in a reasonable theory of semantic interpretation. Finally, the example again illustrates the fact that a datum does not carry with it its explanation. There is no way, a priori, to know whether the deviance of definite noun phrases after "there is" is syntactic or semantic in origin. Only a theory of grammar can determine this, just as in the case of idealization of grammar as distinct from other cognitive structures, discussed earlier.

The various examples discussed here involving plurality — plural noun phrases in predicates, indefinite plurals and their interpretations, definite plurals, plurals as "sentence properties," the problems with generics — suggest, I believe, that we cannot expect linguistic theory to associate syntactic and semantic rules very closely. There may well be interesting correlations between the class of formal structures generated and the expressions of an appropriate "broader-minded logic," but it seems doubtful that these correlations can be reduced to a point-by-point correlation among rules. The same conclusion is suggested by a consideration of the syntactic and semantic variety among the quantifier words that fall within the rough categories "universal" and "existential." Rather, I think, detailed examination of a range of examples suggests the plausibility of the general approach outlined by Jespersen.

Whether or not the latter speculation is correct, we have still found nothing to challenge the absolute thesis of autonomy of syntax.

Lakoff has outlined a rather general argument against a version of an autonomy thesis which he attributes to my *Syntactic Structures* (1957).[55]

---

[53] These observations again suggest that surface structure contributes directly to semantic interpretation. See footnotes 11, 51. On the same grounds, one can explain the status of *"there is being a man robbed," *"there is trying to be a man funny," *"there tried to be a man funny," without any special conditions on the rule of *there*-insertion, e.g., a constraint limiting it to the leftmost occurrence of *be*, which would require quantifiers in the formulation of the structural condition of the transformation.

[54] Or to exclude the cases cited in footnote 53.

[55] George Lakoff, "Linguistics and natural logic," in Davidson and Harman, eds., *op. cit.*

Consider the following two theses:

(I) "the rules that generate the grammatical sentences in English, separating them from the ungrammatical sentences and assigning them their grammatical structure, are distinct from the rules that relate English sentences to their corresponding logical forms"

(II) "In some cases, the rules which determine which sentences are grammatical or ungrammatical are identical to rules relating the surface form of an English sentence to its logical form."

He argues that (II) is correct, so that the version of the autonomy thesis expressed in (I) is false. To demonstrate that (II) is correct, he considers the rule of adverb-preposing, which operates as indicated in (6):

(6) a. Sam smoked pot last night → Last night, Sam smoked pot
    b. I think Sam smoked pot last night → Last night, I think Sam smoked pot

But some matrix sentence verbs block the rule, as indicated in (7);

(7) I realize that Sam will leave town tomorrow → * Tomorrow, I realize that Sam will leave town

Thus adverb-preposing "must be a rule of grammar, since it plays a role in distinguishing grammatical from ungrammatical sentences."

Another verb that does not permit adverb-preposing is "mention," as we can see from (8):

(8) a. I mentoned that Sam will smoke pot tomorrow
    b. *Tomorrow, I mentioned that Sam will smoke pot

But now consider (9):

(9) a. I mentioned that Sam smoked pot last night
    b. Last night, I mentioned that Sam smoked pot

Both are grammatical, but they differ in meaning. Thus a single rule, adverb-preposing, plays a role in generating grammatical sentences and in determining meaning (i.e., it blocks the meaning (9a) for (9b)). The rule has "two functions: to generate the grammatical sentences, filtering out the ungrammatical sentences, while at the same time relating the surface forms of sentences to their corresponding logical forms, while blocking any incorrect assignments of logical form to surface form." We thus establish thesis (II), and must reject (I). The conclusion is that "The rules of grammar, which generate the grammatical sentences of English, filtering out the ungrammatical sentences, are not distinct from the rules relating the surface forms of English sentences to their corresponding logical forms." The only way to avoid this conclusion would be to formulate two distinct rules of adverb-preposing, one for syntax and the other for relating syntax to semantics, "thus missing a significant generalization".[56] Thus, Lakoff argues, the standpoint of *Syntactic Structures* must be rejected.

But is it necessary, under thesis (I), to construct two distinct rules in such cases as these? Surely not. The rule of adverb-preposing, constrained as Lakoff suggests, will give the results (6)–(8) and (as he notes) will generate (9b) only from "I mentioned last night that Sam smoked pot." The structures assigned to the various sentences considered are exactly those that give the right semantic interpretations. There is only one rule of adverb-preposing, a syntactic rule. The underlying forms[57] determine the meaning, by whatever principles apply independently to the examples with no preposing. The argument does not bear at all on (I), or on any other version of the autonomy thesis, or on any position developed in *Syntactic Structures.*

One might challenge the autonomy thesis in a different way, by showing that certain syntactic generalizations can be explained only by direct introduction of semantic considerations and rules into formal grammar. I know of only a few serious proposals in the literature that might be relevant.[58] Robert Rodman points out that elements of relative clauses cannot be relativized, and that they also have narrower quantificational scope than the NP head of the relative clause.[59] Thus in (10), he observes, the scope of "every" includes that of "a," although (11) is ambiguous with regard to scope:

[56] Lakoff presents other arguments as well concerning adverb-preposing, but the logic is more or less the same. The paper presents many very interesting examples and analyses, but nothing that bears on the autonomy thesis, as far as I can see, even in its absolute form.

[57] Or, the surface structures, if we assume a trace to be left by movement rules. See footnote 28. In this connection, see also Thomas Wasow, *Anaphora in Generative Grammar,* mimeographed, 1973 (a revision of an M.I.T. Ph.D. dissertation, *Anaphoric Relations in English,* 1972) where it is shown that some interesting problems in the interpretation of questions noted originally by Paul Postal can be overcome by the trace theory of movement rules; and Elizabeth Selkirk, *The Phrase Phonology of English and French*, Ph.D. dissertation, M.I.T., 1972, where a similar theory is applied in the explanation of a number of phonological problems.

[58] It should be noted that these were not suggested to be relevant to the autonomy thesis, though indirectly, they might prove to be.

[59] Robert Rodman, "The proper treatment of relative clauses in a Montague grammar," in Rodman, ed., *op. cit.*

54

(10) John dates every woman who loves a fish

(11) every woman loves a fish

And an item appearing in the context of "a fish" in (10) cannot be relativized, to give, e.g., (12):

(12) the fish which John has dated a woman who loves — walks

He suggests that no "standard" theory of transformational grammar can "associate two such facts so closely," and he offers an explanation under a principle of binding of variables in relative clauses, employing a grammatical theory that relates semantic and syntactic rules in a more intimate way, in accordance with the "fundamental assumption" presented by Partee. (Cf. p. 45.)

But the argument seems to me to have little force, since quite generally quantifiers within an embedded sentence are within the scope of "higher" quantifiers, and are in fact bound within the embedded sentence itself. Compare "someone realizes that everyone is here," "everyone knows that Bill caught a fish".[60] Similarly, (13) does not have the meaning of (14):

(13) John said that everyone had left

(14) for every $x$, John said that $x$ had left

From (13), it does not follow that John said that Bill had left, but from (14) it does (assuming that Bill is in the domain of the variable). Thus John may have just seen that the room is empty, knowing that there were people there but not knowing who was there. On the other hand, we can perfectly well relativize an element within a clause: compare (15):

(15) the man that John said that Mary had seen — left

Thus it seems that very different principles are at work. The quantificational property that Rodman notes is a special case of a much more general principle, and the impossibility of relativization within a relative, I believe, also falls under a far more general, but quite different principle, namely, that all transformational rules are restricted to adjacent cyclic nodes.[61] Thus the argument is inconclusive.

---

[60] Judgments tend to vary (particularly with certain "higher verbs" such as "think," "guess," which can sometimes be used more or less as "sentence operators"), but I do not think that the situation is essentially different in the case of relative clauses.

[61] See my "Conditions on transformations." [The third essay in this book.]

Still the kind of argument that Rodman suggests is quite important. Implicit in his argument is the correct and important assumption that the significance of any linguistic theory will lie in its explanatory power. There is little doubt that a fair degree of descriptive adequacy over a broad class of cases can be attained in many different ways. Clearly, the serious questions concerning linguistic theory turn on the possibility of providing general explanations for the arrangement of data.

A number of proposals have been put forth as to why grammars have certain types of rules, not others, or why there are certain conditions on rules, or why languages seem to select among a narrow class of syntactic devices to perform certain functions, or why a certain variety of modes of expression is available in natural language. In some cases, explanations have been suggested on semantic grounds.[62] This is, in general, an important line of investigation. Just as the formal devices of language will surely have semantic import, so it might be expected that certain more general constraints on possible formal grammars will have some kind of functional analogue or perhaps explanation. Again, it is worth emphasizing that the results will be interesting when they establish "biological possibility," and do not simply follow from considerations of logical possibility. Whatever the results of such investigation may be, they do not bear on the issue we have been discussing, the absolute autonomy thesis.

I have by no means exhausted the arguments in the literature, but this is, I think, a good sample.[63] It seems to me fair to conclude that although there are, no doubt, systematic form–meaning connections, nevertheless the

---

[62] See, for example, Edward L. Keenan, "Logical expressive power and syntactic variation in natural language," E. L. Keenan, ed., *Formal Semantics of Natural Language*, Cambridge Univ. Press, 1975. For some remarks bearing on the semantic function of the variety of linguistic devices, see Michael Dummett, *Frege: Philosophy of Language*, Duckworth, 1973, chapter 2.

[63] I have not discussed the question of lexical decomposition, which has given rise to quite a considerable literature. I think that the problems in the attempt to introduce lexical items by transformation of more abstract underlying structures are severe, and the arguments against such an approach, quite persuasive. See my *Studies on Semantics in Generative Grammar*, chapter 3, Mouton, 1972, for some discussion; also, J. A. Fodor, "Three reasons for not deriving 'kill' from 'cause to die'," *Linguistic Inquiry*, 1970, no. 1. On the matter of the status of selectional features, see also the references of footnote 38. The empirical questions at stake in connection with the autonomy thesis were a matter of serious concern from the outset of work in transformational generative grammar, and for this reason detailed considerations of selection were avoided, where possible, in the attempt to justify transformations (in contrast, such considerations were at the core of the argument in Harris's theory of transformations; see Z.S. Harris "Cooccurrence and transformations in linguistic structure." *Language* 33, 283–340, 1957). Thus it was argued that to justify postulating the passive transformation it would suffice for a grammar to be able to distinguish proper from abstract nouns, or perhaps even singular from plural (see *Syntactic Structures*, pp. 78–79), and it seems reasonable to expect at least such features to be explicable within the domain of formal grammar (which is not to deny that they have semantic import, along with other concepts of this domain). In

theory of formal grammar has an internal integrity and has its distinct structures and properties, as Jespersen suggested. It seems to me reasonable to adopt the working hypothesis that the structures of formal grammar are generated independently, and that these structures are associated with semantic interpretations by principles and rules of a broader semiotic theory. The hypothesis has led to the discovery of principles of considerable generality and explanatory power concerning the form and organization of rules and the conditions under which they apply, and it is — and could only be — justified by this consequence.

In discussing the notion "related word," I mentioned one respect in which the absolute thesis might be qualified. Namely, in evaluating a formal grammar it seems reasonable to consider the complexity of the characterization of sets of related words in terms of semantic primitives. Similar considerations may apply elsewhere in grammar as well. Thus where one term of the structural condition of a transformation is a lexical category, the transformation may be sensitive to the choice of lexical items within this category. Where this is the case, formal grammar can only resort to the device of "rule features," that is, an arbitrary bifurcation of the lexicon in terms of applicability of the transformation to items of the lexical category that "governs" the transformation,[64] or some graded notion.[65] In any such case, we might hope that the syntactically arbitrary feature can be given some semantic characterization, and that the complexity of this characterization in terms of core notions of semantics (say, Katzian semantic markers) might be a factor in choice of grammar. If this proves to be the case in general, we can take the arbitrary syntactic features to be, in effect, parameters to be determined elsewhere, thus

the case of categories of this sort, at least, it seems that selection is related to the heads of noun phrases. Thus in the expression *"the boy who was turned by magic into a swarm of bees will soon disperse," it is the selectional relation of "disperse" to "boy" that determines the status of the utterance (correspondingly, we take the noun phrase to be referring to the boy, not to what the boy now is, viz., a swarm of bees). Since lexical properties of deep structure configurations, not compositionally determined readings, are involved in such selectional relations, it is not clear whether there is any substance to the dispute as to whether these relations are syntactic or semantic. See my *Aspects of the Theory of Syntax*, pp. 154f.

[64] See George Lakoff, *Irregularity in Syntax*, Holt, Rinehart and Winston, 1970.
[65] For example, consider the passives of structures of the form NP – V + Particle – NP. The "lexicizability" of the Verb + Particle determines the acceptability of such passives. See my *Aspects of the Theory of Syntax*, pp. 217–219. A full analysis of "lexicizability," in the appropriate sense, might involve factors of various sorts. From this fact, one obviously cannot conclude that it is necessary to recast the notion "grammatical transformation" as a mapping on semantically interpreted structures, as has been suggested. Rather, the proper move is to retain the familiar theory of transformations, and to define "lexicizability" as required; the resulting theory is far more constrained in expressive power than an alternative in which transformations are defined on semantically interpreted structures. As in other cases mentioned here, the problems seem localizable to the dictionary.

rejecting the absolute autonomy thesis in favor of a parametrized theory of the sort discussed earlier. As noted before, it seems quite possible that the "openness" of the theory of formal grammar might be localized in the dictionary, just as it seems plausible to make the same proposal in the case of the idealization of "grammar" in the first place.

Further clarification of these rather murky empirical questions can only come from careful investigation of specific linguistic theories and the grammars constructed in accordance with their principles. As noted earlier, it is here that the most important questions lie. I cannot possibly survey here the many different ways in which this question is being investigated in current work. It need hardly be stressed that there are many open questions, and that one can reach only the most tentative conclusions as to which (if any) of these approaches will prove to be correct as research progresses.

At the moment, it seems to me that the so-called "extended standard theory" offers the most promise for dealing with these questions in a satisfactory way. This theory postulates that the syntactic component of formal grammar contains base rules of two types: context-free rules of the "categorial component" and rules of the lexicon, including "lexical transformations" that introduce lexical items into configurations generated by the categorial component. The latter may be narrowly constrained, I think, as a "projection" from the category features $[\pm N]$, $[\pm V]$ (and further subfeatures) by general schemata. Base-generated structures are associated with surface structures by transformational rules. There are certain well-formedness conditions on surface structures. Base-generated structures associated with well-formed surface structures we may call "deep structures." There is, I think, good evidence that one central element in semantic interpretation is determined by deep structures and the lexical items that appear in them,[66] namely, "thematic relations" such as Agent, Goal, Instrument, and so on. One can look forward, I think, to a convergence of proposals of Katz, Gruber, Fillmore, Jackendoff, Davidson and others in this domain. Apart from thematic relations, it seems to me that semantic interpretation relates only to surface structure, or perhaps to what Postal has called "shallow structure." If so, we may assume that thematic relations are "carried over" under transformation, so that surface structure, in this extended sense, completely determines semantic interpretation, including matters of anaphora, scope, presuppo-

[66] Some of these may be introduced into the positions relevant to determining thematic relations by rules of the grammar that raise them from embedded structures; this will be the case, for example, if we adopt the analysis of relatives cited in footnote 49, suggested originally (to my knowledge) by Michael Brame. See Vergnaud, *op. cit.*, and the references cited there, particularly Paul Schachter, "Focus and relativization," *Language* 49, 19–46, 1973.

sition, predication, topic and focus, illocutionary force, and perhaps more. Under the trace theory of movement rules, which seems to me well-motivated, a surface structure is in some respects similar to a logical formula with bound variables.[67] We might, then, loosely think of a transformational grammar from a semantic point of view as a mapping of a structure of thematic relations onto a kind of "logical form." A crucial issue, from this point of view, is the nature of semantic constraints on well-formedness of surface structure (see above, pp. 50–51, for one example). Recent work, which I cannot review here,[68] suggests that a number of the important open questions and problems in the theory of transformational grammar may be resolved by such considerations.

Whether this or one of the other approaches now being actively pursued proves to be correct, I think it is fair to say that the work of recent years tends generally to support the basic ideas that Jespersen outlined 50 years ago, and extends and advances the program that he outlined. The relation between notional and syntactic categories is, by now, a major topic of investigation in the study of language, and hardly a day goes by without some new and provocative ideas and insights, deriving from several points of view. Many intriguing questions are on the agenda, and the prospects for substantial progress in our understanding of these questions seem very bright.

[67] For discussion see the references of footnotes 28, 49, 51, and 57.
[68] See Robert Fiengo, *Semantic Conditions on Surface Structures*, Ph.D. dissertation, M.I.T., 1974.

# On the Nature of Language

# On the Nature of Language*

Imagine a creature so magnificently endowed as to be in a position to regard humans rather in the way that we regard fruit flies. Faced with the problem of determining the nature of language, this creature might exploit a variety of means. It might undertake the study of genetic mutations or intrusive experimentation of various sorts. Or, it might investigate the variation in knowledge of language attained as experience available is experimentally controlled. Under the latter approach, the genetically determined human language faculty, which specifies the nature of language, is considered as a function associating knowledge attained with experience available. Taking the "grammar of a language" to be a representation of the knowledge attained, or at least a fundamental component of such knowledge, the language faculty may be regarded as a fixed function, characteristic of the species, one component of the human mind, a function which maps experience into grammar. The method of concomitant variation is a natural way to study such a function directly.

We may construe a general linguistic theory or a theory of "universal grammar" as a hypothesis concerning this acquisition function. A priori, one might imagine a range of possibilities. Thus it might be that "generalized learning strategies" involving procedures of induction, analogy, and generalization in some dimensional system exhaust the contents of the language faculty. Or, the course of

---

* This article is reprinted with permission from the New York Academy of Sciences and the editor of Annals of the New York Academy of Sciences, Vol. 280, *Origin and Evolution of Language and Speech,* in which it originally appeared.

language acquisition might reflect cognitive growth in other domains, say, constructions of "sensori-motor intelligence." It has been proposed in the past that "taxonomic" procedures of iterated segmentation and classification suffice to determine the grammar of particular languages and thus express "the nature of language."

Alternatively, one might argue that languages have a partially determinate structure as a matter of biological necessity, much as the general character of bodily organs is fixed for the species. Such structure must therefore be spelled out in the theory of the language faculty. The theory of distinctive features is perhaps the most familiar case. It has been proposed that a certain set of features are available in principle for phonetic representation; each language must make its selection from among these, observing certain implicational principles governing such systems. Cf. Jakobson, Fant, and Halle (1963) and much subsequent work. The theory of distinctive features can be regarded as a hypothesis concerning the acquisition function for language. In my view, work of the past years has provided considerable support for a conception of the language faculty along these lines, as a schematism that narrowly constrains the form of the grammar attained, rather than a system of generalized inductive and taxonomic procedures for acquiring knowledge. Thus it seems to me not unreasonable to approach the study of language as we would the study of some organ of the body.

Suppose that a hypothesis is advanced asserting that grammars must have the property $P$; that is, having the property $P$ results from the structure of the language faculty itself rather than from experience, though relevant experience may be required to "trigger" the proper growth and functioning of a system with the property $P$. In principle, the hypothesis might be tested in various ways, say, by designing an environment neutral with regard to $P$, and determining whether grammars invariably have the property $P$ rather than not-$P$, no less compatible with presented experience, in such an environment. Or, one might design an environment with experience inconsistent with $P$ to verify the prediction that the language violating $P$ is not learned under normal conditions of time and access to data, or used with normal facility, and so on.

Of course, no such course of inquiry is available to humans investigating human language. Part of the intellectual fascination of the study of human language derives from the fact that it is often necessary to devise intricate and complex arguments to support, or reject, the hypothesis that grammars must meet some condition $P$ as a matter of biological necessity. This unavoidable contingency of inquiry in no way deprives the study of language of its empirical character, though it does bear on the force and persuasiveness of particular empirical theories.

Given the actual conditions of inquiry, a natural line of argument is the following. Suppose we find that a particular language has the property $P$; that is, speakers' judgments and other behavior conform to $P$ where clear and reliable, constructions violating $P$ are rejected, and so on. Suppose, furthermore, that $P$ is sufficiently abstract and evidence bearing on it sufficiently sparse and contrived so that it is implausible to suppose that all speakers, or perhaps any speakers, might have been trained or taught to observe $P$ or might have constructed grammars satisfying $P$ by induction from experience. Then it is plausible to postulate that $P$ is a property of the language faculty, that languages conform to $P$ as a matter of biological necessity. We are assuming, then, that the environment—which we cannot control—is neutral with respect to $P$, and we seek properties for which this assumption is plausible.

A familiar and very simple example of this kind of reasoning concerns the property of "structure-dependence" of linguistic rules. In this case, the argument, which I will not review (cf. Chomsky (1965; 1975b)), seems to me quite compelling, and there is a theory of linguistic rules with other virtues as well that accounts for the facts. Thus the argument is that the structure-dependent property of rules is not something that has to be learned, but is a precondition of learning. The language faculty requires that rules be formulated in these terms, though for an organism differently designed a system violating this principle could serve the functions of language no less well.

Note that in such cases as these we may plausibly postulate that $P$ is a property of universal grammar on the basis of investigation of a single language. There is no paradox here. The argument rests on the alleged fact that something is known without relevant experience so that knowledge must be attributed to the language faculty itself, a faculty common to the species. Deep analysis of a single language may provide the most effective means for discovering nontrivial properties of universal grammar.

Of course, the argument is nondemonstrative and is therefore open to refutation by broader inquiry into the same language or other languages. Consider the following case, patterned on the familiar argument concerning structure-dependence of rules.

We find in English two kinds of relative clauses, restrictive and nonrestrictive. In (1), the italicized relative clause is restrictive; in (2), nonrestrictive:

(1)    People *who go to MIT* like math.
(2)    John, *who goes to MIT,* likes math.

These two types of relatives have quite different syntactic and semantic properties. In particular, restrictives can "stack," giving such sentences as (3), whereas nonrestrictives cannot, so that (4) is ruled out:

(3)    People who go to MIT who like math will get jobs.
(4)    John, who goes to MIT, who likes math, will get a job.

It seems implausible that all people capable of these distinctions have sufficient confirmatory evidence to establish the principle governing stacking of relatives. Following the line of argument just outlined, it is therefore reasonable to postulate that as a property of universal grammar, biologically necessary, nonrestrictive relatives cannot stack.

Reasonable, but apparently incorrect. It seems that in Korean and Japanese, for example, such sentences as (4) are quite acceptable. Therefore the hypothesis, though reasonable, is untenable.

Bearing in mind that experience to ground the distinction between (3) and (4) does not seem generally available, we might propose a more abstract hypothesis. Perhaps some other linguistic property, which must itself be learned, determines whether nonrestrictives can stack by virtue of a general principle of universal grammar. We observe, for example, that Korean and Japanese do not distinguish two types of relatives, restrictive and nonrestrictive, and that speakers of these languages often find difficulty in discerning the difference of sense. Cf. Kuno (1973) and Andrews (1975). We might therefore postulate that in languages that distinguish two types of relatives, restrictive and nonrestrictive, only restrictives can stack. We are postulating, then, that the language learner must determine from experience whether the language to which he is exposed distinguishes restrictives and nonrestrictives. Given this information, he can appeal to a general principle of universal grammar to establish which relatives can stack, without any experience with stacked relatives. He need not be taught that (4) is excluded and (3) grammatical. Rather, given that English regularly distinguishes (1) from (2), it follows by a general principle that it excludes (4). The conclusion is reasonable, since otherwise we would be hard put to explain why people do not generalize from the stacked relative (3) to the stacked nonrestrictive (4). I note in passing that other learned properties of the language might be suggested as the key to bringing a general principle to bear, in this case.

Our new, more abstract hypothesis is no less empirical than the earlier, simpler one. We know just what evidence would refute or confirm it. Though the direct test of controlling the environment is excluded, we may nevertheless search for relevant evidence among the existing languages or in observation of language acquisition, and perhaps in other ways.

Pursuing a similar line of argument, we may seek universal conditions in any domain of grammar. Suppose, say, that some principle of rule ordering serves to explain some phonetic properties of English. Then — particularly if the evidence is "exotic" — we may reasonably propose that the principle belongs to universal grammar, and then ask whether this conclusion is supported by further inquiry into English and other languages. We will not be surprised to discover, again, that a learned property of language determines when and how the universal principle is applied.

Or, consider the domain of interaction of syntax and semantics. It seems to be a property of certain types of common nouns that they can be used with either abstract or concrete reference. Consider the sentences (5) and (6):

(5)   John wrote a book.
(6)   The book weighs 5 pounds.

In (5), the reference of *book* is abstract. Thus, John may have written the book in his head, committing nothing to paper, but (5) would still be appropriate. Or, if there are two copies of the book before me, I may say of each, "John wrote this book," but I do not conclude that John wrote two books. In contrast, the reference of *book* in (6) is concrete. A specific material object weighs 5 pounds. If a hardcover and paperback copy of the book that John wrote lie before me, I may say that this book weighs 5 pounds and that book, 3 pounds.

We have here what appears to be a systematic ambiguity over a certain category of words, as distinct from the idiosyncratic ambiguity of such words as English *trunk,* which may refer to an oversized suitcase or an appendage of an elephant. Typically, in such cases of systematic ambiguity, we can combine the two senses in a relative construction, as in (7) or (8):

(7)   a.   John wrote a book that weighs 5 pounds.
        b.   The book that John wrote weighs 5 pounds.

(8)  a.  John wrote a book, which weighs 5 pounds.
     b.  This book, which John wrote, weighs 5 pounds.

Such combinations are excluded in other cases of ambiguity. For example, in sentence (9), the phrase *flying planes* may be construed as referring to objects that fly, which are dangerous, or to the act of piloting, which is dangerous:

(9)  Flying planes can be dangerous.

In this case, the ambiguity of *flying planes* is syntactically ·determined, not a general property of phrases with a certain semantic function or character. In this case, of course, we cannot combine the two senses in a relative construction. Sentence (10) is excluded, and in (11), we must construe the head of the relative to be *planes* rather than *flying planes*:

(10)    *Flying planes, which is a nuisance, are dangerous.
(11)     Flying planes, which are a nuisance, is dangerous.

   In general, relativization seems to be free in the case of systematic ambiguity, as in (7) and (8). Consider, for example, such words as "temperature" which designate functions of some sort. Thus we can say (12), meaning that the function is increasing over a certain interval including the present:

(12)  The temperature is rising rapidly.

But such terms can typically be used also to designate a value of the function at a given time and place, as in (13):

(13)  The temperature was 70° here at sunrise.

There are problems in determining the meaning of such expressions; cf. Chomsky (1975a, note 12) and Hacking (1975). But again we find that the two senses can be combined, as in (14):

(14)  The temperature, which was 70° here at sunrise, is rising rapidly.

   Presumably the systematic ambiguity of words such as *book, temperature,* and others (cf. Chomsky (1972, pp. 19f) for some

68

examples) is determined in the lexicon, perhaps by means explored in Katz (1972) or Jackendoff (1972). Thus, we have a single formal element with a fixed range of meaning, and relativization is possible, despite a shift of sense. But in the case of *flying planes* (syntactically determined ambiguity) or *trunk* (idiosyncratic ambiguity) we have two formal elements, in each case, with the same phonetic form. Relativization is impossible in such cases.

One might imagine that the constraint has something to do with "semantic incoherence" or the like, but this is far from clear. Notice that nonrestrictives have a sense rather like conjunction. Thus the pairs (a) and (b) of (15)–(17) are close in meaning:

(15) a.  John, who goes to MIT, likes math.
     b.  John likes math and John goes to MIT.

(16) a.  The temperature, which was 70°, is rising.
     b.  The temperature is rising and the temperature was 70°.

(17) a.  This book, which John wrote, weighs 5 pounds.
     b.  This book weighs 5 pounds and John wrote this book.

Why, then, does not (18a) have approximately the meaning of (18b), and (19a) approximately the meaning of (19b):

(18) a.  *Flying planes, which is a nuisance, are dangerous.
     b.  Flying planes are dangerous and flying planes is a nuisance.

(19) a.  Jumbo waved his trunk, which was full of clothes.
     b.  Jumbo waved his trunk (of an elephant) and the trunk (container) was full of clothes.

There is nothing incoherent about (18b) and (19b). We might ask, then, why we do not generalize from (15)–(17) to the absurd (18)–(19). It seems that a general principle of syntax–semantics interaction is involved, and again it seems plausible to attribute it to universal grammar, though much remains obscure in this case.

Let me turn now to some more complex cases. Consider the operation of question-formation. A rule of "*wh*-movement" forms the sentence (20) by preposing the *wh*-word of (21):

(20)  Who did John see
(21)  John saw who

We ignore here a number of irrelevant details. The *wh*-word may be deeply embedded, as in (22) deriving from (23):

(22)  Who did Mary believe that Bill wanted her to see
(23)  Mary believed that Bill wanted her to see who

But if the *wh*-word is in a sentence embedded within a noun phrase, it cannot be extracted. Thus we cannot derive (24) from (25):

(24)  Who did Mary believe the claim that John saw
(25)  Mary believed the claim that John saw who

The latter fact follows from a general condition that Ross calls the complex noun phrase constraint (CNPC; cf. Ross (1967)), which implies, in particular, that a word cannot be extracted from a sentence embedded within a noun phrase, to a position outside that noun phrase.

Again, it is difficult to imagine that everyone has received relevant instruction or been exposed to relevant experience. Nor is there any "semantic incoherence" or other similar defect in (24); were it a well-formed sentence, we would know exactly what it means. Thus it seems plausible to attribute CNPC to the language faculty itself. Otherwise, it is hard to see why some, or all speakers would not simply generalize the rule of *wh*-movement to the case of a sentence within a noun phrase.

In this case, the constraint CNPC seems so special and artificial that we might search for some deeper and more natural principle from which it follows. I have argued elsewhere (Chomsky (1973; 1975b)) that we can explain this and other constraints on the assumption that all transformational rules are *bounded* and *cyclic*; that is, they apply within a sentence or noun phrase or across adjacent phrases of the type sentence, noun phrase, but not across more widely separated domains. It can be shown that many crucial instances of CNPC follow from this general principle of rule application if we add an empirical observation: that sentences, but not noun phrases, have a *complementizer* position that can be filled by the *wh*-word or by other words such as *that* (*that John left surprised me*) or *for* (*for John to leave would be a mistake*); cf. Bresnan (1970; 1972).

The explanation is controversial. If it is on the right track, as I believe, it illustrates again the expected interaction between general principles that belong to the language faculty and that determine the nature of language, and specific facts that must be learned. In this case, the general principle is the principle of bounded cyclicity, and the fact that must be learned is that English sentences have a complementizer position that can be filled by a *wh*-word, as in (20), (22), or (26) (from (27)), although we cannot, of course, derive (28) from (29), noun phrases having no complementizers:

(26)  I wonder [who John saw]
(27)  I wonder [COMP John saw who]
(28)  I saw [who John's picture of]
(29)  I saw [John's picture of who]

Let us explore the domain of syntax–semantics interaction a bit further. Consider English reciprocal constructions. We have, basically, two types, as in (30) and (31):

(30)  Each of the men saw the others
(31)  The men saw each other

These seem close to synonymous at first glance. In general, we can replace the pair (*each of the men, the others*) by the pair (*the men, each other*) with little if any change of sense. Such substitution gives (31) from (30) in the context (32):

(32)  . . . saw . . .

But such substitution without change of sense is not always possible. Consider the two discourses (33) and (34):

(33)  Each of the women saw some of the films. Each of the men saw the others.
(34)  Each of the women saw some of the films. The men saw each other.

In (33), the phrase *the others* may refer to the films not seen by the women. In (34), the phrase *each other* must refer to the men. Thus substitution of the pair (*the men, each other*) for (*each of the men, the others*) in (33) radically changes the sense. The point is that the phrase *each other* must have its antecedent within the same sentence, while the phrase *the others* need not. The sentences (30) and (31) may have close to the same meaning, but (30) has a broader range of meaning. The reference of *each other* is fixed by a principle of (sentence-) grammar, but the reference of *the others* is not, though the principle governing it may apply within a sentence.

This distinction has an interesting range of consequences. Consider, for example, the sentence (35):

(35)   Each of the candidates wanted [John to vote for the others]

Suppose that we replace the pair (*each of the candidates, the others*) by the pair (*the candidates, each other*). Then we derive (36):

(36)   The candidates wanted [John to vote for each other]

But (36) is no sentence of English. Again, the problem is not semantic. If compelled to assign it a sense, we would, presumably, select the perfectly sensible (35). We might suppose that the problem is that *each other* must find its antecedent within the same sentential structure, that is, within the brackets in (36). But this condition is too strong, as we can see from (37):

(37)   The candidates wanted [each other to win]

In the sentences (35), (36), and (37), the bracketed phrases are sentential (cf. Bresnan (1972)). But only (35) and (37) are well-formed. (36) is not. It is fair to ask why not. Why does the speaker not generalize, noting that the substitution of phrases is permissible in (30) and (31) or in (38) and (37):

(38)   Each of the candidates wanted [the others to win]

Why is the substitution impermissible in (35), contrary to the natural generalization. It is difficult to believe, again, that this is the result of specific training or experience, in each (or any) case. Language learners are not corrected for such mistakes as (36); nor do they in fact make such mistakes. In fact, relevant examples are rare, and a person might well live most or all of his life without coming across any, though he would make the proper distinctions on first presentation with a relevant example, so it appears.

The answer to the problem, I believe, lies in still another general condition on grammar that I have called elsewhere the specified subject condition (SSC; cf. Chomsky (1973; 1975b)). The condition entails that a phrase $X$ within a phrase $P$ cannot be related to a position outside of $P$ if $P$ contains a subject distinct from $X$ (or, in fact, distinct from the occupant of the outside position, in a well-defined sense; cf. Chomsky (1973; 1975b)). Thus if the bracketed expression in (39) is a *P*, then *Y* cannot be related by rule to *X* if *Z* is the subject of *P*:

(39)   . . . *Y* . . . [ *Z* . . . *X* . . . ]

In (36), *the candidates* is *Y, John* is *Z* and *each other* is *X*. Therefore the rule of reciprocal interpretation cannot apply to the pair (*the candidates, each other*), by SSC. But the principle SSC is a principle of (sentence-) grammar. Therefore it does not apply to the case (35). Similarly, it is inapplicable in (37) because *each other* is itself the embedded subject.

The principle SSC applies much more broadly. Consider again *wh*-movement. We have (40) but not (41):

(40)   Who did you hear stories about
(41)   Who did you hear [John's stories about]

((40) may also be blocked in a style that imposes more stringent conditions on "stranded prepositions," but this is irrelevant here). The reason, I think, is that the bracketed noun phrase of (41) has a subject, *John*, while the phrase *stories about who*, which underlies (40), has no subject. Therefore SSC blocks *wh*-movement in (41), but not (40). We are relying here on a generalization of the notion "subject" of traditional grammar, a generalization which I believe is independently well motivated. Cf. Chomsky (1972). Both this extended notion of "subject" and the general principle SSC are fair candidates for universal grammar. That is, it seems to me quite reasonable to propose that they are determined by the language capacity itself.

Consider one final case, one step more complex. Consider the sentences (42) and (43).

(42)   John seemed to each of the men to like the others.
(43)   *John seemed to the men to like each other.

Here again, substitution of (*the men, each other*) for (*each of the men, the others*) in (42) is impossible. Why is this so?

Notice that the verb *like* in (42) and (43) does not have a subject before it as it does in (44):

(44)   The men wanted [Bill to like each other]

Thus (44) has the form of (39); the rule of reciprocal interpretation is blocked because of the presence of the subject *Bill* (= $Z$ of (39)). But in (43), there is no subject corresponding to *Bill* of (44). Nevertheless, (43) is no more grammatical than (44).

In traditional terms, the verb *like* in (43) does indeed have a subject, namely, an "understood subject." *John* is the "understood subject" of *like* in (43). Apparently, this mentally present but physically absent subject behaves just as the physically present subject *Bill* does in (44), bringing SSC into operation. Thus we may think of (43) as having the abstract structure (45):

(45)    John seemed to the men [$Z$ to like each other]

Here $Z$ is the null subject, interpreted as referring to John. But (45) has the structure (39), so that SSC blocks the reciprocal rule.

Again, there is no logical necessity for a language to be designed in such a way that phonetically null mentally present subjects behave just as physically present subjects do. If language were designed differently, (43) would have approximately the meaning of (42), just as (31) has approximately the meaning of (30) and (37) approximately the meaning of (38). The language would be no less well-designed for communication or expression of thought (for a creature designed to handle this language). Again, a person might live most or all of his life without ever being exposed to relevant evidence (let alone training) that would indicate to him that the natural generalization is (for some reason) blocked in (43). Thus, it seems absurd to claim that experience provides the basis for these judgments. Nor do they seem to be explicable in "functional" terms on grounds of communicative efficiency or the like.

Rather, it seems that once again, the facts reflect a biologically given precondition for learning. The child learning English simply imposes the requirement that mentally present subjects function as though they were physically present. He does this even in the absence of relevant evidence, so it appears. A theory of universal grammar — that is, a theory of the language faculty — must seek an explanation as to why this is so. The answer, I think, lies in the "trace theory of movement rules," which requires that when a phrase is moved by transformation it leaves behind a phonetically null but syntactically real element "trace" that functions semantically as a kind of bound variable. Other rules of syntax and morphology have no way of knowing that this element will (ultimately) be phonetically null. Hence it operates as a specified subject, and in other ways in the system of rules, while playing an essential role in semantic interpretation.

Space does not permit a discussion of syntactic and semantic consequences of the trace theory. Cf. Chomsky (1973; 1975b); Wasow (forthcoming); Fiengo (1974). I will describe briefly a curious phonetic effect of trace, which gives independent evidence that it is syntactically nonnull. Consider the sentences (46), (47), and (48):

(46)  Who do you want to hit
(47)  Who do you want to see Bill
(48)  Who do you want to choose

These derive, respectively, from (49), (50), and (51):

(49)  You want to hit who
(50)  You want who to see Bill
(51)  a. You want who to choose
      b. You want to choose who

Thus (48) is ambiguous as between the two interpretations (51a), (51b).

It has been observed by a number of people that in (46) and sense (51b) of (48), the sequence *want to* can be elided to *wanna*; but this is impossible in (47) or in sense (51a) of (48). Thus consider (52), (53), (54):

(52)  Who do you wanna hit
(53)  Who do you wanna see Bill
(54)  Who do you wanna choose

Sentence (54) can only mean (51b), and (53) is impossible. Why is this so?

Notice that under the trace theory, we have the abstract structures (55), (56), and (57), corresponding to (49), (50), and (51), respectively:

(55)  Who do you want to hit *t*
(56)  Who do you want *t* to see Bill
(57)  a. Who do you want *t* to choose
      b. Who do you want to choose *t*

In each case, *t* is the trace left by *wh*-movement. There is a rule attaching *to* to a preceding occurrence of *want* in certain styles. The resulting phonological word then reduces to *wanna*. Obviously, the rule will not apply if there is intervening lexical material, as in (58):

(58)   John will want Bill to go

For exactly the same reason, the attachment rule will not apply in (56) and (57a). It follows that *wanna* can appear in (46) but not (47), and that when it appears in (48), we know that (48) was derived from (57b) rather than (57a) and therefore means (51b) rather than (51a).

Although the trace is phonetically null, it is syntactically real and enters into the computations that determine the form and meaning of sentences no less than the zero plural of *sheep*. Cf. Selkirk (1972) and Lightfoot (1975) and references cited there. Note that I have not explained why the understood subject of *hit* does not block elision in (46), or the understood subject of *choose* in (51b). Here lies another tale.

The trace theory too is controversial and not without its problems. But it does serve to explain quite a range of apparently unrelated facts and it lays the basis for other promising developments in linguistic theory, I believe. If it proves to be correct, or perhaps to be a special case of a still more adequate theory, then again we will have evidence concerning the intrinsic structure of the language faculty, a species property that fixes the essential nature of language.

Examples such as these only scratch the surface of the problem, needless to say. I offer them to illustrate a certain pattern of argument that has proven quite productive and that offers a great deal of promise for the future as well, in that its potentialities have barely been tapped. We might wish that more direct tests could be devised for hypotheses concerning universal grammar. But even in their absence, strictly linguistic investigation can lead us to some plausible general principles of some subtlety, principles that we may hope to relate to the results of other lines of investigation into the nature of language.

## REFERENCES

Andrews, A. 1975. Studies in the syntax of relative and comparative clauses. Doctoral dissertation, MIT.

Bresnan, J. 1970. On complementizers: towards a syntactic theory. *Foundations of Language* 6: 297–321.

––––––. 1972. The theory of complementizers in english syntax. Doctoral dissertation, MIT.

Chomsky, N. 1965. *Aspects of the Theory of Syntax*. Cambridge, Mass.: MIT Press.

————. 1972. *Studies on Semantics in Generative Grammar*. The Hague: Mouton.

————. 1973. Conditions on transformations. In *A Festschrift for Morris Halle*. S. Anderson and P. Kiparsky, Eds. New York: Holt, Rinehart and Winston. Essay 3, below.

————. 1975a. Questions of form and interpretation. *Linguistic Analysis* 1: 75–109. Essay 1, above.

————. 1975b. *Reflections on Language*. New York: Pantheon.

Fiengo, R. W. 1974. Semantic conditions on surface structure. Doctoral dissertation, MIT.

Hacking, I. 1975. All kinds of possibility. *Philosophical Review* 84(3): 321–37.

Jackendoff, R. S. 1972. *Semantic Interpretation in Generative Grammar*. Cambridge, Mass.: MIT Press.

Jakobson, R., Fant, G., and M. Halle. 1963. *Preliminaries to Speech Analysis*. Cambridge, Mass.: MIT Press.

Katz, J. J. 1972. *Semantic Theory*. New York: Harper & Row.

Kuno, S. 1973. *The Structure of the Japanese Language*. Cambridge, Mass.: MIT Press.

Lightfoot, D. 1975. Traces and doubly moved NPs. Mimeograph, McGill University, Montreal, Quebec.

Ross, J. R. 1967. Constraints on variables in syntax. Doctoral dissertation, MIT.

Selkirk, E. 1972. The phrase phonology of English and French. Doctoral dissertation, MIT.

# Conditions on Transformations

# Conditions on Transformations*,1

**1.** From the point of view that I adopt here, the fundamental empirical problem of linguistics is to explain how a person can acquire knowledge of language. For our purposes, we can think of a language as a set of structural descriptions of sentences, where a full structural description determines (in particular) the sound and meaning of a linguistic expression. Knowledge of a language can be expressed in the form of a system of rules (a grammar) that generates the language. To approach the fundamental empirical problem, we attempt to restrict the class of potential human languages by setting various conditions on the form and function of grammars; the term "universal grammar" has commonly been used to refer to the system of general constraints of this sort. With a narrow and restrictive formulation of the principles of universal grammar, it may become possible to account for the remarkable human ability, on the basis of limited and degenerate evidence, to select a particular grammar that expresses one's knowledge of language and makes possible the use of this knowledge.

For heuristic purposes we may distinguish two aspects of universal grammar: (a) conditions on form, and (b) conditions on function — that is, (a) conditions on the systems that qualify as grammars, and (b) conditions on the way the rules of a grammar apply to generate structural descriptions. In the terminology of Chomsky (1965, Chapter 1) and earlier work, these are, respectively, conditions on the class $G_1, G_2, \ldots$ of admissible grammars and on the function f that assigns the structural description $SD_{f(i,j)}$ to the sentence $S_i$ generated by the grammar $G_j$. The distinction is one of convenience, not

* From *A Festschrift for Morris Halle*. Edited by Stephen R. Anderson and Paul Kiparsky. Copyright © 1973 by Holt, Rinehart and Winston, Inc. Reprinted by permission of publisher and editors.

[1] For very helpful comments on an earlier draft of this paper, I am indebted to Ray Dougherty, Morris Halle, Richard Kayne, and Howard Lasnik, among others. I am indebted to the Guggenheim Foundation for a fellowship grant that enabled me to complete the work presented here.

principle, in the sense that we might choose to deal with particular phenomena under one or the other category of conditions. The distinction might be carried over to particular grammars as well. That is, while it has generally been assumed that particular grammars contain specific rules whereas conditions on the functioning of rules are assigned to universal grammar, there is no logical necessity to make this assumption. It is possible that particular grammars differ in conditions of application, just as it is possible that some specific rules actually belong to universal grammar.[2]

To illustrate, we can consider the enumeration of distinctive features or the specification of the form of phonological rules to be conditions of the first sort, that is, conditions on the form of grammars. Or consider the definition of a grammatical transformation as a structure-dependent mapping of phrase markers into phrase markers that is independent of the grammatical relations or meanings expressed in these grammatical relations. This definition makes certain operations available as potential transformations, excluding others. Thus an operation converting an arbitrary string of symbols into its mirror image is not a grammatical transformation, and transformations generally apply to phrase markers that meet some condition on analyzability with no regard to other associated properties.

To take a standard example, the Passive transformation (reducing it to essentials) applies to any phrase marker that can be "factored" into five successive substrings in such a way that the second and fourth are noun phrases, the third a verb of a particular category (perhaps determined by some semantic property), and the first and fifth anything at all (including nothing). Thus the structural condition defining the transformation can be given in the form $(Z, NP, V_x, NP, Y)$. The transformation rearranges the noun phrases in a fixed way. It will, therefore, apply to the phrase markers underlying the sentences of (1), converting them to the corresponding passive forms:

(1) a. Perhaps–John–read–the book–intelligently
  b. John–received–the book
  c. John–regards–Bill–as a friend
  d. John–painted–the wall–gray
  e. John–expects–the food–to be good to eat

Evidently, the semantic and grammatical relation of the main verb

---

[2] For discussion of limited generality of conditions, see Ross (1967), Chomsky (1968), and Postal (1971).

to the following noun phrase varies in these examples (there is no relation at all in (e)), but these relations are of no concern to the transformation, which applies blindly in all cases, producing *Perhaps the book was read intelligently by John, The book was received by John, Bill is regarded as a friend by John, The wall was painted gray by John, The food is expected to be good to eat by John.* By requiring that all transformations be structure-dependent in this specific sense, we limit the class of possible grammars, excluding many imaginable systems.

I will presuppose here, without further discussion, a set of additional conditions on the form of grammar constituting what I have called the "extended standard theory" (see Chomsky (1970b; 1972a)). Other conditions on the choice of possible transformations that also seem to me plausible and suggestive, if controversial, are outlined in Emonds (1970).[3]

The conditions on the form of grammar mentioned so far are quite abstract and still permit much too wide a range of potential grammars. One might therefore look for much more specific restrictions. An example, to which I return, is the "Complementizer Substitution Universal" in (2):[4]

(2)  Only languages with clause-initial COMP permit a COMP-substitution transformation.

This principle presupposes that COMP is a universal element that may appear in various sentence positions and asserts that an item can be moved into COMP position only when COMP is initial. In particular, "*wh*-words" — the relativized constituents in relative clauses or questioned constituents in interrogatives — can be moved only to the left, such movement being permitted only when there is an initial COMP in the phrase to which the transformation is being applied.

It would be quite natural to explore further along these lines. Thus one might try to enumerate "major transformations" such as Question Formation, Imperative, and so on from which languages may draw, with some permitted variation and minor "housekeeping rules" (Bach (1965; 1971)). It may well be that transformations fall into various categories meeting quite different conditions. By constructing

---

[3] As already noted, the distinction between conditions on form and conditions on function is, in part, one of convenience. Thus Emonds' constraints could be formulated as conditions on the applicability of arbitrarily chosen transformations.

[4] J. Bresnan's reformulation (1970) of L. Baker's "Q-Universal" (Baker (1970)).

a more intricate, more highly articulated theory of grammar in such ways as these, we can perhaps move toward a solution of the fundamental empirical problem.

A second approach attempts to constrain the functioning of grammatical rules and thereby to limit the generative power of grammars of a given form. The earliest suggestions appear in Chomsky (1964)[5] (namely, the condition of "Recoverability of Deletion,"[6] the *A*-over-*A* Condition," and so on). Another example, to which I will return, is the Insertion Prohibition suggested in Chomsky (1965), which prevents transformations from inserting morphological material into sentences that have already been passed in the cycle. Many examples are discussed in a very important study by Ross (1967), where a number of specific conditions are proposed. These conditions are formulated in such a way as to restrict severely the operation of the rules of grammars while not affecting their form. Thus such conditions contribute toward a solution of the fundamental empirical problem.[7]

In this paper I want to consider conditions on the functioning of grammars once again, specifically, conditions on how transformations apply. As noted, I assume here the general framework of the extended standard theory and, in particular, the lexicalist theory of base structures and nominals discussed in Chomsky (1970a). The work leading to the extended standard theory suggested constraints on base structures and on the relations between derivations and semantic representations but said little about transformations. Here, I will explore some conditions on the application of transformations within the framework of the extended standard theory.

As an example of a possible condition on transformations, consider

---

[5] This work appears in three versions, which differ in their treatment of these problems. The first is in H. G. Lunt, ed. (1964), *Proceedings of the Ninth International Congress of Linguists, 1962,* The Hague: Mouton; the second is in J. A. Fodor and J. J. Katz, eds. (1964), *Structure of Language,* Englewood Cliffs, N.J.: Prentice-Hall; the third is listed in the bibliography. A further revision, in lectures given at Berkeley in January, 1967, appears in Chomsky (1968).

[6] On the difficulty of defining this properly and the importance of the issue, see Peters and Ritchie (1973).

[7] Another approach toward solving this problem would be to refine the evaluation measure for grammars. As explained in Chomsky (1965), it seems to me that only limited progress is likely along these lines. It has been suggested in recent work that no evaluation measures are necessary, and this is surely a logical possibility (see Chomsky (1965, pp. 36–37)). Those who offer this suggestion, however, typically propose theories of grammar that make infinitely many grammars available compatible with any imaginable data, so that an evaluation measure is necessary in these cases. The point is, I suspect, that "natural" evaluation measures are generally presupposed, without analysis.

the "*A*-over-*A*" principle, stated in (3):[8]

(3) If a transformation applies to a structure of the form

$$[_\alpha \ldots [_A \ldots ] \ldots ]$$

where $\alpha$ is a cyclic node, then it must be so interpreted as to apply to the maximal phrase of the type $A$.

Consider again the Passive transformation with a structural condition imposing a factorization into $(X, NP, V, NP, Y)$. So formulated, the rule would apply to the examples in (4), with the factorization indicated by –, giving the impossible forms in (5):

(4) a. John and–Bill–saw–Mary
  b. The man who saw–Mary–bought–the book
  c. John's winning–the race–surprised–me

(5) a. *John and Mary was seen by Bill
  b. *The man who saw the book was bought by Mary
  c. *John's winning I was surprised by the race

But the misapplication of the rule in these cases is blocked by the *A*-over-*A* Condition (3). This principle requires that *John and Bill, the man who saw Mary,* and *John's winning the race* are the factors selected by the first NP in the structural condition of the Passive in the case of (a), (b), and (c), respectively.

Notice that the condition (3) does not establish an absolute prohibition against transformations that extract a phrase of type $A$ from a more inclusive phrase of type $A$. Rather, it states that if a transformational rule is nonspecific with respect to the configuration defined, it will be interpreted in such a way as to satisfy the condition. Thus it would be possible to formulate a (more complex) rule with a structural condition imposing the factorization indicated by – in (4); such a rule might extract *Bill, Mary,* and *the race,* respectively. Alternatively, one might interpret the *A*-over-*A* constraint as legislating against any rule that extracts a phrase of type $A$ from a more inclusive phrase $A$. The former interpretation, which in effect takes the *A*-over-*A* Condition to be an integral part of an evaluation measure, is perhaps more natural, and I will adopt it tentatively here, for this and other conditions to be discussed. Thus the *A*-over-*A* Condition as

---

[8] This is the formulation in Chomsky (1968), where a number of examples and problems are discussed. We may assume here that the cyclic nodes are S and NP.

interpreted here does not prevent the application of *wh*-Movement to form (6) from (7), or the application of Pseudo-Cleft Formation to form (8) from (9), or the application of Conjunct Movement to form (10) from (11):[9]

(6) Who would you approve of my seeing
(7) You would approve of [my seeing who][10]
(8) The only person John admires is himself
(9) [The only person [John admires himself]] is Predicate
(10) John met Bill
(11) [John and Bill] met

In contrast, we interpret the Complementizer Substitution Universal (2) as imposing an absolute restriction against rules that move an item to the right to a COMP position. But the *A*-over-*A* principle, rather than legislating against the existence of certain rules, permits an ambiguous and unspecific formulation of such rules as Passive, constraining their application in a specific way. The logic of this approach is essentially that of the theory of markedness.

Suppose that we were to formulate the Passive with the structural condition (12):

(12) $(X, NP, VY, NP, Z)$

Then the rule will apply to either of the italicized noun phrases in (13) to give (14a) or (14b):

(13) PRO took *advantage* of *Bill*
(14) a. Advantage was taken of Bill
      b. Bill was taken advantage of

The *A*-over-*A* Condition does not prevent the desired ambiguous application in this case. The same formulation of Passive[11] permits "pseudo-passives" such as *The plan was argued about all day* and *The brat insists on being given in to*. For this formulation of the rule

---

[9] In principle. On the dubious status of this rule, see Dougherty (1970).

We will return briefly to such examples as (6) and (8).

[10] The impossibility of *Whose would you approve of seeing John* from *You would approve of whose seeing John* can perhaps be attributed to a principle that requires that if the specifier of a noun phrase or adjective phrase (in the sense of Chomsky (1970a)) is extracted, then the whole phrase must be extracted: thus the same principle would prevent the formation of *Which did you see books* from *You saw which books*, or *How is John tall* from *John is how tall*. See Ross (1967) for relevant discussion.

[11] Again, oversimplified, overlooking auxiliaries, the agent phrase, and the composite nature of the rule discussed in Chomsky (1970a). Using the terminology suggested there, the structural condition should contain a term after the first NP which can be an arbitrary sequence of specifiers.

to apply correctly, it is necessary to add the condition that the third term in the factorization (12) be a semantic unit. For example, the sentence *England was lived in by many people* is more natural than *England was died in by many people*, but only when *live in* is interpreted as "reside" and not as in "we really lived in England" in the sense of "in England, we really lived."[12]

Quite generally, the terms of the structural condition of a transformation are either variables or single nonterminals, the case in question being one of the rare exceptions. A single nonterminal is a semantic unit — it has a "reading," in the sense of Katz and others. Thus we might consider the general condition (15):

(15)  Each factor imposed by a transformation either is a morphological or semantic unit or corresponds to a variable in the structural condition of the transformation.

This condition, along with the *A*-over-*A* Condition (3), permits Passive to be formulated with the structural condition (12), constraining the application of the rule properly in quite a range of cases.

**2.** To pursue the matter further, let us assume (following, in essentials, Bresnan (1970)) that there is a universal element COMP and that the base system of English includes the rules in (16):[13]

$$(16) \quad \text{a.} \quad S \rightarrow \text{COMP NP} \begin{Bmatrix} \text{T(M)} \\ \textit{(for)-to} \\ \textit{'s-ing} \end{Bmatrix} \text{VP}$$

b.  COMP → P NP ±WH

We assume that the NP or P NP of COMP can be replaced by the *wh*-phrase of questions and relatives (Emonds' structure-preserving

---

[12] See Chomsky (1965, pp. 104, 218). Recall that although transformations are independent of grammatical or semantic relations, they do, of course, reflect properties of lexical items and lexical categories.

[13] More precisely, these "rules" may be factored into several rules that provide intermediate structures that need not concern us here. Much of what we shall suggest will hold under certain other assumptions about English grammar as well; I give these, without further justification, for concreteness. In (16), P stands for "Preposition," T for "Tense," M for "Modal"; and *to* and *ing* are the items that appear (excluding tense and modal), respectively, in *for him to remain is a nuisance, his remaining is a nuisance* (where *for* and possessive, respectively, are assigned to the accompanying noun phrases, the presence of *for* depending on the main verb). We may assume that one realization of M is the element *subjunctive* discussed in Culicover (1971) in his analysis of imperatives and related structures (and thus subjunctives are assumed here to be tensed). We return to some more specific rules later.

hypothesis determines which of these positions is filled). Following Baker (1970), I assume that +WH (essentially, his "Q") underlies direct and indirect questions, while −WH underlies relatives.[14] We impose the condition that no lexical item can be inserted into COMP by base rules; that is, we require that the terminal string dominated by COMP in the base is null. If a −WH COMP is not filled by a *wh*-phrase, it will optionally be realized as *that* (otherwise null) if the auxiliary contains Tense. We may assume that *whether* derives from *wh*-Placement on *either* and *wh*-Movement (see Katz and Postal (1964)) and that free relatives such as *I read what he gave me* derive from full relatives with unspecified heads (*I read* [NP PRO[s *he gave me it*]] — see Bresnan (1972) for a detailed analysis). Further details and appropriate rules will be given as we proceed.

Let us return to the Passive transformation which, reduced to essentials, applies to a phrase marker of the form NP–V–NP–*X*, rearranging the NP's. Consider the sentence (17):

(17)   I believe the dog is hungry.

This can be analyzed into the successive substrings *I, believe, the dog, is hungry*, which are NP, V, NP, *X*, respectively, so that the transformation should yield *\*The dog is believed is hungry* (*by me*). In exactly the same way, the sentence *The dog is believed to be hungry* (*by me*) derives from (18), with the analysis indicated:

(18)   [s [NP I] [VP [V believe] [s [NP the dog] [VP to be hungry]]]]

Notice that there is no problem in explaining why the Passive transformation, with its domain defined in terms of a structural condition on phrase markers in the conventional way, applies to (18); the problem, rather, is to explain why it does not apply to (17).[15]

---

[14] Presumably, either may underlie nominal complements, as in *the idea that S, the question whether S*. Conditions for *wh*-Movement vary slightly, particularly in appositive clauses. See Postal (1971, pp. 71–72) for some discussion.

[15] Under any formulation of the theory of transformations so far proposed, it would require an extra condition on the transformation to exclude (18) from the domain of the Passive with the structural condition (*X*, NP, V, NP, *Y*). One might imagine a different theory in which the domain of a transformation is defined not by a structural condition of the familiar sort but rather by a condition on grammatical relations: thus "Passive" in this theory might be defined not in terms of the structural condition (*X*, NP, V, NP, *Y*), but in terms of the total configuration which expresses subject and object as relational terms. Under this revised theory, Passive would not apply to (18) unless the configuration were modified by a transformation raising the subject of the embedded sentence to the object position in the matrix sentence. There is, however, no empirical

The most obvious distinction between (17) and (18) is that the embedded sentence in (17) is tensed (finite) while the corresponding sentence of (18) is nontensed. Suppose, then, that we propose the tentative principle in (19):

(19)   Items cannot be extracted from tensed sentences.

The principle of Insertion Prohibition mentioned earlier states that morphological material cannot be inserted into sentences that have been passed in the cycle. If, in fact, Insertion Prohibition is restricted to tensed sentences, we can generalize (19) to incorporate this principle.

Let us restrict our attention initially to rules of extraction that move an item to the left (as in the case of Passive) and to rules of insertion that move an item from the left into an embedded phrase. With this restrictive assumption, we can generalize (19) to (20), incorporating the Insertion Prohibition; we henceforth refer to (20) as the "Tensed-S Condition":[16]

(20)   No rule can involve $X, Y$ in the structure

$$\ldots X \ldots [_\alpha \ldots Y \ldots ] \ldots$$

where $\alpha$ is a tensed sentence.

To understand the application of the Insertion Prohibition as a special case of this principle, consider the sentences in (21):

(21) a.   The candidates each hated the other(s)
     b.   The candidates each expected the other(s) to win
     c.   The candidates each expected that the other(s) would win

---

motivation for such a revision of the theory of transformations. It would, furthermore, be ill-advised in the case of Passive because of pseudo-passives (see the discussion following (14)), double passives such as (14), indirect object constructions, and so on.

Note that COMP will not block factorization of (18) in accordance with the structural condition of the Passive transformation if the terminal string dominated by COMP is null, as we have assumed.

[16] A weaker assumption would be that $\alpha$ is a language-specific parameter in the condition. In this exploratory study I will do no more than suggest a number of possibilities and investigate their consequences in English.

Notice that one rule that obviously does not satisfy the condition is Coreference Assignment (however it is formulated). Thus the pronoun can be anaphoric in *John said that he would leave*, for example. The same rule also applies within coordinate structures (for example, *John said that he and Bill would leave*) and others that block various other types of rules.

Dougherty (1970) has argued that such a sentence as *The men hated each other* derives from *The men each hated the other(s)* (ultimately, from *Each of the men hated the other one(s)*) by a rule that moves *each* into the determiner position in *the other(s)*.[17] Assuming this, note that the sentences of (21) should be transformed into those of (22):

(22) a. The candidates hated each other
    b. The candidates expected each other to win
    c. *The candidates expected that each other would win

Only the first two cases are permitted; (22c) is blocked, as required, by the Tensed-S Condition.

Before turning to other examples, let us consider some facts that lead us to a supplementary principle. Suppose that (23b) derives from the underlying form (23a):

(23) a. John expected [$_s$ PRO to win]
    b. John expected to win

Now notice that from (24a) we can derive (24b), whereas from (25a) we cannot derive (25b):

(24) a. The candidates each expected [$_s$ PRO to defeat the other]
    b. The candidates expected to defeat each other

(25) a. The men expected [$_s$ the soldier to shoot the other]
    b. *The men expected the soldier to shoot each other

To account for this difference, let us postulate a second principle, the "Specified Subject Condition" (26), where by "Specified subject" we mean a subject NP that contains either lexical items or a pronoun that is not anaphoric:

(26) No rule can involve $X$, $Y$ in the structure

$$\ldots X \ldots [_\alpha \ldots Z \ldots -WYV \ldots] \ldots$$

where $Z$ is the specified subject of $WYV$ in $\alpha$.

---

[17] I presuppose Dougherty's work (1970) here with no further specific reference. Notice that if one were to accept the alternative analysis of Jackendoff (1969), principle (20) would again apply—in this case, not to a movement rule but to a rule of interpretation.

We shall return to this principle later to give a more careful formulation. As set forth here, it suffices to distinguish (25), with the specified subject $Z$ = *the soldier* in the embedded sentence $\alpha$, from (23) and (24), which have no specified subject in that position.[18]

Within the extended standard theory, as developed in the references cited earlier, both NP and S are nodes to which cyclic operations apply, and the notion "subject of" is defined not only in S but also in such NP's as (27), where *John*, in all cases, is the "subject," in an extended sense of this term:

(27) a. John's refusal to leave
     b. John's picture of Bill
     c. John's strategy for victory

Correspondingly, in (26) $\alpha$ can be either NP or S. Examples (24) and (25) illustrate the application of (26) where $\alpha$ = S. The examples in (28)–(31) illustrate the application of this condition where $\alpha$ = NP:

(28) a. The men each saw [$_{NP}$ pictures of the other]
     b. The men saw pictures of each other

(29) a. The men each saw [$_{NP}$ John's pictures of the other]
     b. *The men saw John's pictures of each other

(30) a. COMP you saw [$_{NP}$ pictures of who]
     b. Who did you see pictures of

(31) a. COMP you saw [$_{NP}$ John's pictures of who]
     b. *Who did you see John's pictures of

The rule of *each*-Insertion applies to (28a) but is blocked by the

---

[18] Helke (1971) observes that *each*-Movement is not permitted in such cases as *The candidates each expected the others to clash* (*The candidates expected each other to clash*), *The candidates each expected the others to work together* (*The candidates expected each other to work together*). However, it seems that this results from the operation of independent rules that also exclude *The men walked between each other* from *The men each walked between the others*. What seems to be involved is a restriction on *each*-Movement in the case when the NP *the other* has the features [+totality, −individual] in the system of Dougherty (1970), where some relevant examples are discussed.

Specified Subject Condition in (29). The rule of *wh*-Movement applies to (30a) but is blocked by the same condition in the case of (31).[19]

Let us next turn to the rule of *it*-Replacement that produces such sentences as *John is easy to please*. Consider the examples in (32) and (33):

(32) a. It is pleasant for the rich for poor immigrants to do the hard work
    b. It is a waste of time for us for them to teach us Latin

(33) a. It is pleasant for the rich to do the hard work
    b. It is a waste of time for us to learn Latin
    c. It is easy for us to learn Latin

The rule of *it*-Replacement applies to the examples of (33) to give the corresponding forms in (34), but it does not apply to (32) to give (35):

(34) a. The hard work is pleasant for the rich to do
    b. Latin is a waste of time for us to learn
    c. Latin is easy for us to learn

(35) a. The hard work is pleasant for the rich for poor immigrants to do
    b. Latin is a waste of time for us for them to teach us

These data follow from our previous assumptions if we suppose that the phrases *for the rich* and *for us* in (32) and (33) form part of the predicate of the matrix sentence, with the subject PRO of the embedded sentence deleted in (33), exactly as in the case of (23). (The lexical item *easy* differs from *pleasant* and *waste of time* in that the rule of deletion is obligatory in the case of *easy* in this context.) Thus we take the structures underlying (33) to be of the form (36), as is clearly true (under our general assumptions) in the case of (32):

(36)    It–is Predicate for NP–[$_s$ NP–VP]

---

[19] Some speakers (myself included) find a three-way gradation of acceptability, with (30b) better than *Who did you see the pictures of,* which is in turn preferable to (31b). A refinement of condition (26) incorporating the feature [definite] as well as the property of lexical specification might be proposed to accommodate these judgments. Specified subjects in NP's are [+definite]. If (26) is revised to include [+definite] as well as specified subjects, then (31b) will involve a double violation and *Who did you see the pictures of* only a single violation. This might account for the gradation of acceptability.

This assumption is not unnatural on other grounds as well. Thus the leftmost *for*-phrase in all the cited examples is more readily detachable than the *for*-phrase in (37), for example:

(37)  It is intolerable for John to have to study Latin.

Compare the variants (38) with (39):

(38) a.  For the rich, it is pleasant for poor immigrants to do the hard work
     b.  For us, it is a waste of time to learn Latin
     c.  Latin is a waste of time to learn, for us
     d.  Latin is easier to learn for us than for John
     e.  It is easier to learn Latin for us than for John

(39) a.  For John, it is intolerable to have to study Latin
     b.  It is intolerable to have to study Latin, for John
     c.  It is more intolerable to have to study Latin for us than for John

The examples in (39), if acceptable at all, are interpreted somewhat differently from (37): in (39), it must be understood that John finds it intolerable to have to study Latin, but this is not the case in (37). On the other hand, such examples as (38) seem true stylistic variants of the corresponding forms of (32)–(34). We might capture this fact by limiting stylistic inversion to a *for*-phrase of the predicate of the matrix sentence.

There are, moreover, selectional relations between a predicate that appears in the matrix form (36) and the subject of the embedded S, a property that further differentiates these structures from (37). Compare (40) and (41):

(40) a.  It is intolerable for there to be snow in June
     b.  It is intolerable for the car to be so poorly constructed

(41) a.  *It is easy for there to be snow in June
     b.  *It is easy for the car to be so poorly constructed

These facts, too, might be expressed by assigning the *for*-phrase to the matrix sentence in the examples (33), with deletion of the subject PRO of the embedded S after it is assigned coreference with the NP of the matrix *for*-phrase. (In such cases as *It is easy to learn Latin*, we might assume that the matrix predicate contains a nonspecified phrase *for*-Δ which is deleted, as is the nonspecified agent in agentless passives). We can then restrict the selectional features to the predicate phrase of the matrix sentence.

We return to these structures later.

Consider next the "Unlike Person Constraint" discussed by Postal (1966; 1969). We might formulate this as a rule that assigns the feature * (deviant) to a sentence S dominating $PRO_i-V-PRO_j-X$, where $PRO_i$ and $PRO_j$ are both first person or both second person. Thus we cannot have such sentences as (42):

(42) a. *I saw me
b. *I watched us leaving (in the mirror)
c. *We watched me leaving
d. *You (all) noticed you standing there (by yourself)

The point is clearly more general (see Postal (1969)). Thus in (43) we interpret the two pronouns as different in reference, and in (44) we interpret the NP's as nonintersecting in reference; that is, we assume that the officers are not included among the soldiers doing the shooting (we do not interpret this sentence as referring to a situation in which some of the officers shot others):

(43)   He saw him
(44)   The soldiers shot the officers (among them)

The point seems to be that a rule of interpretation RI applying to the structure NP–V–NP (among others) seeks to interpret the two NP's as nonintersecting in reference,[20] and where this is impossible (as in the case of first and second person pronouns — see (42)), it assigns "strangeness," marking the sentence with *. But consider the sentences in (45):

(45) a.  *We* expect them to visit *me*; *I* expect them to visit *us* (*me*)
b. **We* expect *me* to visit them; *I* expect *us* (*me*) to visit them
c. **We* expect *me* to be visited by them; *I* expect *us* (*me*) to be visited by them
d.  *We* believe *I* may still win; *I* believe *we* (*I*) may still win

---

[20] This particular formulation presupposes the analysis of reflexives in Helke (1971) His approach to reflexives and inherent anaphora (*John lost his mind, John craned his neck,* and so on) fits very well into the present framework.

In (45a) and (45d), the rule RI is blocked (by the Specified Subject Condition and the Tensed-S Condition, respectively). Therefore in these sentences the pair of italicized NP's may intersect in reference; the sentences are not marked with * by RI. But the rule RI applies to (45b) and (45c), assigning *, just as it applies to the examples of (42). Although the matter is more complex, this appears to be a plausible first approximation to a correct analysis. Notice that it is difficult to see how RI can be construed naturally as anything other than a rule of semantic interpretation, operating at a fairly "superficial" level (at or close to surface structure), at least if we wish to incorporate (44) and (45) under the generalization. Exactly the same considerations apply if we restrict our attention to the Unlike Person Constraint.

Observe that we have now applied the principles to two kinds of rules, namely, syntactic operations moving constituents and rules of semantic interpretation. Some further possibilities are suggested by observations of Lasnik (1971). He points out that the sentences (46a,b) are ambiguous in a way in which (47) is not:

(46) a. I didn't see many of the pictures
     b. I didn't see pictures of many of the children
(47)    I didn't see John's pictures of many of the children

The first (more normal and less sophisticated, I believe) interpretation of (46a) in colloquial English associates *not* and *many*; under this interpretation, the sentence means "I saw few of the pictures," "Not many of the pictures are such that I saw them." Thus the sentence would be false, under this interpretation, if I had seen 50 of the 100 pictures (assuming 50 pictures to be "many" under the contextual conditions of the utterance), while it would be true if I had seen only 3 of the 100 pictures. Some speakers also accept a second interpretation of (46a), with the meaning "Many of the pictures are such that I didn't see them." Under this interpretation, which associates *not* with *see*, the sentence would be true if I had seen exactly 50 of the 100 pictures, since there would be 50 that I hadn't seen.

The same ambiguity arises in the case of (46b). Under the interpretation which associates *not* with *many*, the sentence means "I saw pictures of few of the children," "Not many of the children are such that I saw pictures of them." It would be false if I had seen pictures of 50 of the 100 children, true if I had seen pictures of 3 of the 100 children. Under the second interpretation, the sentence means "Pictures of many of the children are such that I didn't see them," which is true if I had seen pictures of 50 of the 100 children. For speakers who do not accept the second interpretation of (46a) and (46b), it seems that (47) is unacceptable. For speakers who assign both interpretations to the sentences of (46), (47) is acceptable with the unique interpretation that associates *not* with *see*; thus it means "John's pictures of many of the children are such that I didn't see them." The sentence (47), then, has no interpretation under which it is false, given that I had seen John's pictures of exactly 50 of the 100 children.

The observations are moderately subtle, but I believe that Lasnik's judgments are correct. Notice that the facts, as stated, follow from the Specified Subject Condition, which does not permit association of *not* with *many* in (47). If (following Lasnik) we regard the assignment of scope of negation as a matter of semantic interpretation, the Specified Subject Condition again blocks a semantic rule. If, on the other hand, it is claimed that a rule of *not*-Movement extracts *not* from the NP object to give the first (normal) interpretation of the sentences of (46), this syntactic rule is blocked in (47) by the same condition.

Lasnik suggests also the following, slightly different example. Consider the sentences in (48):

(48) a. You didn't understand the proofs of enough of the theorems (for me to be justified in giving you an A)
   b. You didn't understand Euclid's proofs of enough of the theorems (for me to be justified in giving you an A)

The word *enough* differs from *many* in that *not* must be associated with it (rather than with *understand*) in (48a). That is, only what I have called the "normal" interpretation is possible in the case of (48a), which must mean something like "You understood proofs of some (but not enough) of the theorems. . ." It follows, then, that (48b) receives no direct interpretation at all (though an interpretation can be forced, as it can also be, say, in (31b)), just as (47) receives no interpretation for speakers who accept only the "normal" interpretation of (46). This appears correct and is a further example of the application of the Specified Subject Condition.

3. Consider next the sentence (49) which, we assume, derives from (50) by *wh*-Placement (on *something*), *wh*-Movement, and Auxiliary Inversion:

(49)   What did you tell me that Bill saw
(50)   COMP you told me [$_S$ COMP Bill saw something]

The rule of *wh*-Movement in this case appears to violate both the Tensed-S Condition and the Specified Subject Condition.

Before turning to the problem posed by *wh*-Movement, let us consider the notion "transformational cycle" somewhat more carefully. The Insertion Prohibition, now sharpened as a special case of the Tensed-S and Specified Subject Conditions, is a step toward a stricter interpretation of the cycle: it asserts that once a stage of the cycle has been passed, we cannot introduce material into it from the outside under the stated conditions. To further sharpen the notion "transformational cycle," suppose that we impose the general condition (51):[21]

(51)   No rule can apply to a domain dominated by a cyclic node *A* in such a way as to affect solely a proper subdomain of *A* dominated by a node *B* which is also a cyclic node.

In other words, rules cannot in effect return to earlier stages of the cycle after the derivation has moved to larger, more inclusive domains. We will refer to (51) as the "Strict Cycle Condition."

From this condition it follows that *wh*-Movement must be a cyclic rule, since it applies in indirect questions and relatives.[22] The condition (51) seems fairly natural, and we will proceed to investigate its consequences.

Returning now to (50), we first assign *wh* and apply *wh*-Movement on the innermost cycle, which gives (52):

(52)   COMP you told me [$_S$ [$_{COMP}$ what] Bill saw]

On the next cycle, we want to move *what* to the COMP position of the matrix sentence, to give (49).[23] The Specified Subject Condition is

---

[21] The condition should perhaps be restricted to major transformations in the sense of Bach (1965; 1971), excluding his "housekeeping rules." A slightly different formulation of (51) would make it impossible for a rule applying to the domain dominated by *A* to affect solely items that were originally dominated by *B*. These alternatives lead to slightly different empirical consequences in areas that do not concern us here
[22] It has been argued repeatedly that *wh*-Movement cannot be a cyclic rule, but I am aware of no conclusive arguments. To my knowledge, none of the arguments that appear in the literature apply to the formulations given here. However, at a later point I will deal with some considerations that might suggest that *wh*-Movement is post-cyclic.
[23] We shall return to the rule for inserting *that* in (49).

no longer a barrier, but we are left with a violation of the Tensed-S Condition. An investigation of the conditions of the violation indicates that they are quite narrow: an item can "escape" from a tensed sentence if it has been moved into the COMP position on an earlier cycle and is moving into the COMP position on the present cycle. Furthermore, in no case does an item in COMP position move to anything other than the COMP position.[24] These specific properties of COMP may be considered alongside the property formulated as the Complementizer Substitution Universal. With the appropriate reformulation of our conditions (which we give as (55)), *wh*-Movement can apply to (52), giving (53), which becomes (49) by Auxiliary Inversion and *that*-Insertion:

(53)   What you told me [$_s$ COMP Bill saw]

Suppose now that we replace some of the base rules in (16) to obtain the more detailed analysis (54) (following Bresnan (1970)):

(54)   S → COMP S′
        S′ → NP Aux VP
        ⋮

Suppose further that we continue to take S (but not S′) to be the domain of cyclic rules. Under this assumption we can reformulate the Tensed-S and Specified Subject Conditions, together with the narrow restrictions on COMP, as in (55):

(55)   No rule can involve $X, Y$ in the structure

        $\ldots X \ldots [_\alpha \ldots Z \ldots -WYV \ldots ] \ldots$

        where (a) $Z$ is the specified subject of $WYV$
           or (b) $Y$ is in COMP and $X$ is not in COMP
           or (c) $Y$ is not in COMP and $\alpha$ is a tensed S.

This modification of the conditions in effect asserts that an item can be extracted from a tensed sentence or across a specified subject only if there is a rule that moves it into the COMP position. Thus a *wh*-word can be extracted, as in (49)–(50), but the subject of the

---

[24] In fact, this must be stipulated, quite apart from the Tensed-S Condition, to prevent improper passivization of, for example, *John asked what to read* to *\*What was asked to read by John*. On the other hand, *What did John ask to read* is permitted by the conditions.

embedded sentence cannot be passivized in *I believe the dog is hungry*. Notice, however, that *wh*-Movement will not be permitted across a specified subject in (31a), which we restate here as (56), to give the ungrammatical *\*Who did you see John's pictures of*:

(56)   COMP you saw [<sub>NP</sub> John's pictures of who]

The relevant difference between (56) and (50) is that (56) has no COMP node in an NP. Therefore the *wh*-word in (56) cannot escape from the NP.

It is observed in Chomsky (1964) that *wh*-Movement can be applied only once to a constituent of the form S. We cannot, for example, question (or relativize) an item that is within an indirect question to derive (57) from (58):[25]

(57)   *What did he wonder where John put
(58)   COMP he wondered [<sub>S</sub> COMP John put what where]

To derive (57) from (58), we must first place *where* in the COMP position of the embedded sentence. But in that case, *what* cannot enter the COMP position, which is filled by *where*, and thus cannot be extracted on the next cycle. The principles of the cycle presupposed so far in this discussion permit no other ordering of rule applications to give (57).

**4.**   As the rules and conditions now stand, we can derive (59) from (60) because the embedded S is not tensed:

(59)   What crimes does the FBI know how to solve
(60)   COMP the FBI knows [<sub>S</sub> COMP PRO to solve what crimes how]

The item *how* is moved into COMP position in the internal cycle, but *what crimes* can be extracted on the next cycle. This is a dubious result, however. Though judgments vary, there seem to me to be severe restrictions on cases such as (59). Thus, (61) seems to me unacceptable, surely much less acceptable than (59); and from (62) the predicted derived sentences (63) and (64) both seem unacceptable,

---

[25] Some speakers seem to accept such forms as *What did he wonder whether John saw, What crimes did he wonder how they solved*. For me, these are unacceptable. It would be possible to add special rules to allow for these examples by a complication of the particular grammar, given the suggested interpretation of the conditions.

though the immediately underlying forms (65) and (66) are all right:

(61) *What crimes does the FBI know whether to solve
(62) COMP John knows [$_s$ COMP PRO to give what books to whom]
(63) *What books does John know to whom to give
(64) *To whom does John know what books to give
(65) John knows what books to give to whom
(66) John knows to whom to give what books

Notice also that (67) does not derive as predicted from (60), but rather only from (68), analogous to (69a) from (69b):

(67) How does the FBI know what crimes to solve
(68) COMP the FBI knows [$_s$ COMP PRO to solve what crimes] how
(69) a. How does the FBI know the code
　　　b. The FBI knows the code how

It may be, then, that the *know how to* examples such as (59) are unique in permitting further *wh*-Movement from the embedded sentence and that the general case is that the conditions on transformations prevent movement of a *wh*-phrase over a *wh*-COMP.

In fact, the elaboration of the Specified Subject Condition that we will develop later on will suffice to prevent *wh*-Movement in the cases considered here.[26] However, it may be that there is an independent condition that suffices to prevent *wh*-Movement in these cases. Support for this conjecture is provided by the fact that example (70) must be ruled out as ungrammatical:

(70) *John knows what who saw

---

[26] Thus one could, under this modification, permit the unique case (59) by stipulating that (60) is unique in not containing PRO (or the element Δ, as in agentless passives, which also blocks *wh*-Movement by the Specified Subject Condition). One would thus be arguing that this is a special property of the locution *know how*, perhaps related to the fact that *know-how* can be a nominal compound (*He showed a remarkable degree of know-how*) but not *know-what*, *know-why*, *wonder-why*, and so on. A further modification that we shall discuss will not permit this explanation, given that the subject of the embedded sentence is PRO, and will require something like condition (73).

Observe that even with (73), we still need to invoke the strict cyclic interpretation of *wh*-Movement to block such cases as (57). Thus (73) alone would not suffice to prevent movement of *what* in (57) to the COMP position of the matrix sentence followed by movement of *where* to the COMP position of the embedded sentence.

The source, *John knows who saw what,* is grammatical, but (70) and other examples like it indicate that *wh*-Movement cannot move a *wh*-phrase across a *wh*-subject (just as it cannot move a *wh*-phrase across a *wh*-COMP). Notice, however, that *wh*-Movement over a *wh*-phrase P is permissible if P is contained in the predicate phrase, that is, to the right of the verb in the clause in question, as we can see from such examples as (71) and (72):

(71)   John remembers where Bill bought which book
(72)   John remembers to whom Bill gave which book

These examples, to which we shall return, are of a type discussed in Baker (1970). Though judgments vary slightly, such forms are surely more satisfactory than (70). (See also (65), (66).) Thus (71) would have the interpretation (roughly) "John remembers that Bill bought the *i*th book in the *j*th place," and similarly for (72).

Speculating, we might propose a further condition on transformations to accommodate these judgments. The obvious suggestion is based on the observation that the subject NP is "superior" to any phrase in the predicate in the sense that it is closer to the root of the tree structure. More precisely, we say that the category $A$ is "superior" to the category $B$ in the phrase marker if every major category dominating $A$ dominates $B$ as well but not conversely.[27] Suppose that we then add the stipulation (73) to the set of general conditions that we are considering:

(73)   No rule can involve $X$, $Y$ in the structure

$$\ldots X \ldots [\,_\alpha \ldots Z \ldots -WYV \ldots ] \ldots$$

where the rule applies ambiguously to $Z$ and $Y$ and $Z$ is superior to $Y$.

---

[27] We use the term "major category" in the sense of Chomsky (1965, p. 74), that is, N, V, A and the categories that dominate them. See Chomsky (1970a) for a further elaboration of this notion.

To simplify subsequent exposition, we will want to say that in the sentence [*the men each*] *saw the other* and others like it, the word *each* is superior to *the* of *the other*. Let us therefore extend slightly the notion "superior" so that $A$ is "superior" to $B$ if every major category dominating MMC($A$) dominates MMC($B$) as well but not conversely, where MMC($X$) is the minimal major category dominating $X$ ($X$ itself, if $X$ is a major category). We assume now that the NP *the men each* is the minimal major category dominating *each* in the sentence cited. Thus *each* in this sentence is superior to *the*, as intended. Other elaborations are possible, but this will suffice for expository purposes below.

The condition requires that a rule must select the superior term where that rule is ambiguous in application, that is, where the structure given in (73) will satisfy the structural condition defining the rule in question with either $Z$ or $Y$ selected as the factor satisfying a given term of this condition. Like the $A$-over-$A$ Condition, (73) restricts the ambiguity of rule application. Like (51), it provides a stricter interpretation of the notion of the cycle. It should be noted that in all of the cases of the general form given in (73) that we are considering, the category $X$ is superior to $Y$ in the sense just defined; and where $Z$ is the specified subject, it is superior to $Y$.

The condition (73) blocks (70) while permitting (71) and (72). Furthermore, the condition (73) suffices to block the examples (61)–(64), independently of other constraints. Thus consider (62), which we restate here as (74):

(74)  COMP John knows [$_S$ COMP PRO to give what books to whom]

On the first cycle, *wh*-Movement gives either (75) (= (65)) or (76) (= (66)):

(75)  John knows what books to give to whom.
(76)  John knows to whom to give what books.

But on the next cycle condition (73) prevents movement of the embedded phrase *to whom* in (75), just as it prohibits movement of the embedded phrase *what books* in (76). The reason, in both cases, is that the *wh*-phrase in COMP of the embedded cycle is superior to these categories, not being dominated by the major category S'. If *wh*-Movement moves the superior *wh*-phrase *what books* of (75) or *to whom* of (76) to initial position in the sentence, then the sentence will be marked ungrammatical by virtue of the unfilled COMP of the embedded clause and related considerations that we will examine later. This COMP position cannot be filled by subsequent application of *wh*-Movement by virtue of the general condition (51) that provides the strict interpretation of the cycle. Thus all possibilities are excluded except (75), (76).

To further explore structures of the general form given in (73), let us say that if $X$ is superior to $Y$ in a phrase marker P, then $Y$ is "subjacent" to $X$ if there is at most one cyclic category $C \neq Y$ such that $C$ contains $Y$ and $C$ does not contain $X$. Thus, if $Y$ is subjacent to $X$, either $X$ and $Y$ are contained in all the same cyclic categories (and are thus considered at the same level of the transformational cycle) or they are in adjacent cycles. In the sentence of (77), *who* is subjacent to both nodes COMP, but in (78) and (79) it is subjacent only to the node COMP of the embedded sentence:

(77) a. COMP he believes [$_s$ COMP John saw who]
     b. COMP he wonders [$_s$ COMP John saw who]

(78) a. COMP he believes [$_{NP}$ the claim [$_s$ COMP John saw who]]
     b. COMP he considered [$_{NP}$ the question [$_s$ COMP John saw who]]

(79) a. COMP he believes [$_s$ COMP John saw [$_{NP}$ a picture of who]]
     b. COMP he wonders [$_s$ COMP John saw [$_{NP}$ a picture of who]]

From (77a) we can derive *Who does he believe that John saw* by iteration of *wh*-Movement. From (77b) we can derive *He wonders who John saw*. From (79a) we can derive *Who does he believe that John saw a picture of*, again by iteration of *wh*-Movement; from (79b) we derive *He wonders who John saw a picture of*. In the case of (77) and (79), *who* can move to any of the COMP positions; *who* moves ultimately to the external COMP position in (77a) and (79a) and to the internal COMP position in (77b) and (79b). The other four possibilities are excluded, namely, *\*He believes who John saw*, *\*Who does he wonder that John saw*, *\*He believes who John saw a picture of*, and *\*Who does he wonder that John saw a picture of*. We return to this matter when we consider contextual features of lexical items.

Turning now to (78), we observe that only the embedded COMP position can be occupied by *who*. Thus we can derive from (78b) the sentence *He considered the question who John saw*. No such operation is possible in the case of (78a) because of contextual features of the lexical item *claim*, as we shall discuss at a later point.

Given appropriate contextual features for nouns and verbs, we might account for all of these facts by adding the condition (80), which would restrict rules to adjacent cycles or the same cycle:

(80) No rule can involve $X$, $Y$, $X$ superior to $Y$, if $Y$ is not subjacent to $X$.

Certain examples that we will consider suggest that (80) does not apply to *each*-Movement. The examples, however, are somewhat marginal, and it may furthermore be possible to account for them, under the assumption (80), by a sharpening of the notion "cyclic category." Let us tentatively stipulate, however, that condition (80) applies only to extraction rules, that is, to rules that move some item from the position $Y$ to the superior position $X$.

**5.** We can combine conditions (51) and (80) as (81) (slightly reformulating (80)):

(81)  Consider the structure $\alpha$ where $\alpha$ is a cyclic node:

$[_\alpha \ldots X \ldots ]$

Suppose that the structural description $\Sigma$ of a transformation T applies to $\alpha$, where $X$ is the maximally superior category that satisfies some term of $\Sigma$. Then T applies to $\alpha$ only if $\alpha$ is the only cyclic category containing $X$ (condition (51)). If, furthermore, T is an extraction rule moving some category in . . . to the position $X$, then some constant term of $\Sigma$ must hold of a category subjacent to $X$ in $\alpha$ for T to apply to $\alpha$ (modification of condition (80)).

We will tentatively suppose that condition (81) is a general property defining cyclic application of transformations.

The examples of (77) and (79) are not affected by the condition (80) incorporated in (81), and we can thus apply iterated *wh*-Movement as desired. But in (78), though *wh*-Movement can apply on the innermost cycle, it cannot apply on the next cycle since NP does not have a COMP. Furthermore, *wh*-Movement cannot apply on the outermost cycle because of the condition (80) incorporated in (81).[28] In this way, we can explain many of the examples that fall under the Complex Noun Phrase Constraint (Ross (1967)); many others fall under the *A*-over-*A* principle.

Notice that this argument is similar to the one that explains the distinction between (50) and (56). For clarity, we repeat the essential point. The sentences (82) and (83) derive from (84) and (85), respectively:

(82)   Who did he expect Bill to see
(83)   *Who did he find Bill's picture of
(84)   COMP he expected [$_S$ COMP Bill to see who]
(85)   COMP he found [$_{NP}$ Bill's picture of who]

---

[28] If we accept the analysis of factives suggested in Kiparsky and Kiparsky (1970), then, as shown there, the fact that there is no *wh*-Movement from factives will follow from the special case of the Complex Noun Phrase Constraint that follows from (80), (81).

Apart from the element COMP, (84) and (85) are alike, phrase by phrase, from the point of view of rule applicability: *Bill* is the "subject" of *see who* in (84) and of *picture of who* in (85), in our extended sense of the term "subject," and *who* is the "object" in both cases. But (82) is derivable from (84) by iteration of *wh*-Movement, whereas *wh*-Movement cannot apply in (85), on the first cycle because there is no COMP in NP and on the second cycle by virtue of the Specified Subject Condition (55a).

If we are correct in assuming the condition (81), which restricts extraction to adjacent cycles, it follows that although *wh*-phrases can be extracted from such structures as *a picture of_____*, *stories about _____*, *requests for _____*, as in (86), it will not be possible to extract a *wh*-phrase when one of these structures is embedded in another, as in (87), because of the absence of a COMP node in noun phrases. On the other hand, on the same assumptions the forms in (88) are permitted since no extraction rule is involved:

(86) a.  Who did you see a picture of_____
     b.  Who did you hear stories about _____
     c.  What do you write articles about _____
     d.  What do you generally receive requests for _____

(87) a.  *Who did you hear stories about a picture of_____
     b.  *What do you receive request for articles about _____

(88) a.  We heard stories about pictures of each other
     b.  We received requests for articles about each other

Judgments are insecure, but the conclusion seems to me plausible. On the other hand, Ross (1967) cites such examples as (89) as grammatical:

(89)  What books does the government prescribe the height of the lettering on _____

Examples (87) and (89) appear to be parallel from the point of view of rule applicability. I see no obvious explanation for an apparent difference in degree of acceptability.

From the same assumptions it follows that such sentences as (90) involve repeated cyclic application of *wh*-Movement:

(90)  What did John believe that Bill asked Mary to give her sister to read

It also follows that the surface structure position of the *wh*-phrase will be significant for interpretation and for determination of acceptability, as we might expect under the general assumptions of the extended standard theory.

In Chomsky (1968, Chapter 2, note 23) it is suggested that the *A*-over-*A* principle might be extended to the effect that a transformation must select the minimal phrase of the type S as well as the maximal phrase of the type *A* contained in S. This would account, for example, for the fact that from *John was convinced that Bill would leave before dark* we can derive *John was convinced that before dark Bill would leave* but not *Before dark John was convinced that Bill would leave*. Notice that the Subjacency Condition (81) on extraction rules in effect achieves the same results as the proposed extension of the *A*-over-*A* Condition.

**6.** The conditions that we have been examining can be extended to accommodate other examples. Notice that in none of the cases considered so far is the rightmost term *Y* involved in a rule properly contained in the subject of a phrase.[29] But there are additional constraints on items in subject position, as has been noted repeatedly (see Chomsky (1964), Ross (1967)). Thus, consider the sentences (91)–(98), where in each case the (a) structure underlies the corresponding (b) forms:

(91) a.  COMP John heard [$_{NP}$ stories about who]
      b.  Who did John hear stories about

(92) a.  COMP [$_{NP}$ stories about who] terrified John
      b.  *Who did stories about terrify John

(93) a.  COMP you expect [$_S$ COMP PRO to hear [$_{NP}$ stories about who]]
      b.  Who do you expect to hear stories about

(94) a.  COMP you expect [$_S$ COMP [$_{NP}$ stories about who] to terrify John]
      b.  *Who do you expect stories about to terrify John

(95) a.  COMP it surprised John [$_S$ COMP Mary saw what]
      b.  What did it surprise John that Mary saw

---

[29] To be more precise, if we take $Y = the$ as the rightmost term involved in the *each*-Movement rule, then what should be said is that in each case so far considered, where *C* is the minimal major category contained the rightmost term *Y* involved in a rule, then *C* is not properly contained in the subject of a phrase.

(96) a. COMP [$_{NP}$ [$_S$ COMP John saw what]] surprised Mary

    b. *What did that John saw surprise Mary

(97) a. COMP it surprised John [$_S$ COMP PRO to see [$_{NP}$ pictures of who]]

    b. Who did it surprise John to see pictures of

(98) a. COMP [$_{NP}$ [$_S$ COMP PRO to see [$_{NP}$ pictures of who]]] surprised John

    b. *Who did to see pictures of surprise John

We might account for these discrepancies between subject and predicate position by the condition that in structures of the general form (73) $\alpha$ may not be a subject phrase properly containing $Y$. The stipulation that only *proper* inclusion blocks the rule is, of course, necessary to permit a full subject to be extracted, as in *Who did you expect to be here, Who did you suppose would be here*.[30] With this condition, *who* will not be extractable from the subject phrase *stories about who* in (92), (94).[31] The same condition will prevent extraction of the *wh*-phrase to form (96b), (98b). More exactly, in the case of (96a) and (98a), the *wh*-phrase can be moved to the position of the internal COMP but then cannot be extracted further since it is properly contained in a subject phrase. (The ungrammatical status of the intermediate forms so produced is determined by considerations to which we will turn when we consider rules of interpretation.) In the case of (94), the condition just proposed prevents movement of *who* to COMP on the internal cycle (exactly as in the case of (92)), and the Subjacency Condition (81) prevents *who* from being moved to the external COMP on the next cycle. There is a redundancy in this case since the Subject Condition also prohibits the movement of *who* to the external COMP; a similar redundancy applies in the case of (96), (98).

We can eliminate the redundancy by restricting the condition on

---

[30] To incorporate such phrases as *what books, whose books,* we might again use the notion "minimal major category," or we might rely on the considerations of note 9. Again, we must stipulate that proper inclusion of the minimal major category containing $Y$ blocks the application of the rule, for the reasons just noted.

[31] This analysis of course assumes, as throughout, that there is no raising rule assigning the subject *stories about who* of the embedded sentence of (94) to the object position of the matrix sentence. If there were such a rule, *wh*-Movement should apply, giving (94b), analogous to *Who did you see pictures of last night, Who did you tell stories about at the campfire.* These forms, though hardly elegant, seem to me much more acceptable than (94b), as we would expect on the assumption that there is no rule of subject raising to object position.

subjects to the case where $Y$ is subjacent to $X$. This will not affect any examples involving *wh*-Movement, since in any case where $Y$ is not subjacent to $X$ the extraction rule is blocked. We will also assume, as noted, that the relevant conditions apply to the minimal major category containing $Y$ (= MMC($Y$)), not $Y$ itself, an assumption that in this discussion has empirical effects only in the case of *each*-Movement. To simplify exposition, we will therefore modify the definition of "subjacency" exactly as we modified the definition of "superior" in note 27, saying that where $X$ is superior to $Y$, $Y$ is "subjacent" to $X$ if there is at most one cyclic category $C \neq$ MMC($Y$) such that $C$ contains MMC($Y$) and $C$ does not contain $X$ (and therefore does not contain MMC($X$)). With these modifications, the Subject Condition reads as in (99):

(99)   No rule can involve $X$, $Y$ in the structure

   $\ldots X \ldots [_\alpha \ldots Y \ldots ] \ldots$

   where (a) $\alpha$ is a subject phrase properly containing MMC($Y$) and (b) $Y$ is subjacent to $X$

Condition (b) of (99), rather than being merely a device to avoid redundancy, is in fact necessary, as we can see from the examples in (100) (which were pointed out to me by R. Kayne):

(100)   a.   We expect [$_S$ [$_{NP}$ pictures of each other] to be on sale]
       b.   We expect [$_S$ [$_{NP}$ each others' arguments] to be valid]

In such cases the rule of *each*-Movement can apply since the subjacency requirement (99b) prevents the rule from being blocked by the Subject Condition (99a). That is, the position $Y$ to which *each* moves is not subjacent to the position $X$ filled by *each* in the matrix sentence of the structure underlying the examples of (100). Rather, there are two cyclic categories (namely, NP and S) containing MMC($Y$) (= *the other(s)*) and not containing $X$ (= *each*) in the underlying structure. But the definition of "subjacency" implies that in the cases excluded by (99), the subject phrase $\alpha$ is the only cyclic category containing (and by (99a), properly containing) MMC($Y$) and not containing $X$.

Comparing (94) and (100), we observe that *wh*-Movement does not apply under conditions in which *each*-Movement does apply in these cases. We have already noticed this in the case of (87) and (88). The reason, again, is the Subjacency Condition (81) on extraction rules.

108

The rule RI (see the discussion accompanying (43)–(45)) and the copying rule that forms reflexives (see note 20) should apply under the same conditions as *each*-Movement. Therefore the sentences (101) should be marked "strange" by RI and the sentence (102) should be grammatical:

(101) a. We (I) expected pictures of me to be on sale
     b. We (I) expected my arguments to be valid
(102)   I expected pictures of myself to be on sale

To my ear, (101b) is perfectly acceptable, and (101a) and (102) seem acceptable as well. Assuming these judgments, it follows that RI has not applied in (101), although the structures are exactly analogous to (100), in which *each*-Movement has applied. Perhaps the difference might be traced to the *A*-over-*A* Condition, if RI is formulated so that both *pictures of me* and *me* in (101a) and both *my arguments* and *my* in (101b) are subject to inspection for possible overlap of reference by RI; if so, then the *A*-over-*A* Condition will block inspection of *my*, *me*, and RI will not assign strangeness. If this assumption is correct, we should also expect both cases of (103) to be acceptable:

(103) a. I saw a picture of me hanging on the wall
     b. I saw a picture of myself hanging on the wall

My judgments are uncertain in these cases.
Consider next the sentences in (104):

(104) a. They each expect [$_S$ [$_{NP}$ the others] to win]
     b. They each were quite happy [$_S$ [$_\alpha$ for the others] to win]
     c. They each were quite happy [$_S$ [$_\alpha$ for pictures of the others] to be on sale]

The rule of *each*-Movement applies to (104a), giving *They expect each other to win*. The Subject Condition (99) is inapplicable because the subject of the embedded sentence of (104a) does not properly contain the phrase *the others* (= MMC($Y$)). The rule of *each*-Movement also applies to (104c), which is like (100a) in all relevant respects, to give *They were quite happy for pictures of each other to be on sale*.

Consider now the structure (104b). If *each*-Movement were to apply, it would give *They were quite happy for each other to win*. This seems to me ungrammatical. Assuming this judgment, it must be that the Subject Condition (99) prevents the application of *each*-Movement to (104b). This will be the case here only if $\alpha$ is a subject phrase properly containing MMC($Y$) and furthermore $Y$ (= *the*) is subjacent to $X$ (= *each*). Assuming that MMC($Y$) = *the others,* the first of these conditions holds. As distinct from (104a), the subject of the embedded sentence of (104b) does properly contain MMC($Y$) (= *the others*). But it also must be the case that, as distinct from (104c), $Y$ (= *the*) is subjacent to $X$ (= *each*) in (104b). That is, whereas in (104c) there are two cyclic categories properly containing MMC($Y$) and excluding $X$ (namely, $\alpha$ and S), in (104b) there is only one cyclic category properly containing MMC($Y$) and excluding $X$ (namely, S). Thus the rule of *for*-Placement must be formulated so that it does not produce (105), with $\alpha$ = NP and *the others* an NP, but rather produces (106), with $\alpha$ = PP:

(105)  [$_{NP}$ for [$_{NP}$ the others]]
(106)  [$_{PP}$ for [$_{NP}$ the others]]

Notice that if we were to assume that *the others* is not a category within $\alpha$, then the Subject Condition would no longer apply since under this assumption $\alpha$ = MMC(*the*). But assuming the analysis (106), the examples of (104) and others like them will be properly handled by the Subject Condition (99).

Consider next the sentences in (107):

(107)  a.  We like [$_S$ [$_{NP}$ pictures of each other] to be on sale]
       b.  We hate it [$_S$ [$_\alpha$ for pictures of each other] to be on sale]
       c.  We hate it [$_S$ [$_\alpha$ for each other] to win]

Sentence (107a), which is analogous to (100a), is grammatical because of the Subjacency Condition (b) of (99), which prevents *each*-Movement from being blocked in this case. Sentence (107b) is also unaffected by the Subject Condition (99) and for the same reason.

Now we turn to case (107c). If *it*–S is analyzed as an NP in case (c), then the sentence should be grammatical since *the* is no longer subjacent to *each* in the underlying form *We each hate it for the other(s) to win.* If *it*–S is not analyzed as an NP in these structures, then (107c) will be ruled ungrammatical on the same grounds as (104b). To exclude (107c) on the assumption that *it*–S is an NP here, we might modify the definition of "subjacency" to (108):

110

(108) a. Category *A* "L-contains" category *B* if and only if *A* properly contains *B* and for all *C* ≠ *A*, if *A* contains *C* and *C* contains *B*, then *A* = . . . *C* . . . , where . . . contains a lexical item.

   b. *B* is "subjacent" to *A* if and only if *A* is superior to *B* and there is at most one cyclic category *C* such that *C* L-contains MMC(*B*) and *C* does not contain *A*.

This is a fairly natural extension of the former definition of "subjacency," making use of the notion "L-contains" in place of "contains."

Returning to (107c), suppose now that the *it*–S structure is an NP. Then the structure underlying (107c) is (109):

(109)   We each hate [$_{NP}$ it [$_S$ [$_\alpha$ for the others] to win]]

The only cyclic category that L-contains *the others* and excludes *each* is S; therefore, *the* is subjacent to *each*. Furthermore, $\alpha$ properly contains MMC(*the*) (= *the others*); therefore, *each*-Movement is blocked by the Subject Condition (99). Notice that this conclusion does not depend on the assumption that $\alpha$ is analyzed as in (106) rather than (105), but only on the assumption that *the others* is an NP in $\alpha$ and *for* is not a lexical item. Similarly, under the new definition of "subjacency" in terms of "L-contains" (108b), it is no longer necessary to select (106) over (105) in order to prevent *each*-Movement in (104b).

Structures of the form NP *hates it for* . . . seem awkward to me, but many speakers find them quite acceptable and examples are not uncommon in the literature. This discussion suggests that such forms seem to provide no difficulty for the theory so far developed. Since the examples seem to me somewhat questionable, however, I will not try to fix specific suggestions at this point. It would be interesting to find clearer examples on the basis of which to decide among the slightly different alternative analyses and formulations of the conditions that have been examined in this connection.

7.   To review this discussion so far, we assume the *A*-over-*A* Condition and the related condition (73), and we assume that cyclic application of rules is governed by the general convention (81). In addition, we revise (55) to (110), incorporating the Subject Condition (99):

111

(110)    No rule can involve $X$, $Y$ ($X$ superior to $Y$) in the structure

$$\ldots X \ldots [_\alpha \ldots Z \ldots -WYV \ldots ] \ldots$$

where (a) $Z$ is the specified subject of $WYV$
   or (b) $\alpha$ is a subject phrase properly containing MMC($Y$)
        and $Y$ is subjacent to $X$
   or (c) $Y$ is in COMP and $X$ is not in COMP
   or (d) $Y$ is not in COMP and $\alpha$ is a tensed S.

With this revision, (110) incorporates Ross's Sentential Subject Constraint, insofar as the latter does not already fall under the *A*-over-*A* Condition. Other examples might be accounted for by specific properties of certain constructions. In coordination, for example, it is generally the case that operations must apply uniformly through the coordinated terms; for instance, verbal affixes must be assigned uniformly, so that we have *John has flown planes and driven cars* but not *\*John has flown planes and drive cars*. Correspondingly, in a structure such as (110) where $Y$ is a term of a conjunct, no rule, syntactic or semantic, can involve $X$ and $Y$ (but see note 16). For example, there is an echo question *John saw Bill and who*, but *wh*-Movement cannot apply to give *\*Who did John see Bill and* or *The man who John saw Bill and*.

Though there remain many recalcitrant cases and large areas where even the gross phenomena are unexplained, it seems that the approach just outlined offers considerable promise for a unified and systematic treatment of conditions on transformations, if the specific hypotheses that have been proposed in the course of this discussion can be sustained.[32]

---

[32] In some cases it is not at all clear that conditions of the sort we are discussing are the appropriate device for explaining certain distinctions. Consider Ross's (1967) example — *handsome though I believe that Tom is* versus *\*handsome though I believe the claim that Tom is*. The distinction can be explained by the case of Ross's Complex Noun Phrase Constraint that falls under the condition of subjacency on extraction (81). However, other examples that seem to me about as bad are *handsome though they told me that Tom is, handsome though my friends suggested that Mary thinks that Tom is*, and so on. If this is so, it is not clear what considerations apply. Perhaps *I believe*, like *I guess* and a few other items, can be analyzed as pre-sentence qualifiers rather than as matrix phrases. The relative order of pre-sentence elements and COMP raises certain problems: *I wonder whether at sunset they'll still be out sailing, \*I wonder at sunset whether they'll still be out sailing, At sunset who'll still be out sailing, \*Who at sunset will still be out sailing; I wonder why, having offered his support, John then backed down, \*I wonder, having offered his support, why John then backed down, Having offered his support, why did John then back down, Why, having offered his support, did John then back down*. Note also that the preposing rule in such cases seems to

As already noted, under the analysis proposed here there is no necessity for a rule raising the subject of an embedded sentence to the object position of the matrix sentence (and, furthermore, it is questionable whether such a rule could even be added). One might then raise the question whether cyclic transformations should not be constrained so as to forbid operations that never change the terminal string of a phrase marker but only its structure, as in the original formulations of subject raising to object position (see, for example, Kiparsky and Kiparsky (1970)).[33] Perhaps all such operations can be

---

share some but not all the properties of root transformations, in the sense of Emonds (1970).

Observe that to accommodate comparative deletion (which, as D. Vetter noted, obeys the Complex NP Constraint), one might assume that it involves a movement rule with deletion in the position of the COMP *than*. Thus *John is taller than Mary claims that he is* (cf. *\*John is taller than Mary believes the claim that he is*) would derive, by successive movement of *tall* through the indexed COMP's, from *John is taller than$_2$ Mary claims that$_1$ he is tall*, with [*than, tall*] becoming *than*. That *than* is a COMP follows from the parallelism between adjectival and nominal phrases discussed (within the framework of the lexicalist hypothesis) in Bowers (1969) and Selkirk (1970).

Langendoen (1971) suggests that relative pronouns not moved to initial position yield more acceptable sentences in tenseless than in tensed clauses: thus he proposes that *Many people do things to teach children to do which* (namely, those things) *constitutes a crime in California* is preferable to *The vase that John broke which* (namely, the vase) *annoyed Harry had only sentimental value*. This, if correct, might be explained in terms of the proposed conditions, where the rule associating antecedent and *wh*-word is blocked where the relative clause is a finite (tensed) clause with a specified subject. Langendoen also mentions a number of other examples which, it seems, might be covered by an appropriate formulation of the *A*-over-*A* Condition, though it remains for this to be demonstrated. See Ross (1967) and Postal (1971) for relevant and illuminating discussion.

[33] It is pointed out by McCawley (1970) that if English is a VSO language, then raising to subject and to object positions can be formulated as a single rule. There is, however, no persuasive independent evidence for the assumption, so far as I can see. If there is no rule of raising to object position, then there remains no substantial argument for the VSO analysis.

As already noted, it is difficult to incorporate a rule of raising of the familiar sort within the present framework (see (94), (104b), note 31). There are other examples too which indicate that the allegedly raised subject continues to behave as the subject of the embedded sentence rather than the object of the matrix sentence. Thus, consider *The men each were told to expect John to kill the other(s)*. If *John* is raised on an internal cycle, it will no longer be a subject when the matrix cycle is reached so that *each*-movement should apply to give *\*The men were told to expect John to kill each other*. Similarly, we have *We were told to expect John to kill me* but not *\*We were told to expect to kill me*, the former inconsistent with subject raising unless we assume that when the subject is raised a "trace" is left behind, perhaps in the form of a PRO controlled by the raised subject and ultimately deleted. While this is not impossible (in fact, we will suggest it as a possibility for certain cases), such a device would not account for (94) or (104b). Furthermore, it seems pointless in the case of a rule which in any event does not modify the form of the terminal string. Another problem is suggested by some observations of John Kimball, suggests that from *It was easy for Jones to force Smith to recover* we can derive *Smith was easy for Jones to force to*

restricted to the readjustment rule component of the grammar, which relates syntax and phonology (see Chomsky and Halle (1968)). There is no reason to suppose that such rules of regrouping will receive a natural formulation within the theory of grammatical transformations. One might expect such regrouping to apply most regularly to form words from syntactically separate items, and it may be that some languages (Japanese is a case that comes to mind) make much greater use of regrouping rules than of transformations in a stricter sense.

**8.** Putting aside these speculations and returning to the main topic, consider again the Specified Subject Condition, case (a) of (110), which we restate as (111):

(111)   No rule can involve $X$, $Y$ ($X$ superior to $Y$) in the structure

$$\ldots X \ldots [ \ldots Z \ldots -WYV \ldots ] \ldots$$

where $Z$ is the specified subject of $WYV$.

In the cases so far considered, the notion "specified subject" could be taken as "subject specified with lexical entries," where nonanaphoric pronouns are taken as lexical (see, for example, (45a)). Thus the distinction was between (a) lexically specified subjects such as *Bill, the man,* and fully specified referring pronouns, on the one hand, and (b) the deleted and controlled subject PRO, on the other. But consideration of a wider range of examples shows that the notion "specified subject" must be further refined.

W. Leben points out that the example (112), derived from (113), is unexplained if "specified subject" in (111) means "lexically specified subject":

(112)   *We persuaded Bill to kill each other
(113)   We *each* persuaded Bill [COMP PRO to kill *the* other(s)]

In (113) the italicized terms are $X$, $Y$ of (111) and PRO is $Z$. But the rule of *each*-Movement involving $X$, $Y$ is blocked, even though $Z$ is not lexically specified.

---

recover, but from *It was easy for Jones to expect Smith to recover,* we cannot form *Smith was easy for Jones to expect to recover.* Assuming subject raising, the two sentences are identical at the point where *it*-Replacement takes place. If there is no subject raising, the rule of *it*-Replacement can make the required distinction by permitting the NP moved to be followed by S (as in *Bill is easy to persuade that the moon is made of green cheese*).

It might be supposed that the intervening lexically specified object *Bill* blocks *each*-Movement here. However, this is evidently not so, as we can see from (114), which derives from (115):

(114)  We promised Bill to kill each other
(115)  We *each* promised Bill [COMP PRO to kill *the* other(s)]

We might try to explain such cases by imposing on *each*-Movement the condition that it be strictly within a single clause, thus assuming that (114) derives from (116):

(116)  We promised Bill [COMP PRO each to kill the other(s)]

This would require that, say, (117) derives from (118), conflicting with the fact that (119) must be blocked:

(117)  We wanted to kill each other
(118)  We wanted [COMP PRO each to kill the other(s)]
(119)  a. *We each wanted to kill each other
      b. *We would have both wanted to kill each other

Apart from the difficulty of excluding (119), examples like (104) and (107) indicate that *each*-Movement cannot be restricted to a single clause. (Notice that we would not want to assume that *each other* is generated by the base in the embedded subject position in the latter cases since we want to exclude this possibility in general so as to avoid *each other saw Bill* and the like.) Furthermore, it would be highly undesirable to extend the general theory of transformations so as to permit transformations to be restricted to a single clause, and so far as I can see, there are no strong empirical reasons motivating such an elaboration of the theory, given the general framework that we are exploring here.[34]

---

[34] In the absence of other considerations, the general point that the theory of transformations should not be extended to permit this option is compelling, if not decisive. Specific arguments are somewhat inconclusive because there are some unresolved questions about the interpretation of *each other* and of quantifiers in general. Thus I think it is clear that there are general grounds for supposing that quantifiers are interpreted at least in part in terms of surface structure position (see Chomsky (1972a) for some review of this question). Specifically, in the case of *each other* there is independent evidence for this assumption. Thus Dougherty (1970) points out that *each other* does not imply a pairwise relation, as does its presumed source: for example, *The kids met each other at the beach every day last summer* does not strictly imply a pairwise meeting, as does *The kids each met the others at the beach every day last summer* (example from M. Helke). Similarly, consider such examples as *We each*

115

The rule RI imposes disjoint reference patterns in exactly the same way as *each*-Movement, as we can see from (120), where (a) is parallel to (112) and (b) to (114):

(120) a. *I* (*we*) persuaded Bill to kill *us*
 b. *\*I* (*we*) promised Bill to kill *us*

Evidently, the crucial factor in these examples is the question of control of the embedded subject PRO (to use terminology suggested by Postal). In (112) PRO is controlled by the object of the matrix sentence, a term unrelated to the italicized pair $X$, $Y$ involved in the rule. In (114) PRO is controlled by the subject of the matrix sentence, which incorporates the term $X$ of the pair $X$, $Y$.[35] When PRO is not controlled by the minimal major category containing $X$, then the rule involving $X$ and $Y$ is blocked. The same assumption accounts for (120), with grammaticalness reversed, as usual.

On the same assumptions, we would expect that grammaticalness would be reversed in the case of *each*-Movement from the direct objects of *persuade* and *promise*. That this is indeed the case is shown by the examples in (121) and (122), suggested in a different context by Fauconnier (1971) (his examples are the French analogs, but the properties are the same):

(121)　I ordered the boys to have each finished the work by noon
(122)　*I promised the boys to have each finished the work by noon

In (121), PRO in the embedded sentence is controlled by the object phrase *each of the boys* of the matrix sentence, so that *each*-Movement is permitted. (Compare (112), where PRO of the embedded

---

saw a picture of the other(s), We each saw pictures of the other(s), *We saw a picture of each other, We saw pictures of each other*. See also note 40. There has been, to my knowledge, no analysis of quantifiers adequate to account for cases of this sort in a principled way.

If we assume that PRO does not take quantifiers in the base where it is subject to control, it follows that such sentences as *\*I argued with Bill about shaving each other*, *\*I had an understanding with John to kill each other*, *\*I received a letter from John about killing each other* are excluded (along with (119)), although the same sentences with *ourselves* replacing *each other* are grammatical (see Helke (1971)). The conclusion seems plausible to me in this case. However, such sentences as *We worked together to kill each other*, if grammatical, would indicate that PRO in the embedded sentence can take inherent *each*, even when subject to deletion under control. One would suspect that the solution lies in a theory of interpretation of quantifiers in terms of their surface structure positions.

[35] For a very suggestive discussion of how control is determined in such cases, see Jackendoff (1969; 1972). The subject of the matrix sentence is MMC($X$) in this case.

sentence is controlled by the object phrase *Bill* of the matrix sentence and *each*-Movement from the subject is not permitted.) In (122), PRO of the embedded sentence is controlled by the subject phrase *I* of the matrix sentence so that *each*-Movement from the object *each of the boys* is not permitted. (Compare (114), where PRO of the embedded sentence is controlled by the subject phrase *we each* of the matrix sentence and *each*-Movement from the subject is permitted.)

Notice that when the embedded subject is not PRO but is lexically specified, then it is of course not controlled by the category containing $X$. Hence all cases considered here will be accommodated by the principle (111), if we take "specified subject" in (111) to mean "subject not controlled by the category containing $X$."[36]

Making this revision explicit, we restate (110) as (123):

(123)    No rule can involve $X$, $Y$ ($X$ superior to $Y$) in the structure

$$\ldots X \ldots [_\alpha \ldots Z \ldots -WYV \ldots ] \ldots$$

where (a) $Z$ is the subject of $WYV$ and is not controlled by a
                 category containing $X$
       or (b) $\alpha$ is a subject phrase properly containing MMC($Y$)
                 and $Y$ is subjacent to $X$
       or (c) $Y$ is in COMP and $X$ is not in COMP
       or (d) $Y$ is not in COMP and $\alpha$ is a tensed S.

In earlier examples, we took $Z$ to be lexically specified. An NP is lexically specified (in the sense of our earlier discussion) if and only if it is not controlled. Thus in earlier discussion we could just as well have referred to $Z$ as the subject of $WYV$ which is not controlled. The modification incorporated into (123a), then, broadens the scope of the condition to include all cases in which $Z$ is not controlled by a category containing $X$, including, as a special case, a subject $Z$ which is not controlled at all, that is, is lexically specified in the earlier sense.

**9.**    Examples of the sort that we have been considering have been

---

[36] Bresnan (1971) points out the contrast *Such things are not good [for there to be children involved in]* versus the grammatical *Such things are not good for children [to be involved in]*, where the brackets bound the embedded phrases. Note that this distinction follows from the Specified Subject Condition as here formulated since the transformationally introduced element *there*, though not a lexical item, is not controlled by any outside category and therefore blocks *it*-Replacement. The distinction will also follow, on other grounds, if one adopts the rule of PRO-Replacement to be taken up later (see the discussion accompanying (170)–(179)).

used to motivate various pruning conventions in earlier work. Thus, in the sentences of (124), the rule of *each*-Movement does not apply; and in (125), the rule RI of semantic interpretation does not apply (so that the sentences are grammatical):

(124) a. The men *each* expected him to want to kill *the* others
 b. The men *each* expected to want him to kill *the* others
 c. The men *each* wanted to hear his stories about killing *the* others

(125) a. *I (we)* expected him to want to kill *us*
 b. *I (we)* expected to want him to kill *us*
 c. *I (we)* wanted to hear his stories about killing *us*

But if *him, his* do not appear, *each*-Movement can apply in (124) and RI will apply in (125) (assigning *).

We have explained these facts by means of the Specified Subject Condition (123a). Alternatively, one might suggest that *each*-Movement and RI apply only in a single clause,[37] adding the convention that when the subject *him, his* does not appear, the S node is pruned so that only a single clause remains and the rules apply. However, examples such as (112), (114), (120), as well as (124c) and (125c), indicate that it is control of the subject by the term $X$ of the matrix phrase, rather than a pruning convention of the kind discussed in the literature, that is the determining factor. Indeed, it may be that pruning can be dispensed with. If so, it may be that the only deletion of S nodes is by late rules that delete repeated phrases (for example, Ross's "sluicing," or VP deletion, that is, optional deletion of an intonationally marked VP), rules that are possibly the final ones of the grammar. I will not pursue the matter here, but it may well be that the results on cycling functions in Peters and Ritchie (1972) can be applied, under these assumptions, to demonstrate that transformational grammars are quite limited in weak generative capacity. At the

---

[37] Assuming that the difficulties noted earlier (see discussion following (119)) have been overcome. Note that the Specified Subject Condition accounts for the facts just noted in a uniform manner. In contrast, a pruning convention could at best account for cases (a) and (b) of (124)–(125). Clearly, the NP node cannot be pruned if *his* is deleted in *his story about killing the others, his story about killing us* since these phrases continue to function as NP's with respect to further operations. Notice that application of *each*-Movement to (124c) with *his* deleted is much more natural if *hear* is replaced by *tell*, so that the subject of *kill* is understood to be *the men,* and there is a relation similar to semantic agency between *the men* and *stories.* The Specified Subject Condition as stated does not suffice to account for the full range of such facts. We shall return briefly to the matter of agency.

very least, this might be true of the interesting sublanguages generated prior to optional final ellipsis.

Notice that the modification (123a) does not affect the cases of *wh*-Movement so far discussed, apart from examples such as (62)–(64). Due to the fact that *wh*-Movement, being cyclic, moves the *wh*-phrase to the COMP position of the clause in which the *wh*-phrase appears, the specification of the subject $Z$ in (123) has no bearing on *wh*-Movement in these cases. Thus both cases of (126) are grammatical, as distinct from the pairs (112), (114) and (120a,b):

(126)  a.  Who did they persuade Bill to kill
       b.  Who did they promise Bill to kill

Thus we have the pattern in (127):

(127)  a.  *We expect John to see each other   (*each*-Movement does not apply)
       b.  We expect John to see us   (RI does not apply)
       c.  Who do we expect John to see   (*wh*-Movement applies twice)
       d.  *We heard John's stories about each other   (*each*-Movement does not apply)
       e.  We heard John's stories about us   (RI does not apply)
       f.  *Who did we hear John's stories about   (*wh*-Movement does not apply)

In all cases of (127), if *John* (the specified subject $Z$ of (123a)) is dropped, then the rules apply, reversing the asterisk except in case (127c).

The modification (123a) has some implications for examples of a different sort. Consider the sentences (128) and (129):

(128)  We heard about plans to kill Bill
(129)  We received instructions to kill Bill

Sentence (128) means that we heard about plans for some indeterminate person(s) to kill Bill. Sentence (129), in its more natural interpretation, means that we received instructions that we should kill Bill, though perhaps it also has an interpretation analogous to (128), namely, that instructions for someone to kill Bill arrived in our possession. Clearly, (128) cannot have the interpretation analogous to the more natural interpretation of (129), namely, that we heard about the plans that we should kill Bill (it is not, of course, excluded that the indeterminate killer(s) in (128) should be among those designated by *we*). We can express these facts by postulating the underlying forms (130)–(132) and excluding (133). The element $\Delta$ in (130) and (132) is an indeterminate subject which deletes; PRO is controlled by the subject *we* and deletes by Equi-NP Deletion.

(130)  We heard about [plans [$\Delta$ to kill Bill]]
(131)  We received [instructions [PRO to kill Bill]]
(132)  We received [instructions [$\Delta$ to kill Bill]]  (?)
(133)  We heard about [plans [PRO to kill Bill]]  (*)

Consider then the sentences (134) and (135):

(134) a.  We heard about plans to kill each other  (*)
      b.  We received instructions to kill each other

(135) a.  We heard about plans to kill me
      b.  We received instructions to kill me

If the underlying source for (134a) is analogous to (130) (with *we each* replacing *we* and *the other* replacing *Bill*), then (134a) should be blocked by (123a) since $\Delta$ is not controlled by the NP *we each* containing *each*.[38] And (135a) should be grammatical since RI is blocked for the same reason. Sentence (134b) should be grammatical with the interpretation expressed by (136) (analogous to (131)) but not with that expressed by (137) (analogous to (132)); and (135b) should

---

[38] This assumes that deletion of the indeterminate subject follows *each*-Movement. Similarly, as the examples in (135) show, deletion of the indeterminate subject follows RI. If this line of reasoning is correct, then "deletion of $\Delta$" should be construed as a principle of interpretation. That is, we can think of $\Delta$ in these examples as being a null element; there is no rule of deletion. The rules of interpretation will assign a null element dominated by an NP subject the interpretation of an indeterminate subject.

If (129) cannot be interpreted as meaning "Instructions for someone's killing Bill arrived in our possession," then the rules of interpretation (or of selection) will have to be formulated to block (132). Notice that if the judgments given in this discussion are correct, then selection of PRO or $\Delta$ in the embedded sentence will involve both the head noun to which it is complement and the verb of which the phrase N-complement is the object, as is indicated by (134), (135), and (140).

It might be asked why *plans* and *instructions* in these examples are not preceded by the indeterminate subject $\Delta$, as determiner, blocking *each*-Movement and RI in all cases. The reason is that NP's, as distinct from sentences, do not have obligatory subjects. This fact is noted by Wasow and Roeper (1972), who use it to give an explanation of some properties of action nominals (*the singing of songs*) as distinct from gerundive nominals (*singing songs*), in an interesting corroboration of the lexicalist hypothesis concerning the structure of complex noun phrases.

be grammatical with the interpretation expressed by (138) (analogous to (132)) but not with that expressed by (139) (analogous to (131)). These conclusions seem to me correct.

(136)   We each received [instructions [PRO to kill the other]]
(137)   We each received [instructions [Δ to kill the other]]
(138)   We received [instructions [Δ to kill me]]
(139)   We received [instructions [PRO to kill me]]

Consider next (140):

(140) a.   We received plans to kill Bill
      b.  *We received plans to kill each other
      c.   We received plans to kill me

Sentence (140a) is unlike (129) in that it cannot have the interpretation "We are to kill Bill"; thus it cannot have the source analogous to (131) (with *plans* replacing *instructions*). Accordingly, (140b) is ungrammatical and (140c) is interpretable, in contrast to (134b) which is grammatical under the interpretation (136) and (135b) which is uninterpretable with the underlying source (139). Judgments are somewhat uncertain, but it seems to me that these conclusions are correct. If so, these cases, too, indicate that it is the Specified Subject Condition (123a) rather than a standard pruning convention that is operative here.

The conditions we have suggested have certain other consequences. Consider the sentences in (141)–(143) (compare (86)–(88)):

(141) a.   We heard a story about some pictures of me   (?)
      b.   Who did you hear a story about some pictures of   (*)
      c.   The men heard a story about some pictures of each
           other   [G]

(142) a.   We heard interesting claims about pictures of me   (?)
      b.   Who did we hear interesting claims about pictures of   (*)
      c.   The men heard interesting claims about pictures of each
           other   (G)

(143) a.   We heard interesting claims about me   (?)
      b.   Who did we hear interesting claims about   (G)
      c.   The men heard interesting claims about each other   (G)

The conditions suggested so far imply the judgments given in

121

brackets (* = ungrammatical, G = grammatical). In the case of the examples (a), the judgment should be G if RI is formulated so as to be subject to the *A*-over-*A* principle, * otherwise (see discussion of (101)). In the case of the examples (b), the Subjacency Condition (81) blocks *wh*-Movement in the case of (141b) and (142b), but not (143b). In the case of the examples (c), the rule of *each*-Movement is permitted in each case. While judgments are not entirely trustworthy, the conclusions seem to me plausible.

R. Dougherty notes a variety of other examples that can be explained along similar lines in terms of the Specified Subject Condition. Consider the underlying structures (144) and (145):

(144)   They will obey [any request [COMP PRO to kill *X*]]
(145)   They will okay [any request [COMP PRO to kill *X*]]

From (144) we derive *They will obey any request to kill* X; from (145) we derive *They will okay any request to kill* X. In the former case, under its most natural interpretation, they are to kill *X*; but in the latter, someone indeterminate is to do so. That is, in (144), but not (145), the matrix subject *they* controls PRO. Correspondingly, we have the examples in (146) and (147):

(146) a.  *Who will they obey any request to kill
      b.  *Who will they okay any request to kill
      c.   They will obey any request to kill each other
      d.  *They will okay any request to kill each other

(147) a.  *We will obey any request to kill us
      b.   We will okay any request to kill us

Examples (146a,b) are excluded by virtue of the Subjacency Condition on extraction and the lack of COMP in the NP *any request to kill* X. Example (146c), however, is not blocked by these circumstances since it is not formed by an extraction rule. But (146d) is again excluded, in this case by the Specified Subject Condition since the matrix subject *they* does not control the subject of the most deeply embedded S. For the same reason, the rule RI is blocked in the case of (147b) and the sentence is grammatical, but RI is applicable in the case of (147a) and the sentence is marked "strange."

Similarly, consider the underlying forms (148) and (149):

(148)   It appeared to John [COMP they to like *X*]
(149)   They appealed to John [COMP PRO to like *X*]

By *it*-Replacement, (148) yields (150), while (149) is transformed finally into (151):

(150)   They appeared to John to like $X$
(151)   They appealed to John to like $X$

In (149) the embedded subject PRO is controlled by *John*. In (150), on the other hand, *John* does not control the subject of the embedded sentence. (Rather, either there is no subject after *it*-Replacement or there is a "trace" controlled by the matrix subject *they*, under an analysis that we will consider later.) Correspondingly, we have the distribution of data in (152) and (153):

(152)   a.   Who did they appear to John to like
        b.   Who did they appeal to John to like
        c.   They appeared to John to like each other
        d.   *They appealed to John to like each other

(153)   a.   *We appeared to John to like us
        b.   We appealed to John to like us

Iterated *wh*-Movement gives (152a) and (152b). The rule of *each*-Movement from the matrix subject *they each* is permitted in (152c); but it is blocked in (152d) by the Specified Subject Condition since *John*, rather than *they each*, controls the subject of the embedded sentence. Similarly, the rule RI is blocked in the case of (153b) by the Specified Subject Condition but is applicable in (153a) where it assigns *.

Dougherty (1970) also notes that the *respectively* Interpretation Rule appears to obey the same constraints. Thus consider the examples in (154):

(154)   a.   We will obey any request to kiss our respective wives
        b.   *We will okay any request to kiss our respective wives
        c.   We appeared to John to like our respective wives
        d.   *We appealed to John to like our respective wives

Association of *respective* with the matrix subject *we* is permitted in cases (a) and (c) but blocked in cases (b) and (d) by the Specified Subject Condition since the subject of *kiss, like* is not controlled by the matrix subject *we*.

In all of these cases, it is control of the embedded item PRO that determines applicability or nonapplicability of rules. In particular, it seems quite impossible, in these cases too, to rely on any familiar notion of pruning to make the appropriate distinctions.

Before leaving this topic, I will merely mention examples which indicate a possible further refinement of the notion "specified subject," without pursuing the matter. Y. Bordelois notes the following examples (with (155) from Kayne (1969)):

(155)   Why are John and Mary letting the honey drip on each other's feet
(156)   *Why are John and Mary letting Bill drip honey on each other's feet
(157)   Why are they letting the baby fall on each other's laps
(158)   *Why are they letting Bill drop the baby on each other's laps

The rule of *each*-Movement is blocked in examples (156) and (158) by the Specified Subject Condition. However, (155) and (157) seem considerably more acceptable, even though they too contain a specified subject that should block *each*-Movement. The examples suggest that a notion of "agency" is involved and that perhaps the notion "specified agent" is the critical one rather than formal subject. Notice, incidentally, that this conclusion, if correct, would not affect the hypothesis that transformations do not refer to semantic relations but only to bracketing of phrase markers (see the opening discussion) even if the semantic notion "agency" plays a role in determining applicability of transformations. Similarly, reference in (123) to the semantic notion of "control" does not affect this conclusion.

**10.**   The Specified Subject Condition, as we have now formulated it in (123a), asserts that in a structure of the form (159), no rule can involve $X$ and $Y$ if $Z$ is the subject of the phrase $WYV$ and $Z$ is not controlled by the category containing $X$:

(159)   $\ldots X \ldots [ \ldots Z \ldots -WYV \ldots ] \ldots$

The condition on $Z$ has the two subcases (a) and (b) of (160):

(160)   a.  $Z$ is not controlled at all[39]
        b.  $Z$ is controlled by a category not containing $X$

---

[39] Specifically, $Z$ is a lexical item, an item (such as *there*) introduced by a transformation and not subject to control, a nonanaphoric pronoun, or the indeterminate element $\Delta$. See note 38.

124

Notice that if $X$ (or the minimal major category containing it) is not a possible controller, then case (160b) will always hold in examples of the sort we are discussing, given that $Z$ is the anaphoric item PRO. We might therefore consider adding to (160b) the provision (161):

(161)   where the minimal major category containing $X$ (i.e., $MMC(X)$) is a possible controller

A possible argument against this modification is provided by such sentences as (162):

(162) a.  John made a fortune by cheating *his friends*
      b.  John made a fortune while living *in England*

A *wh*-phrase in the italicized position of (162) is not subject to *wh*-Movement, although *each*-Movement into this position is permissible. Thus we have the examples in (163):

(163) a.  *Who did John make a fortune by cheating
      b.  *Where did John make a fortune while living
      c.   They get their kicks by cheating each other
      d.   They were apprehended while shooting at each other[40]

These judgments regarding grammaticalness follow from the Specified Subject Condition (159), (160). In all four cases of (163), the subject PRO of the embedded phrases *by . . .* and *while . . .* is controlled by the matrix subject. In cases (c) and (d), the matrix subject fills the position $X$ of (159) (more precisely, the position $MMC(X)$), so that case (160b) is inapplicable and the rule of *each*-Movement applies. In cases (a) and (b) of (163), however, $X$ of (159) is COMP, not the subject *John* which controls $Z$ ($=$ PRO). Therefore (160b) applies and the rule of *wh*-Movement is blocked, as indicated in (163a,b). But if we add the provision (161) to (160b), then the Specified Subject Condition no longer applies since COMP is not a possible controller. We are thus left without an explanation for the ungrammaticalness of (163a,b). Condition (161) is, then, unacceptable unless there is an alternative explanation for (163a,b).

Let us assume that there is an alternative explanation in this case and consider the provision (161). We have discussed two cases in

---

[40] Not synonymous with "Each was apprehended while shooting at the other," since for (d) to be true they must have been apprehended simultaneously. See note 34.

which $X$ is not a possible controller and in which (161) will therefore be relevant, namely, the rule of *it*-Replacement, where $X = it$, and the rule of *wh*-Movement, where $X = $ COMP. Let us examine each of these, under the tentative assumption that (160b) is qualified by (161).

In discussing *it*-Replacement previously (see (32)–(41)), we argued that (164b) derives from (164a), whereas the corresponding form (165b) cannot be derived from (165a) because of the Specified Subject Condition (160a):

(164) a. It is pleasant for the rich [$_S$ COMP PRO to do the hard work]
   b. The hard work is pleasant for the rich to do

(165) a. It is pleasant for the rich [$_S$ COMP poor immigrants to do the hard work]
   b. *The hard work is pleasant for the rich for poor immigrants to do

This earlier discussion preceded our extension of the Specified Subject Condition to include (160b) alongside of (160a). But notice that (160b) prevents *it*-Replacement in (164) as well since PRO of the embedded sentence is controlled by the phrase *the rich* rather than by $X = it$.[41] The problem would be resolved by the modification of the Specified Subject Condition just proposed, namely, the provision (161) added to case (160b).

Notice, incidentally, that we cannot assign the provision (161) to both cases of the Specified Subject Condition for if (160a) is qualified in this way then (165b) will no longer be blocked.

The same point is illustrated by the examples (167), deriving from (166) (from Postal (1971)):

(166) a. It is tough for me [COMP PRO to stop [COMP Bill's looking at Harriet]]
   b. It is tough for me [COMP PRO to stop [COMP PRO looking at Harriet]]

(167) a. *Harriet is tough for me to stop Bill's looking at
   b. Harriet is tough for me to stop looking at

---

[41] I am indebted to R. Kayne for bringing this fact to my attention.

If we were to accept the analysis of such phrases proposed by Bresnan (1971), this problem would not arise since the embedded structure is analyzed as VP rather than as S in the underlying structure. This approach necessitates a richer system of interpretive rules to determine the subject of the embedded structure and corresponding modifications of most of the material presented here. I have not investigated the consequences of such modifications.

126

If the provision (161) qualifies (160b) but not (160a), then (167b) can be derived from (166b) but (167a) cannot be derived from (166a), explaining the distinction.[42]

Notice that (168) does yield (169) under *it*-Replacement:

(168)   It is tough for me [COMP PRO to stop Bill from [COMP PRO looking at Harriet]]

(169)   Harriet is tough for me to stop Bill from looking at

The distinction between (169) and (167a) (which would be a near paraphrase of (169) were it grammatical) is that in (168), but not (166a), the most deeply embedded subject is PRO; thus, the provision (161) applies, rendering the Specified Subject Condition inapplicable and permitting *wh*-Movement.

This analysis is weakened, however, by the fact that extraction of *Harriet* in (166b) and (168) violates the Subjacency Condition (81) on extraction rules. To preserve this general convention, we must suppose that *Harriet* is moved to the position of *it* in (166b) and (168) by two cyclic rules, one applying in the cycle containing the main verb *stop* and the second applying in the matrix cycle.

In fact, there is another approach to the analysis of these structures that preserves the general convention (81) and at the same time dispenses with the provision (161), thus further weakening the hypothesis that the latter is required. Recall that the acceptable sentence (164b) is prohibited by the extension (160b) of the Specified Subject Condition unless the provision (161) is added. Now note that (164b) would be permitted if the NP *the hard work* were moved into a

---

[42] It might be argued that the most deeply embedded cyclic category in (166) is an NP (see the discussion of (202)). In that case, the *A*-over-*A* Condition should prevent extraction of *Harriet* in (166), although *it*-Replacement would produce *Bill's looking at Harriet is tough for me to stop* from (166a) and *Looking at Harriet is tough for me to stop* from (166b). (Notice that the alternative form *To stop (Bill's) looking at Harriet is tough for me* is irrelevant to this discussion.) However, the issue is complicated by the fact that extraction of NP's from such nominal structures seems marginally possible (see the discussion of (6) and (186b)).

The *A*-over-*A* Condition should prevent the derivation of *\*John is fun to see pictures of* from *It is fun [COMP PRO to see [pictures of John]]* (permitting only *Pictures of John are fun to see*), despite the fact that there is no specified subject in the underlying NP *pictures of John*. Similarly, consider the sentence *It is fun to take pictures of John*. This is ambiguous: it can be interpreted with the NP *pictures of John* as object of the verb *take* (meaning "remove" or "steal") or with the NP *John* as object of the verbal expression *take pictures* (meaning "photograph"). Under the former interpretation we can derive *Pictures of John are fun to take* but not *\*John is fun to take pictures of*. The latter is derivable only when *take pictures* is analyzed as the verbal expression so that the *A*-over-*A* Condition does not block extraction of *John*, there being no NP *pictures of John*.

position not preceded by PRO on the internal cycle. Then, exactly as in the case of *wh*-Movement, the NP *the hard work* could be extracted on the next cycle, irrespective of the control of PRO, since the structure would not in any event be of the form (159) to which the Specified Subject Condition applies. It cannot be that the NP *the hard work* moves to the position of the embedded COMP in (164a) (as a *wh*-phrase would) or (165b) would not be blocked; furthermore, (123c) would prevent *it*-Replacement by *the hard work* on the next cycle under this assumption. The only remaining possibility, then, is that the NP *the hard work* replaces PRO itself by a new rule of PRO-Replacement, analogous to the rule of *it*-Replacement itself, giving the intermediate form (170):

(170)   It is pleasant for the rich [$_s$ COMP the hard work to do]

The assumption that there is such a rule of PRO-Replacement is not unreasonable. Notice that we already require a rule that will move the NP *the hard work* from (170) to the subject position of the matrix sentence to replace *it,* namely, the rule that gives (172) from the corresponding cases of (171):

(171)   a.   It is likely [$_s$ COMP John to leave]
        b.   It seems [$_s$ COMP John to be a nice fellow]

(172)   a.   John is likely to leave
        b.   John seems to be a nice fellow

Adding the new rule of PRO-Replacement permits, at very little cost, generalization of the obligatory rule that gives (172). It must be stipulated that if PRO-Replacement has applied, say, in the most deeply embedded structure of (166b), then further application is obligatory (as it is with the rule of *it*-Replacement with which PRO-Replacement can probably be merged). We must then make this combined rule obligatory when the NP that is to replace *it* is in subject position in the embedded sentence.[43]

---

[43] If the subject position of the embedded sentence is filled by a lexical item, then the general condition of Recoverability of Deletion will block the rule of PRO-Replacement. This will, then, suffice to prevent illegitimate *it*-Replacement to give (165b) from (165a). Notice that the rule of *it*-Replacement must be formulated so that while obligatory in (171) and (170), it is inapplicable to (165a), which cannot yield *\*Poor immigrants are pleasant for the rich to do the hard work.* Thus we must assume that (170) is structurally distinguishable from (165a). The simplest proposal is that the rule of PRO-Replacement, which yields (170), does not replace PRO with *the hard work* but rather combines the two, assigning the feature PRO to the NP *the hard work* which moves into the position of PRO. Then the rule of *it*-Replacement will be obligatory with matrix predicates of the sort that appear in (171) and with all matrix predicates when

It is possible that some of the limitations on *it*-Replacement may be explicable in these terms. For example, J. Kimball has noted that there are very few examples of sentences of the form (164b) derived from passives in the embedded sentence. (One of the few examples, noted in Chomsky (1964), is *Such flattery is easy to be fooled by*; there are others with closely related verbs.) For example, we cannot form such sentences as *\*The poor are pleasant for the rich to be served by* from *It is pleasant for the rich [to be served by the poor]*. To express this fact, it would be sufficient to have PRO-Replacement precede Passive, or, more exactly, precede the subrule of Passive that preposes NP, the latter being actually a special case of PRO-Replacement, in effect.

An additional argument in support of PRO-Replacement is that it accounts for some observations of Bresnan (1971) regarding stress contours. Bresnan points out that if the rules of stress assignment are part of the transformational cycle (as she convincingly argues), then it would be necessary to exclude from the cycle the categories marked with brackets in such cases as (164a), (166b), and (168); otherwise, the Nuclear Stress Rule will incorrectly assign primary stress to the term that replaces *it*. Her proposal is to take the bracketed expressions as VP's, an approach which, as noted earlier, has far-reaching effects on the formulation of many rules. Within the present framework, we can achieve the same result by continuing to take the bracketed categories in these examples to be S and postulating the cyclic rule of PRO-Replacement.

There are, however, certain problems that arise if we assume the rule of PRO-Replacement. Consider the sentences in (173), which derive ultimately from the corresponding cases of (174):[44]

---

the subject of the embedded S, which replaces *it*, contains the feature PRO. Under all other circumstances, the rule of *it*-Replacement is inapplicable. This complication is the cost of the rule of PRO-Replacement. We will see in a moment that, under the analysis we are now considering, the assumption that the NP *the hard work* retains the feature PRO in (170) might serve an additional function as well.

Notice that the Tensed-S Condition will in any event block *Books are difficult to believe that Tom reads,* although *This is the book that it is difficult to believe that Tom read* is derivable, by iteration of *wh*-Movement.

I will not explore the many further problems in characterizing the domain of applicability of *it*-Replacement.

[44] Compare (173a) with *\*The men are happy for each other to leave,* blocked for reasons discussed earlier (see (104b)). Notice that in the latter case, the *for*-phrase is presumably part of the embedded sentence, whereas in the case of (173a), it is part of the predicate of the matrix sentence. Thus we cannot form *\*The men were happy to leave, for Bill* as a variant of *The men were happy for Bill to leave* although *The men were easy to kill, for Bill* is a possible variant of *The men were easy for Bill to kill.* (See the discussion of (32)–(41).) Similarly, the other properties of *easy*-constructions discussed earlier distinguish these from *The men were happy to leave,* and so on.

(173)  a.  *The men are easy for each other to please
       b.  *John seems to the men to like each other
       c.  Toys are fun for the kids to give each other   (?)

(174)  a.  It is easy for the others [COMP PRO to please each of the men]
       b.  It seems to each of the men [COMP John to like the others]
       c.  It is fun for each of the kids [COMP PRO to give toys to the others]

Of the sentences in (173), (b) is the worst and (c) seems to me better than (a). Assuming tentatively the classification given in (173), consider the implications. In the case of (174a), the phrase *each of the men* replaces *it* on the external cycle. The rule of *each*-Movement then gives (173a). One way to block the latter would be to order the rule of *each*-Movement before the rule of *it*-Replacement.[45] Let us assume this ordering of rules, tentatively.

Turning then to (174b), we see that the phrase *John* replaces *it*, after which *each*-Movement would give (173b). But (173b) is blocked, as required, if *each*-Movement precedes *it*-Replacement, as we are tentatively assuming.[46]

Consider then (174c). On the inner cycle, Indirect Object Movement gives (175):

(175)  It is fun for each of the kids [COMP PRO to give the others toys]

If there is no rule of PRO-Replacement, then we turn to the external cycle. The rule of *each*-Movement applies, followed by *it*-Replacement, giving (173c). Application of *each*-Movement is permitted by the condition on control since *each of the kids* controls PRO. The qualification (161) on case (160b) of the Specified Subject

---

[45] Other avenues might be explored in attempting to account for the questionable or ungrammatical status of (173a). Thus a relation analogous to that of antecedent-anaphoric pronoun holds between the phrases *each of the men* and *the others* in the underlying structure (174a), and there might be conditions preventing an antecedent from being subjacent to and to the right of a term associated with it by such a relation. Also, one might explore a variant of some Crossover Principle of the type discussed by Postal (1971). These approaches seem to me dubious, however, if not completely impossible, because of such examples as (178) and (179), which require *it*-Replacement from (174a).

[46] Notice that in the case of (174b), we do not have the alternative possibilities for explanation noted in the preceding footnote for the case of (174a).

130

Condition makes this condition inoperative, thus permitting *it*-Replacement, giving (173c).

Suppose, however, that we rely on the rule of PRO-Replacement instead of the qualification (161). Then PRO-Replacement, applying on the inner cycle, gives (176), which is then subject to obligatory *it*-Replacement on the next cycle:

(176)   It is fun for each of the kids [COMP toys to give the others]

Assuming the analysis of note 43, the item *toys* is actually a complex structure containing the feature PRO. Assuming still that *each*-Movement precedes *it*-Replacement, then *each*-Movement must apply to (176) at this point if we are to derive (173c). However, *each*-Movement will apply only if the position of PRO in (175), now occupied by the complex structure [toys, PRO] (= *toys*) in (176), is still controlled by the phrase *each of the kids* of the matrix sentence of (176); otherwise, *each*-Movement will be blocked by the Specified Subject Condition, which is no longer rendered inoperative by (161). In effect this means that we regard control as an enduring property of the paired positions in such cases (relying, presumably, on the continued presence of PRO in the complex structure [toys, PRO]). Furthermore, we must reformulate the Specified Subject Condition slightly so that a position is not considered to be lexically specified, thus falling under the condition, if it is controlled. These consequences, while not intolerable, nevertheless do not seem to me particularly desirable.

Suppose then that we were to drop the assumption that *each*-Movement precedes *it*-Replacement. Now there is no problem with (174c), assuming the rule of PRO-Replacement or not. We might account for (173b) by assuming that when the NP *John* replaces *it* in (174b), it leaves behind a "trace" which it controls. The trace might be PRO, or it might be the null element if we think of the transformation as moving only the terminal symbol *John* to the NP subject position of the matrix sentence, leaving unaltered the nodes that originally dominated it (see note 38). If the trace is PRO, it will be deleted by a final rule that deletes controlled PRO in such sentences as *We expected to leave*. The controlled trace blocks *each*-Movement, so that (173b) is ungrammatical.

This approach will not work in the case of (173a), however. Applying PRO-Replacement on the inner cycle in (174a) and then *it*-Replacement on the outer cycle, we derive (177):

(177)   Each of the men is easy for the others [COMP PRO to please]

There is, however, no reason why *each*-Movement should not apply to this to give the unwanted (173a). If *each*-Movement does not apply in (177), we derive (178), which seems acceptable:

(178)   Each of the men is easy for the others to please

Thus, if we assume (173a) to be ungrammatical and (173c) to be grammatical, it would appear that PRO-Replacement entails that *each*-Movement precedes *it*-Replacement and that it is necessary to carry out the modifications suggested after (176). This conclusion might be regarded as an argument against PRO-Replacement, hence an argument in support of the provision (161) on (160b), which seems necessary if there is no rule of PRO-Replacement. (Indirectly, it is also an argument against the Subjacency Condition (81) on extraction rules, which appears to be violated if we do not presuppose PRO-Replacement.) The argument is no stronger than the assumptions regarding the status of (173a) and (173c) and also depends on the assumption that there is no other way to prevent *each*-Movement to the *for*-phrase in (177). The latter assumption might in fact be challenged. Consider (179):

(179)   The men are each easy for the others to please

It seems to me that (179) is as acceptable as (178), and better than (173a). But if our general assumptions about *each*-Movement are correct, then (179) derives from (178) by one of the cases of *each*-Movement (see (121), (122)). If so, then *each*-Movement must be able to apply after *it*-Replacement. Then we can account for (173b) and (173c) as already explained, and we are left with the unexplained distinction between (179) and (173a). We must, in short, suppose that some other consideration makes the *for*-phrase in (174a), (173a) immune to insertion of *each*. If this is correct, then these considerations provide no argument against PRO-Replacement and in support of (161).

I have explored the interconnections among various assumptions, reaching no firm conclusion. It seems reasonable to make the tentative assumption that PRO-Replacement operates and that *it*-Replacement in (174b) leaves a "trace," and, finally, that we can dispense with the qualification (161) and preserve the principle (81) of Subjacency. On this assumption, we leave unexplained the ungrammaticalness of (173a) (as compared with (179)), but all of the other cases examined fall into place.

Let us turn now to the second general case to which the provision (161) applies, namely, the case of $X$ in COMP, where $X$ again is not a possible controller.

Consider the sentences (180)–(182):

(180)   COMP they expected [COMP Bill to kill who]
(181)   COMP they expected [COMP PRO to kill who]
(182)   COMP they each expected [COMP who to kill the others]

In the case of (180), cyclic iteration of *wh*-Movement gives *Who did they expect Bill to kill*. The cyclic property of *wh*-Movement prevents violation of the Specified Subject Condition, case (160a). In the case of (181), the same process gives *Who did they expect to kill*. However, with the subcondition (160b) of the Specified Subject Condition qualified by provision (161), we no longer need to appeal to the cyclic property of *wh*-Movement to explain why application of *wh*-Movement to (181), placing *who* in the external COMP, is not a violation of the Specified Subject Condition.

Recall that we cannot extend provision (161) to case (160a) of the Specified Subject Condition, that is, to the case of a lexically specified subject. We have already noted this with regard to *easy-to-VP* constructions (see (165)–(167)). Depending on the status of such examples as (6), we may be able to illustrate the same point directly in the case of *wh*-Movement itself. Consider the structures (183)–(186):

(183)   a.   +WH you counted on [COMP PRO going to college]
        b.   +WH you counted on [COMP your son's going to college]

(184)   a.   +WH you counted on [COMP PRO doing what]
        b.   +WH you counted on [COMP your son's doing what]

(185)   a.   Did you count on going to college
        b.   Did you count on your son's going to college

(186)   a.   What did you count on doing
        b.   What did you count on your son's doing   (?)

Overlooking details that are irrelevant here, the structures (183) yield the corresponding cases of (185), as expected. The rule of *wh*-Movement applied to (184a) gives (186a). Sentence (186b) is analogous to (6). As noted earlier, it constitutes a violation of an "absolute" interpretation of the *A*-over-*A* Condition, though not of the interpretation we have tentatively adopted. If, in fact, COMP is empty in such structures as (183), (184), as we will suggest directly, then (186b) is also a violation of the Specified Subject Condition since *wh*-Movement will then not apply on the internal cycle. Such examples as (6), (186b), and others (for instance, *What did you talk about Bill's doing, What did you insist on Bill's doing, What did you stop Bill's reading*) seem marginal, for the most part. If they are ungrammatical (perhaps with a few idiomatic exceptions, as permitted by the interpretation of the conditions suggested with regard to (6)–(14), then the array of data (183)–(186) again illustrates the impossibility of adding provision (161) to subcondition (160a) of the Specified Subject Condition since this would now permit all such cases as (186b).

Let us return now to (182). Iteration of *wh*-Movement gives (187):

(187)   Who they each expected to kill the others

But then *each*-Movement should be applicable, giving (188) ultimately (this example from R. Kayne):

(188)   *Who did they expect to kill each other

But (188) does not have the interpretation of (187). Rather, it can derive, if at all, only from *They expected [each of who to kill the other]*, by *each*-Movement on the internal cycle (analogous to the questionable *Who did Bill expect to kill each other*). The example is analogous to the case of (173a,b), where we considered (but ultimately rejected) the assumption that *each*-Movement precedes *it*-Replacement as an explanation for the ungrammaticalness of the forms. The analogous assumption that *each*-Movement precedes *wh*-Movement would suffice to account for (188), but the assumption does not suffice in general, as we can see from the derivation (189):

(189) a.   COMP Bill wanted [COMP they each to expect [COMP who to kill the others]]
      b.   COMP Bill wanted [COMP they each to expect [who to kill the others]]
      c.   COMP Bill wanted [COMP they to expect who to kill each other]
      d.   COMP Bill wanted [who they to expect to kill each other]
      e.   *Who did Bill want them to expect to kill each other

On the innermost cycle, *wh*-Movement applies to (a) of (189), giving (b). On the second cycle, assuming *each*-Movement precedes *wh*-Movement, we derive first (c) by *each*-Movement and then (d) by *wh*-Movement. Finally, on the last cycle we derive (e) by *wh*-Movement and the obligatory rules of Auxiliary Inversion and Case Assignment.[47] Therefore the assumption that *each*-Movement precedes *wh*-Movement does not suffice to exclude the unwanted derivations in such cases.

In investigating *it*-Replacement, we noted that to exclude (173b) we might assume either that *each*-Movement precedes *it*-Replacement or that when an NP replaces *it* by *it*-Replacement it leaves behind a trace which is controlled by the moved NP; we finally opted tentatively for the latter conclusion. Although the device of rule ordering does not suffice in the analogous cases just discussed, the device of leaving a trace does. Suppose, then, that we assume that the rule of *wh*-Movement leaves a controlled PRO (or a null symbol dominated by its former categories — see the discussion that precedes (177)) in the position from which it moves. Then *each*-Movement cannot apply to give (189c) from (189b) because of the Specified Subject Condition, subcase (160b). Similarly, (188) cannot be derived from (187).[48] As we shall see, this assumption permits a fairly simple rule of interpretation for *wh*-Questions and might be supported on other grounds as well.[49]

---

[47] We have not explicitly formulated the latter. The simplest assumption would appear to be that pronouns are always in the objective case, except in the subject position of a tensed sentence where a special rule marks them with the appropriate "nominative" inflection.

[48] The final rule of PRO-Deletion must now delete PRO in *They expected* PRO *to leave, Who did they expect* PRO *to leave,* and *Who did they expect* PRO *would leave* (assuming that PRO rather than null is the "trace"), but not in *John expected that* [PRO, singular, masculine] *would win the prize,* where the set of bracketed features is read *he*. The latter may or may not be controlled by *John*. The technical problem of making the appropriate distinction can be handled in a number of fairly obvious ways, and I will not explore the matter here.

[49] For example, assuming that *wh*-Movement leaves a trace PRO, we might then stipulate that every rule that moves an item from an obligatory category (in the sense of Emonds (1970)) leaves a trace. If the trace is not specified as PRO in the movement rule itself, then the trace is *, in which case the sentence will be blocked as ungrammatical unless the position with * is filled by some subsequent rule. It is easy to show that on this assumption Emonds' observations on the obligatory character of NP-preposing in Passive in sentences and its optional character in noun phrases follow directly on the basis of the assumption that in simple N–V–N sentences the subject position is filled by a full NP in the underlying structure. In Emonds' analysis, the subject position is empty in the base and is filled by a rule that moves NP from the agent position. (This rule then replaces the rule of Subject Postposing, one component of Passive). He then stipulates that an obligatory category, such as "subject," must be filled somewhere in a derivation, thus explaining the difference between Passive in NP and S. But the assumption that the obligatory category "subject" is obligatorily null in the base seems curious. And there are further difficulties. As R. Kayne points out, this

There is one other alternative that immediately comes to mind in the case of (188) and (189e), namely, that the rule of *wh*-Movement be extracted entirely from the cycle of transformational rules and applied only after all of the cyclic rules have applied. Under this assumption, it will follow at once that (188) cannot be derived from (187) or (189e) from (189a) by virtue of the Specified Subject Condition, case (160a), which will block *each*-Movement. Thus the assumption would be that there are two independent and ordered cycles, the first containing all cyclic rules apart from *wh*-Movement and the second containing *wh*-Movement.[50] We must still suppose *wh*-Movement to be cyclic, in particular because of such examples as (180), which will otherwise violate the Specified Subject Condition, case (160a).

Although the possibility just suggested is attractive in some respects, I will not pursue it further here and will assume in the following discussion that the rule of *wh*-Movement leaves behind a trace in the sense discussed.

**11.** The Specified Subject Condition has a certain naturalness. Note that in several (though not all) of the cases in which it applies to a structure of the form (190), the rule involving $(X, Y)$ might also have involved $(Z, Y)$, were $Z$ appropriately selected:

---

assumption requires us to relate adverbials to an item in agent position, as in *The offer was sent by John with great glee*. But in general, adverbials relate only to items in subject position: compare *John received the offer with great glee, John was sent the offer with great glee*, where the latter, if interpretable at all, does not associate the adverbial with *John*.

A further step would be to distinguish, in some principled way, between the rules that leave PRO and * as a trace. I will not pursue here the various possibilities that suggest themselves.

To relate this discussion to other currently debated issues, note that the device of leaving a trace which functions in subsequent rules amounts to admitting a certain "derivational constraint" into the grammar. As the notion "derivational constraint" has been used in recent work, there would appear to be no condition on derivations, hence no grammatical rule operating within a derivation, that is not a derivational constraint. The only interesting problem, clearly, is to discover what specific kinds of rules (that is, derivational constraints) are empirically motivated. For my views on this matter, see Chomsky (1972a).

[50] The latter cycle might also contain the root transformation of Topicalization and perhaps various rules of preposing of adverbials and other structures. See note 32.

Bresnan (1971) suggests that the rules of stress assignment (hence, presumably, all the rules of the phonological component) belong to the transformational cycle, and she discusses the implications of this view with respect to the ordering of *wh*-Movement. The question also bears on the description of Pronominalization, as has been frequently pointed out. (See particularly Postal (1971).) To my knowledge, the considerations just discussed provide the only reason for supposing that *wh*-Movement may not be part of the regular cycle of transformational rules, assuming that the general framework discussed here can be sustained.

(190)   $\ldots X \ldots [ \ldots Z \ldots -WYV \ldots ] \ldots$

Thus (191) derives from (192):

(191)   The men expected [the police to arrest each other]
(192)   The men expected [the police each to arrest the other(s)]

The Specified Subject Condition implies that (191) must have the interpretation indicated by (192), not that given by the underlying representation (193), which cannot be transformed into (191) because of the Specified Subject Condition:

(193)   The men each expected [the police to arrest the other(s)]

Thus the Specified Subject Condition, in some cases, has the effect of reducing ambiguity, or, to put it differently, of increasing the reliability of a reasonable perceptual strategy that seeks the nearest NP to a verb (or the head noun of a nominal phrase) as its subject. Similar observations apply in the case of the $A$-over-$A$ condition (3). (See also the discussion of (203).) The foregoing of course assumes that the deep structure position of *each* plays some role in interpretation. See, however, notes 17, 34. If deep structure position plays no role, then the considerations just mentioned in effect guarantee a correspondence between deep structure position and scope as determined by surface structure interpretation rules, a rather natural consequence.

**12.** The rules we have discussed so far involve an item $Y$ in an embedded phrase and an item $X$ superior to it and to its left, as in the structure (190). We have noted various conditions under which $X$ and $Y$ may or may not be involved in a rule in this case. Suppose that we generalize these conditions, eliminating the left-right asymmetry. Thus we simply drop from (123) the requirement that $X$ be to the left of the embedded phrase $[_\alpha$ and leave all conditions otherwise unchanged. I do not know of many convincing examples that bear on the correctness of this generalization. For example, one consequence will be that the Specified Subject Condition will block (194) but not (195):

(194)   *John's pictures of each other intrigued the children
(195)   Pictures of each other intrigue the children

Although (194) surely is much worse than (195), leftward movement of *each* still seems at best clumsy, so that the example is perhaps not too illuminating. However, there are more interesting cases when we consider the Subjacency Condition (81). This condition implies (196):

(196)   No rule can move an item from position $Y$ to position $X$ in the structure

$$\ldots [_\beta \ldots [_\alpha \ldots Y \ldots ] \ldots ] \ldots X \ldots$$

where $Y \neq \alpha$ and $\alpha$, $\beta$ are cyclic categories, unless some constant term of the structural description of the rule holds of a phrase in $\beta$ that is subjacent to $X$.

In particular, we cannot derive sentences such as those in (197):

(197)  a.  John believes [$_\beta$ that [$_\alpha$ a man _____] was here . . . ] despite the evidence to the contrary *who comes from Philadelphia*
   b.  [$_\beta$ [$_\alpha$ one _____] of the men . . . ] will meet you at the station *who is a friend of mine*
   c.  the girl [$_\beta$ to whom [$_\alpha$ it _____] was obvious . . . ] slapped the dean *that he was after her*[51]

In (197), _____ indicates the position from which the italicized item is extracted by various types of extraposition, and . . . indicates the position to which the italicized item can properly be moved. These examples are of the form (196), where the italicized phrase is in the position $X$, having been moved illegitimately from the position $Y$ marked by _____.

On the other hand, consider such sentences as (198):

(198)  a.  [[$_\beta$ the only people [$_\alpha$ they really like _____]] are Bill and Mary
   b.  [[$_\beta$ the only people [$_\alpha$ they really like _____]] are each other

On the assumption (proposed in Chomsky (1970a) and developed in detail in Akmajian (1970)) that (a) and (b) of (198) derive from a source with a subject containing *They really like Bill and Mary, They really like each other,* respectively, by substitution of the object of $\alpha$ into the predicate position of the matrix sentence, the derivation is permissible, under (196), if the structural description of the rule that forms (198) makes explicit reference to the position occupied by *the only people* in (198).

If the analysis given so far is correct, then, there appears to be no

---

[51] Example from Bach (1971). If, as Emonds (1970) proposes, there is no rule of extraposition of the assumed form, then the issue does not arise in the case of (197c).

left-right asymmetry for extraction rules. Though relevant examples are few, to my knowledge, it seems plausible to offer the general working hypothesis that there is no left-right asymmetry at all with respect to the conditions that have been discussed here.

Left-right asymmetry of rules is not unknown, of course, anaphora being the most obvious example, and the Complementizer Substitution Universal (2) being another one. Ross (1967) has suggested that leftward movement rules and rightward movement rules differ in that the former can move an item arbitrarily far to the left, crossing arbitrarily many clause boundaries, whereas the latter cannot extract an item from a clause. Notice that this asymmetry of boundedness follows from the asymmetry of the Complementizer Substitution Universal. That is, we have proposed that leftward and rightward extraction rules are bounded by the Subjacency Condition, but items that move to COMP position will escape this limitation, for reasons that we have discussed. Assuming that complementizer substitution is only leftward (that is, the Baker-Bresnan Complementizer Substitution Universal (2)) and that an item in the COMP position can move upward to (and only to) another COMP position, unhindered by the Specified Subject and Tensed-S Conditions, it follows that there can be, in effect, unbounded movement to the left by iteration of Complementizer Substitution. Thus the two cases of asymmetry are not independent. Rather, the asymmetry of boundedness follows from the asymmetry of the Complementizer Substitution Universal, in the special case of rules that substitute an item in the COMP position. The available data would appear to bear out this limitation.

**13.** Let us now turn to the transformational rules. We have so far assumed the cyclic rules that I restate as (199) and the root transformations (200):

(199)  a.  *wh*-Placement on NP, PP, AP, or *either*
      b.  *wh*-Movement: in the structure

$$[_S [_{COMP} X_1, X_2, X_3, \pm WH], X_5, wh, X_7]$$

        the sixth term fills the position of $X_2$ and is replaced by PRO
      c.  [*wh*, NP] becomes null in the context

$$[_{NP} NP \underline{\quad\quad} \ldots ] \text{ (i.e., in relatives)}^{52}$$

---

[52] I assume here that a relative structure, at this stage of derivation, has the form NP S. This is not obviously correct, and if the structure is in fact different, the condition for (c) will have to be correspondingly reformulated.

d. −WH becomes *that* in the context

$$\begin{cases} [_\alpha X[_S \underline{\qquad} YT \ldots ] \ldots ] & \text{(i)}^{53} \\ [_\sigma Z[_{\bar N} N \underline{\qquad} S']] \text{ (obligatory)} & \text{(ii)} \end{cases}$$

where $X$ or $Y$ = NP and $\alpha$ is the adjacent cyclic node

e. NP becomes NP's in the context _____*ing* VP and becomes *for* NP in the contest _____ *to* VP (obligatory)

f. *for* becomes null after *expect*, . . . (obligatory)

g. Passive, etc.

(200) a. Auxiliary Inversion

b. *whether* becomes null[54]

I assume that *wh* is a feature that can be placed on a node (and, by convention, on all nodes it dominates — see Dougherty (1970) on the matter of "feature percolation"). By (199a) we can assign *wh* either to *someone* or to *to someone* in the sentence *I gave the book to someone*. The rule of *wh*-Movement (199b), which we may take to be optional, will form either *Whom did I give the book to* or *To whom did I give the book,* depending on whether *wh* is applied to the PP or the NP.[55] The structure-preserving condition will insure that P and NP move into the proper position in COMP.

---

[53] Notice that this rule and the preceding one, as formulated, exploit the interpretation of conditions discussed earlier (see discussion of (6)–(14)). That is, the change effected by the rules is internal to a cycle already passed. It is, in any event, unclear whether the relevant conditions apply to "housekeeping rules" such as (c) and (d).

[54] Both cases of (200) are obligatory and restricted to the matrix sentence. Note that there is no way to generate *that* as the COMP of a matrix sentence. Thus we cannot have either *that* S' or *whether* S' as full sentences. I will assume here that *yes-no* questions derive by (199a,b) from something of the form +WH *either* . . . , along the lines of Katz and Postal (1964). The assumption is in no way crucial.

[55] Here and in what follows, I omit discussion of echo questions. Note that rule (199a) is hardly more than a notational device. We might eliminate it, assuming rather that *wh* is assigned by base rules or dispensing with the element *wh* entirely and reformulating (199b) so that the contexts of *wh*-placement appear in place of *wh* in the structural description. This approach would involve slight modifications of later rules.

The fact that *wh*-Movement, though optional, must apply in indirect questions and relatives follows from considerations to which we turn in a moment. Notice that if *wh*-Placement is applied to the PP *to someone* in the sentence *You expected to give the book to someone,* then after the internal cycle we have COMP *you expected* [[*wh, to whom*] PRO *to give the book*], where [*wh, to whom*] is the structure *to whom* dominated by the feature complex [*wh*, PP]. The *A*-over-*A* principle prevents extraction of *whom* on the next cycle, blocking \**Whom did you expect to to give the book,* with the "dangling preposition" *to*. This observation is redundant, however, since the rules of interpretation to be given will in any event block interpretation of sentences with

Rule (199c), which is optional, permits the *wh* noun phrase introducing a relative to be deleted (*the man whom I met, the man I met*). Some conditions on the application of this rule follow from the operation of a surface filter to which we return.

Case (i) of (199d), which is also optional, permits *that* as a realization of COMP when the auxiliary contains tense. The requirement that *X* or *Y* must be NP permits *The book that fell on the floor, What did you tell me that Bill read* while excluding *\*What did you tell me that fell on the floor*. It is ad hoc and presumably indicates some error in the analysis since one would expect this distinction to be predictable on other grounds. After certain verbs, −WH in the circumstances of case (i) must be *that*. Compare *John said (that) he had to do his homework this evening, John complained that he had to do his homework this evening, \*John complained he had to do his homework this evening*. As noted by Dean (1967), such verbs as *complain, quip,* which require a following *that* as COMP, also block *wh*-Movement; that is, we do not have *\*What did John complain that he had to do this evening, \*What did John quip that Mary wore*. There are a number of ways that come to mind for expressing this generalization, but I see no interesting explanation. Again, this lack may indicate a defect of the analysis.

Case (ii) of (199d) excludes such forms as *\*the claim John is here* (while permitting *We claim John is here* — $\overline{\mathrm{N}}$ is to be understood in the sense of Chomsky (1970a)). This is one of a set of such conditions (for example, *I am glad John is here, I am sure John is here, \*I am delighted John is here, \*It surprises me John is here, \*I am aware John is here* — again, there is undoubtedly more to this, perhaps an entirely different analysis).

Rules (199e), (199f) must also be given in a more general form (incorporating as well *John's refusal, John's book,* and so on). They provide, for example, for such distinctions as *I expected John to leave, What I expected was for John to leave* and *What we hoped for*

---

dangling prepositions in COMP. The same will be true if we eliminate the notational device of *wh*-Placement entirely.

Notice that in the formulation of rules given here, there may be nodes P and NP in COMP that dominate no terminal string and therefore play no role in interpretation or in factoring terminal strings for transformation. There are other conventions and correspondingly different formulations of the rules that might be adopted in these cases. Note that *wh*-Movement of "intransitive" prepositions also gives structures that are uninterpretable by the rules to be given. We overlook here the interesting and important question of the full set of rules of rewriting of COMP, sufficient to account for all cases of *wh*-Movement.

*was for John to win, We hoped for John to win* (with PP simplification — there is much variation in judgment in such cases).[56]

We assume further the base rules (54) (a refinement of (16)).
Following essentially Emonds (1970), we assume that of the COMP-
Aux pairs, only a null COMP with the auxiliary *-ing* appears as an
NP. Thus we assume, at the deep structure level, the following
analyses:

(201) a. I–expect–[COMP John will leave]   (NP–V–S)
        (I expect (that) John will leave)
      b. I–expect–[COMP John to leave]   (NP–V–S)
        (I expect John to leave)
      c. we–argued–about–[COMP John ing leave so early]   (NP–
        V–P–NP)
        (We argued about John's leaving so early)

In fact, *-ing* nominals can appear quite freely as noun phrases, though
*that*-S and *for*-NP-*to*-VP cannot (for example, alongside of (201c),
*We argued about that John left so early, *We argued about for John
to leave so early*). Noting this, let us add the base condition (202):

(202)  In the structure [$_{NP}$ [$_S$ COMP NP Aux VP]], Aux = *ing* and
       (16b) does not apply. In effect, then, S = S' when S is
       immediately dominated by NP.

There will a number of other conditions of this sort.[57]

---

[56] Alternatively, we might drop (f) and reformulate (e) so that insertion of *for* depends
on the governing lexical item. Another possibility would be to distinguish two cases of
*to*, determined by selectional rules relating to the governing lexical item, one of which
requires *for*, the other of which excludes *for*. I will not pursue these questions here.

Derived nominals with complements of the form (*for* NP) *to* VP do not correlate
entirely with such complements in the corresponding sentence (*We believe John to be a
nice fellow, *Our belief (for) John to be a nice fellow; *We desire (for) John to win, Our
desire for John to win*). It seems that derived nominals take *for* only when they also
take prepositional phrases with *for* (*our desire for victory (for John to win), (to win)* —
similarly, *wish, hopes, plans*, and so on). In Chomsky (1972a) I suggested that the
impossibility of *John's belief of Bill to win* was a consequence of the lexicalist
hypothesis regarding derived nominals. The considerations just mentioned, however,
indicate that the example was irrelevant to that issue since *John's belief for Bill to win*
is also impossible.

[57] We might go on, following Emonds (1970), to hold that instead of extraposition
there is a rule of *it*-Replacement that gives *For John to leave would surprise me, That
John left surprised me*, and so on; we might also hold that the Passive transformation
does not apply to such forms as (201a,b) to prepose the embedded S. Forms such as
*That John left is* (*widely*) *believed* then derive by *it*-Replacement from *It is* (*widely*)

**14.** We have so far listed the relevant conditions, base rules, and transformations. To ensure that only the right forms are generated, we add the Surface Exclusion Filter (203):[58]

(203) The structure [$_{NP}$ NP $V_T$ . . . ] is excluded, where $V_T$ is an element containing tense (T)

Before illustrating the rules, let us consider the status of the filter (203). Bever (1970) has made the interesting suggestion that certain formal properties of grammar might be functionally motivated, in the sense that their effect on strings is to facilitate perceptual strategies. (As we have already observed, the Specified Subject Condition (123a) might be regarded in this way.) As one example, Bever discusses some of the rules that determine the presence or absence of *that* as a complementizer. The filter (203) accommodates several cases of this sort. By virtue of (203), a left-right analytic routine can operate reliably on the assumption that a noun phrase–verb phrase structure, unless it is preceded by *that* or morphologically marked, is always a full sentence, not a noun phrase. This is a natural candidate for a performance strategy. It would also be rather natural for performance strategies to affect grammars at the level of surface structure filters. So few persuasive examples exist that no firm conclusions can be drawn, but the question that Bever raises is an intriguing one, and (203) is a suggestive example.[59]

---

*believed that John left* (which we shall refer to as "sentence (a)") under these assumptions. If this is a root transformation, in Emonds' sense, it follows that we cannot have *I wonder whether that S' is widely believed,* though *I wonder whether the fact that S' is widely believed* is all right. Speculating as to the sentence (a), we might take it to be in effect a base form, if VP → $\bar{V}$, where Aspect → (Perfect)(Progressive)(Passive). This analysis would require that both components of Passive are obligatory if Aspect contains Passive (and, of course, NP-Preposing is inapplicable if there is no NP following the verb, as in (a)); that a rule of interpretation relates *it* and sentential complements (thus there is no interpretation for *\*It is died by John,* but there is for (a)); that *believe* and so on must have a subject at the deep structure level, either a lexical subject or Δ, which will delete (by the rule of Agent Deletion) if it moves to the agent position (excluding *\*It believes that* S); that *it* appears in the position of an otherwise unfilled subject.

[58] In the terminology of Chomsky (1972a), $V_T$ contains the features [+verb] and also [+tense], that is, it is a tensed verb or auxiliary. The proposal here is similar to but not quite identical with that of Perlmutter (1971).

[59] Bever's other examples do not involve conditions on the form of grammars. Thus he observes that acceptable adjective order (which is inexpressible in any natural way in a transformational grammar) can be determined in accord with a natural perceptual strategy, and he suggests an alternative to a proposal of Miller and Chomsky (1963) concerning embedded sentences (The question is irrelevant here, but his alternative seems to me considerably more ad hoc than the proposal he rejects. He states that the

**15.** We illustrate the rules (199)–(200) by a few sample derivations (in which irrelevant details are omitted).

Consider the base structure (204):

(204) $[_{NP}$ the person $[_S [_{COMP}$ P NP $-$WH$] [_S$ Bill saw the person$]]]$

On the innermost cycle, *wh*-Placement (199a) applies to the NP *the person*, which replaces the NP of the COMP by *wh*-Movement (199b). Turning to the next cycle, namely, the cycle of the whole NP

---

latter does not explain the distinction between single and multiple self-embedding, but in fact it does when supplemented by the very natural proposal that there are perceptual strategies for the analysis of such structures as relative clause and that in the case of any analytic procedure it is difficult to call upon this procedure in the course of executing it. See Chomsky, (1965, p. 14).)

Bever's paper has been widely interpreted as questioning the distinction between competence and performance and as denying that grammatical rules relating deep and surface structure are involved in language use. In fact, he presupposes a relation between "internal structure" and "external structure" in language use, and if in fact knowledge of language includes a specification of a pairing between deep (internal) and surface (external) structures determined by transformational rules, it would be surprising to discover that this is not the pairing involved in language use. In any event, Bever's discussion provides no reason for doubting this identity. As to the competence–performance distinction, Bever presupposes it throughout, with his reference to "epistemological systems" (in particular, grammars that describe competence). In fact, his discussion provides independent support for the appropriateness of the competence–performance framework, as conventionally formulated, precisely because the properties of acceptable sentences that he accounts for in terms of performance strategies are grammatically inexpressible (in any natural way). For discussion, see Chomsky (1965; 1971). Bever's comments on the nature of the evidence for transformational grammars seem to me misleading, and in part incorrect, for reasons elaborated in Chomsky (1965).

It is difficult to imagine a coherent alternative to the conventional competence–performance distinction. However, it is possible that grammatical transformations are not the appropriate device for expressing the relationship between "external structures" and "internal structures." Thus one might imagine that this relationship is captured by some set of "perceptual strategies," now unknown. Were knowledge of language to be more adequately expressed in such a system, we could dispense with the theory of transformational grammar. This possibility seems to me quite remote, given present knowledge or conjectures, but it is conceivable. It has been occasionally suggested that transformational grammar is a system of "strategies of prediction" used in determining grammaticalness but not otherwise involved in language use (see Langendoen (1970)). Though possible in principle, this is a most implausible hypothesis. It amounts to the belief that there are separate systems for expressing, on the one hand, strategies of perception and production and, on the other, strategies of prediction; only the former are used in the normal experience of a speaker-hearer, but the latter come into operation when an informant is asked to perform such tasks as judging the acceptability of sentences. The obvious question is why the second system should exist at all since it is rarely if ever used by nonlinguists. Surely the more natural assumption is that there is a mentally represented grammar expressing knowledge of language and used in production, perception, and prediction. One would surely want strong evidence before abandoning this very conservative hypothesis.

structure (204), we first replace the *wh*-phrase *the person* by *who* and then turn to (199c), the first applicable rule of those in (199).[60] If this optional rule does not apply, then (199d) is inapplicable and we derive *the person who Bill saw*. If (199c) deletes *who*, then (199di) is applicable. If it applies, we derive *the person that Bill saw*; if not, *the person Bill saw*.

Consider next the base structure (205):

(205)  [$_{NP}$ the person [$_S$ [$_{COMP}$ P NP $-$WH] [$_S$ the person saw Bill]]]

Again, on the innermost cycle *wh*-Placement and *wh*-Movement apply, giving (206):

(206)  [$_{NP}$ the person [$_S$ [$_{COMP}$ P[*wh*, the person] $-$WH][$_{S'}$ saw Bill]]]

On the next cycle, if (199c) is not applied, we derive *the person who saw Bill*. If (199c) does apply, then (199d) is applicable. If (199d) applies, we derive *the person that saw Bill*; if not, we derive *\*the person saw Bill*, which is excluded by the Surface Exclusion Filter (203). Hence there are only two possible surface forms corresponding to (205), as compared to three in the case of (204).

Now consider the underlying structure (207):

(207)  [$_{NP}$ [$-$WH Bill is here]] is surprising

On the innermost cycle no rule applies to (207). On the NP cycle, rule (199di) can apply, giving *that Bill is here is surprising*. If this optional rule does not apply, the resulting form, *\*Bill is here is surprising,* is excluded by the Surface Filter (203). This is a case of (203) that is different from the one in the derivation initiated by (205). The example here, of course, is beside the point if, as suggested earlier, the sentence in question is derived by *it*-Replacement.

Consider next the base form which, after *wh*-Placement, becomes (208):

(208)  [$_{COMP}$ NP $+$WH] [you will tell me [$_α$ [$_{COMP}$ NP $-$WH] [Bill saw who]]]

On the innermost cycle $α$, *who* moves to the NP position in the

---

[60] On notations for expressing the obligatory character of Relativization, see Chomsky (1965).

COMP, before −WH. This gives (209):

(209)  [$_\text{COMP}$ NP +WH] [you will tell me [$_\alpha$ [$_\text{COMP}$ who −WH] [Bill saw]]]

Unless there is further *wh*-Movement on the next cycle, this structure will be excluded by the rule of interpretation (to be given later) that obligatorily interprets a *wh*-phrase in a −WH COMP as a relative; this is impossible here since $\alpha \neq$ NP and there is no antecedent. Suppose, however, that *who* is moved on the next cycle, giving (210):

(210)  [who +WH] [you will tell me [−WH [Bill saw]]]

The first applicable rule is (199d). (Note that $Y =$ NP). If it applies, we derive (with Auxiliary Inversion) *Who will you tell me that Bill saw*; if it does not apply, *Who will you tell me Bill saw.*[61]

Suppose that we had −WH as the initial COMP instead of +WH in (209). Then the result corresponding to (210) will also be uninterpretable since the obligatory relative interpretation of a *wh*-phrase in a −WH COMP is inapplicable.

Suppose that we have *Who saw Bill* instead of *Bill saw who* in (208). Then the only possible outcome is *Who will you tell me saw Bill.* Rule (199di) is inapplicable in this case since $Y \neq$ NP.

The base structure (211) will yield *I believe (that) John saw Bill*, with the presence of *that* depending on whether or not (199di) applies:

(211)  I believe [−WH John saw Bill]

In contrast, consider (212):

(212)  I wonder [+WH Bill saw who]

Applying *wh*-Movement on the innermost cycle, we derive *I wonder [who Bill saw]*. If the initial COMP of the matrix sentence is −WH, this stands as a grammatical sentence. But if the initial COMP is +WH, then no interpretable sentence is generated. (Recall that on our present assumptions, *Do I wonder who Bill saw* comes from a different source, with *either* in the matrix sentence; see note 54). The

---

[61] There are further considerations determining the applicability of (199di). Thus, it seems to me that omission of *that* is unacceptable in *What did you persuade Bill ____ John should see* or *What did you urge ____ I see*, for example.

rules of interpretation that we shall discuss provide that a +WH COMP is interpretable (namely, as a question) just in case the COMP is filled with a *wh*-phrase. If *wh*-Movement does not apply on the outermost cycle in (212), then the initial +WH COMP is not filled by a *wh*-phrase and the sentence is uninterpretable. If *wh*-Movement does apply, giving, with Auxiliary Inversion, *Who do I wonder* +WH *Bill saw,* then the embedded +WH COMP contains no *wh*-phrase and the sentence is again uninterpretable.

Compare (211), (212) with (213), (214):

(213)   I believe [−WH John saw who]
(214)   I wonder [+WH John saw Bill]

In the case of (213), *wh*-Movement on the innermost cycle gives *I believe* [*who* −WH *John saw*]. This cannot stand as is because, as already noted, a *wh*-phrase in a −WH COMP must be interpreted as a relative, which is impossible in this case. But if the initial COMP of the matrix sentence contains +WH, we can derive *Who do I believe* (*that*) *John saw* by *wh*-Movement on the external cycle. In the case of (214), no grammatical sentence is generated since we have a +WH COMP not containing a *wh*-phrase. The words *believe* and *wonder* differ lexically in that, as the sense indicates, the former requires −WH COMP and the latter requires +WH COMP, leading to the grammatical consequences just noted.

Consider finally the verb *ask,* which appears in a variety of structures. In the first place, like *wonder,* it appears in (215), analogous to (212):

(215)   John asked [+WH Bill saw who]

As in the case of *wonder,* we can derive *John asked who Bill saw* from (215) if the initial COMP is −WH, but no grammatical sentence results if the initial COMP is +WH (in particular, not \**Who did John ask* (*that*) *Bill saw*).

The verb *ask,* however, can take −WH COMP in the embedded sentence if the latter is subjunctive, as in *John asked that Bill leave early.* Consider, then, (216):

(216)   John asked [−WH Bill see who]

This case is analogous to (213) rather than (212). Thus we can derive *Who did John ask that Bill see* but not \**John asked who Bill see.*

The verb *ask,* as distinct from *believe* and *wonder,* can take controlled PRO in the embedded sentence, as in *John asked to see Mary* from (217):

(217)   John asked [−WH PRO to see Mary]

Suppose, however, that we have +WH rather than −WH in (217). Then, exactly as in the case of (214), no grammatical sentence can be derived. But suppose that we have +WH in place of −WH and *who* instead of *Mary,* that is, (218):

(218)   John asked [+WH PRO to see who]

This is now analogous to (212) and (215). For the reasons already noted, from (218) we can derive (219) but not (220):

(219)   John asked who to see
(220)   Who did John ask to see

Of course, *ask* can also take −WH COMP, as in (216), (217). Thus we have the underlying form (221):

(221)   John asked [−WH PRO to see who]

From (221) we can derive (220) but not (219). Thus (219) and (220), though both grammatical, derive from different sources: (219) derives from (218), and (220) derives from (221), with matrix-initial +WH. The answer to (220) might be *John asked to see Mary,* which derives from (217). As is generally the case with answer–question pairs of the simplest sort, (217) is identical to (221) except that it contains *Mary* instead of *who*.

The preceding examples illustrate uses of *ask* with only S as complement, but *ask* can also take NP S as complement: *John asked me why Bill left.* Consider, then, the underlying forms in (222)–(226), analogous to (215), (216), (217), (218), (221), respectively:

(222)   John asked me [+WH Bill saw who]
(223)   John asked me [−WH Bill see who]
(224)   John asked me [−WH PRO to see Mary]
(225)   John asked me [+WH PRO to see who]
(226)   John asked me [−WH PRO to see who]

In the case of (222), we derive *John asked me who Bill saw* but not *Who did John ask me (that) Bill saw*. (In fact, as in the case of (215), there is no grammatical sentence derivable if the initial COMP of the matrix sentence in (222) contains +WH.)

Consider next (223). As in the case of (216), we should be able to derive *Who did John ask me that Bill see,* but not **John asked me who Bill see*. For me, the first is also excluded, but in this case because the verb *ask* with NP S complement does not take subjunctive in the embedded sentence, as we can see from the ungrammaticality of **John asked me that Bill leave early* (compare *John asked that Bill leave early*).

The next example, (224), is analogous to (217). Thus we can derive *John asked me to see Mary* (*see* in the rough sense of "visit," as in *John asked me to see the head nurse when I arrive*). Notice that in this case PRO is controlled not by the subject of the matrix sentence but by the NP following the verb *ask*, as in *John asked me to throw the ball* and so on.

Consider next the example (225), analogous to (218). From (225) we can derive (227) but not (228):

(227)   John asked me who to see (visit)
(228)   Who did John ask me to see (visit)

As in the analogous case of (221), from (226) we can derive (228) but not (227).

As before, these conclusions are semantically correct. We can see this particularly clearly in the present case by considering the matter of control of PRO. As already noted, in the case of (224) PRO is controlled by *me*: I am to see (or visit) Mary. This is in general the case when *ask* takes NP S complement where the COMP of S is −WH. But where the COMP of S is +WH, the subject of *ask*, rather than the NP following it, controls PRO. We can see this in the case of (229), as contrasted with (230) in which the embedded COMP is −WH:

(229)   John asked me whether to visit Mary
(230)   John asked me to visit Mary

In the case of (229), John is to visit Mary; in the case of (230), I am to visit Mary. Similarly, in the case of (227) John is to see (visit) someone, whereas in the case of (228) I am to do so. This result is as predicted, given that (227), like (229), derives from an underlying structure with +WH in the embedded COMP, whereas (228), like (230), derives from an underlying structure with −WH in the embedded COMP.

Summarizing, *ask* takes an S complement or an NP S complement. In the latter case, a lexical property indicates that the embedded COMP can be −WH only if the subject of the embedded sentence is PRO. Where the subject of the embedded S is PRO, PRO is controlled necessarily by the subject of *ask* if the complement is merely S; PRO is controlled by the subject of *ask* if the complement is NP S and the COMP of the embedded S is +WH; PRO is controlled by the NP following *ask* if the COMP of the embedded S is −WH. (We might seek a further explanation of these facts, but that is another matter). Given the idiosyncracies noted, the distribution of grammatical and ungrammatical sentences and their interpretations follows from the rules already given.

In (199) we assumed, without argument, that Passive follows *wh*-Movement. Supposing this to be true, consider the sentence (231):

(231)   Who is John believed to like

The underlying source, after *wh*-Placement, is (232a), and the rule of *wh*-Movement on the first cycle gives (232b):

(232) a.   COMP Δ believe [COMP John to like who]
      b.   COMP Δ believe [who John to like]

The rule forming passives will not apply to (232b). But if *wh*-Movement precedes Passive, placing *who* in the initial COMP, then Passive will apply, forming (231) ultimately.

However, this argument for ordering *wh*-Movement before Passive fails because there is another possible derivation of (231). Since *wh*-Movement is optional, we may assume that it does not apply on the internal cycle. Turning to the outer cycle, we might form (231) by Passive followed by *wh*-Movement, if *wh*-Movement is not blocked under these circumstances by some version of the Specified Subject Condition, as discussed earlier.

The issue is clarified if there is an extra cycle. Thus consider the underlying structure (233):

(233)   COMP Δ expected [COMP John to try [COMP PRO to win the race]]

Passive can apply to (233) on the external cycle to give (234):

(234)   John was expected to try to win the race

Suppose that in (233) we have *which race* in place of *the race*. Then *wh*-Movement on the internal cycles will given (235):

(235)   COMP Δ expected [which race John to try [COMP PRO to win]]

Turning to the outermost cycle, if *wh*-Movement precedes Passive, we derive (236) by applying both rules (followed by Agent Deletion and Auxiliary Inversion):

(236)   Which race was John expected to try to win

If Passive precedes *wh*-Movement, however, we cannot derive (236), which is grammatical. Notice that in this case the alternative analysis suggested in the case of (231) is excluded. If *wh*-Movement has not already produced (235) by the time we reach the external cycle, then it will not be applicable at all, by the Subjacency Condition (81) on extraction. Therefore the ordering of (199) is correct, on the assumption that the hypotheses proposed so far (some rather tentatively) are correct. Notice that the same example indicates that the "trace" left by *wh*-Movement must not be a non-null terminal symbol. Therefore, it must either be null (see the discussion that precedes (177)) or, if PRO, a feature of a complex nonterminal symbol.

Notice that Passive must also apparently be permitted to precede *wh*-Movement if such sentences as *Who was John killed by* are to be derived in the most natural way. It may be, then, that the two rules are unordered relative to one another, that is, that they may apply in either order.

**16.** It remains to discuss lexical subcategorization and rules of interpretation. We suppose (again following Bresnan (1970)) that lexical items are subcategorized with respect to the choice of COMP and Aux in embedded complement sentences. For example, the item *ask* in the sense of "ask a question," as in *You asked me who John saw,* must take a +WH COMP in the embedded sentence; but in the sense of "request" it will take a −WH COMP with subjunctive, as in *I ask that you leave at once.* (See examples (215)–(221)). On the other hand, the verb *tell* can freely take ±WH as COMP in the embedded sentence.[62] Thus we have the indirect question (237), the free relative (238a), and the sentential complement (238b):

(237) I told him who would leave
      (I told him [+WH someone would leave])

(238) a. I told him what Bill asked me to tell him
         (I told him [PRO [−WH Bill asked me to tell him some-thing]])
      b. I told him that it is raining
         (I told him [−WH it is raining])

To be more precise, only cases (237) and (238b) are determined directly by the lexical subcategorization of *tell*. Case (238a) is a special case of the base structure NP–*tell*–NP′–indirect object, where NP′ happens to be a relative with an unspecified antecedent, analogous to *I told him the story he likes, I told him something*. (In these cases, as in (238a), Indirect Object Movement has applied.)

Notice that further specifications are necessary to determine under what conditions indirect questions are appropriate. For example, the examples in (239) seem preferable to those in (240):

(239) a. I will know whether I pass as soon as he walks in
      b. I will tell him whether you'll apply
      c. I didn't tell him whether it would rain

(240) a. I knew whether I would pass
      b. I told him whether you will (would) apply
      c. I told him whether it would rain

Lexical specifications account for such facts as the following. Although (241a) cannot be derived from (241b), as we have seen earlier, (242a) can be derived from (242b), though not from (242c); and (243a) derives properly from (243b), though not from (243c):

(241) a. *What did you tell him who saw
      b.  +WH you told him [+WH someone saw something]

---

[62] When it has an indirect object, as in (237), (238). Otherwise, as Bresnan notes, it can take only +WH (*Susie didn't tell whether they had eaten, *Susie didn't tell that they had eaten, Susie didn't tell us that (whether) they had eaten*).

(242) a.   What did you tell him (that) Bill saw
      b.   +WH you told him [−WH Bill saw something]
      c.   +WH you told him [+WH Bill saw something]

(243) a.   You told him what Bill saw
      b.   −WH you told him [+WH Bill saw something]
      c.   −WH you told him [−WH Bill saw something]

Sources (242c) and (243c) are ruled out for (242a) and (243a), respectively, by the principles of interpretation to which we now turn.[63]

In all cases other than those enumerated, the sentence receives no interpretation.

A +WH COMP is interpreted only when it contains a *wh*-phrase. A −WH COMP containing no terminal string is interpreted as a clause introducer; if it introduces a relative clause (that is, after application of (199c)), the interpretation is that of relatives. A −WH COMP with a terminal string other than a *wh*-phrase might be interpreted as topicalization; we have not dealt with this process here, but it appears to be similar to *wh*-Movement except for the condition that there is an interpretation only in a root sentence in the sense of Emonds (1970).

Consider next the rules of interpretation for *wh*-phrases. First, in a −WH COMP, the interpretation is always as a relative clause,[64] with the antecedent appropriately associated with the position marked by the trace left by *wh*-Movement. (Details of relative clause interpretation need not concern us here; it is sufficient to note that the formal structures that provide a full interpretation are appropriately determined.) A free relative (for example, *I read what you gave me*) is derived when the antecedent is the indeterminate element, which deletes.

Let us look at the item *urge*, which takes a −WH COMP and subjunctive in Aux, as in (244):

(244)   I urge that Bill visit the museum

---

[63] Compare (238a) with (243) from *You told him* [PRO [−WH *Bill saw something*]]. The latter is excluded on the same grounds that exclude *I told him the picture of Mary*, and so on.

[64] We assume that noun phrases with relative clauses have a different structure than those with sentential complements to nouns. Thus we have been assuming such structures as the following, at the surface level: $[_{NP} [_{NP}$ *the man*$][_{S}$ *that I saw*$]]$, $[_{NP}$ *the* $[_{\bar{N}}$ *claim*$[_{S}$ *that John saw Bill*$]]]$, $[_{S}$ *we*$[_{VP}[_{\bar{V}}$ *claim*$[_{S}$ *that John saw Bill*$]]]]$, where $\bar{N}$ and $\bar{V}$ are as in Chomsky (1970a) (and NP = $\bar{\bar{N}}$, VP = $\bar{\bar{V}}$).

Since $[_{NP} NP[wh +WH] \ldots]$ cannot be interpreted as a question, only −WH can introduce a relative.

Consider now the underlying structure (245) (where *wh*-Placement has applied on the internal cycle):

(245)   COMP I urge [[NP −WH][Bill visit *what*]]

On the first cycle, *wh*-Movement will apply, giving (246):

(246)   COMP I urge [[what −WH][Bill visit]]]

Turning to the external cycle, if the initial COMP is +WH, *wh*-Movement must apply (or we will have an unfilled +WH COMP). This yields, ultimately, (247):

(247)   What did I urge that Bill visit

If the initial COMP is −WH in (245), *wh*-Movement will be impossible on the external cycle because the initial −WH COMP is uninterpretable as a relative. If no *wh*-Movement takes place, the resulting form is (246), and there is again no interpretation since here too there is a −WH COMP containing a *wh*-phrase but not interpretable as a relative. Therefore a grammatical sentence (one which is generated by the rules, is not assigned * in the course of the derivation, and receives an interpretation) is generated from (245) only if the initial COMP is +WH and *wh*-Movement takes place on both cycles.

Consider next the rules for interpreting a *wh*-phrase in a +WH COMP. There are several cases, depending on the choice of *wh*-phrase. (Perhaps the cases can be combined, but this will not concern us here.) Thus [*whether* +WH] will be interpreted as "is it the case that" (as in NP *wondered whether it would rain*). The NP's *who* and *what* are interpreted in accordance with (248):

(248)   The phrase [$_\alpha$ [*wh*, NP] +WH] . . . PRO . . . ] is interpreted with PRO a variable bound by the node [*wh*, NP] and . . . the semantic interpretation determined by the derivation of $\alpha$[65]

Thus, for example, *I wonder who John saw* would mean "I wonder

---

[65] We leave open, as irrelevant here, the question of which aspects of the derivation (deep structure, surface structure, both, and so on) determine the semantic interpretation. In the case in question, PRO is controlled by the complex symbol [*wh*, NP] which has moved from the position occupied by PRO by *wh*-Movement; that is, PRO is the "trace" remaining from *wh*-Movement, in the terminology used earlier. The principle (248) can be generalized to other cases where a controlled PRO functions as a variable.

for which $x$, John saw someone $x$." The principle can be extended to other *wh*-phrases, such as *how, when, which, what* (as in *which (what) books*), and can be formalized, but we will carry the matter no further here.

The only remaining case is that of a *wh*-phrase that is not in a COMP. Again overlooking here the matter of echo questions, we can interpret such phrases with the principle (249):

(249)   Assign a *wh*-phrase not in COMP to some higher structure [$_{COMP}$ . . . +WH] and interpret as in (248) where the interpretation is uniform in this COMP node.

Thus the sentence (250) will have the interpretation (251), and (252) will have the interpretation (253):

(250)   I wonder who saw what
(251)   I wonder for which $x$, for which $y$, someone $x$ saw some- thing $y$
(252)   I remembered what John had given to whom; I remembered to whom John had given what
(253)   I remembered for which $x$, for which $y$, John had given something $x$ to someone $y$

But sentence (254) will receive no interpretation at all since (248) cannot apply uniformly in the node containing *whether* (since it does not apply to *whether*):

(254)   I wonder whether Bill saw what

In fact, (254) is interpretable only as an echo question.

Notice that principle (249) in effect overcomes the formal restriction against moving two *wh*-phrases into the same COMP position. That is, it permits interpretations that proceed as if this double movement had taken place.

In the examples just cited, the *wh*-phrase not in COMP position was assigned, for interpretation, to the immediately dominating COMP. However, principle (249) is not restricted to this case.[66] An

---

[66] Notice that (249), as formulated, explicitly violates (123), just as the rule of Coreference Assignment does (see note 16). Recall again that under the proposed interpretation of universal conditions (see discussion of (6)–(14)), it is possible to formulate particular rules to which they do not apply. If this formulation of (249) is correct, then there should be an interpretation, analogous to (250), for such sentences as *I wonder who heard John's stories about what, I wonder who wrote which textbook and which novel.*

155

example discussed by Baker (1970) illustrates additional possibilities. Consider the sentence (255):

(255)   Who remembers where we bought which book

Principle (249) (appropriately extended to *which book, which place = where*) permits either of the interpretations in (256) and only these:

(256) a.   For which $x$, $x$ remembers for which $z$, for which $y$, we bought $y$ at $z$
     b.   For which $x$, for which $y$, $x$ remembers for which $z$ we bought $y$ at $z$

A possible answer, under the interpretation (a), would be *John remembers where we bought which book*. A possible answer under the interpretation (b) would be *John remembers where we bought the physics book and Bill remembers where we bought the novel.*[67]

Notice that in the case of (256b), principle (249) in effect overcomes the restriction against moving a *wh*-phrase from a phrase to which *wh*-Movement has already applied into a higher phrase of the phrase marker, just as in the case of (250)–(253) (and, in fact, both cases of (256) as well) principle (249) overcomes the formal restriction against moving two *wh*-phrases into the same COMP position.

Observe also that with no artificial notational devices, we can interpret sentences directly in terms of the surface structure position of the *wh*-phrase and the nature of the COMP in which it appears.[68] This would seem to be the simplest possible situation. It is also what one would expect, given the framework of the extended standard theory.

There are further complexities when we consider a richer array of cases similar to (255). Moreover, there are other cases that we have still not dealt with. To mention one, consider the fact (noted by Bresnan (1970)) that we cannot have such forms as *\*I don't know who Bill to ask _____* or *\*It is not known who to see _____*, although *I don't know who to ask _____* is acceptable (where _____ indicates the position from which *who* was moved). These are indirect ques-

---

[67] Such examples as (255) appear, with the same ambiguity, in indirect questions, whether or not they are dominated by a "question word"; *I wonder who remembers where we bought which book, It is uncertain who remembers where we bought which book*. Notice, therefore, that there is no generalization to be gained by supposing that an obligatorily deleted "performative" question verb appears in the structure underlying (255) as the matrix verb, as has occasionally been suggested.

[68] Notice, in particular, that there is no necessity for any additional devices to exclude other possible interpretations (for example, "For which $x$, for which $z$, $x$ remembers for which $y$, we bought $y$ at $z$" in the case of (255).

156

tions with a +WH COMP. It appears that when a +WH COMP takes an S' with the auxiliary *to,* deletion of the subject of the S' by Equi-NP Deletion is obligatory (and there is an interpretation roughly as "should"—for example, *I wondered whether to leave (how to answer)).* We might express this by adding a Surface Exclusion Filter barring +WH NP *to.* Notice that we might also express the obligatory character of the interpretation rules by surface filters, in various ways which I will not elaborate.

**17.**    Though many questions have been left open and, obviously, many problems remain, nevertheless it seems to me that the approach explored here is quite plausible. Given the extended standard theory, with its restrictions on the possibilities for base structures, on the ordering of lexical and nonlexical transformations, and on the relations between semantic interpretations and derivations, we have been able to sharpen some earlier proposals and to accommodate a number of particular suggestions concerning universals, as well as a fairly wide range of data, under some fairly natural and simple assumptions. The illustrative examples exploit all of the devices available in this theory to determine grammaticalness, namely, rules of the categorial component of the base, lexical insertion transformations involving contextual features, nonlexical transformations of various sorts, surface filters, and rules of interpretation involving deep and surface structures.[69] Only if a derivation satisfies all of these conditions does its final terminal string qualify as a grammatical sentence. We have considered the possibility that surface filters might be regarded as a point of contact between a performance theory and a competence theory, as might some of the conditions on transformations. One might look into the effects of enriching one or another component of the theory. (For example, would more extensive reliance on rules of interpretation suffice to characterize the grammatical sentences without the distinction between +WH and −WH or, say, permit us to eliminate *wh*-Movement in favor of an expansion of COMP in the base?)[70] There is, furthermore, little doubt that additional restrictions

---

[69] It remains an open question whether rules of interpretation and filters must also apply to what have been called "shallow structures."

[70] The latter suggestion, though attractive in some respects, faces difficulties in the case of such examples as *Which pictures of each other were the men looking at, The pictures of each other that the men were looking at.* The latter might be used to support the view that the antecedent of a relative is actually raised from the relative by a movement rule, with an appropriate *wh*-phrase left behind. I believe that this possibility was first suggested by M. Brame, to explain why it is possible to have such noun phrases as *the headway that he made* though *headway* is otherwise impossible as a noun phrase, and similarly in the case of many other idioms.

and conditions must be discovered if the fundamental empirical problem mentioned at the outset is to become a realistic topic of inquiry.

## REFERENCES

Akmajian, A. 1970. Aspects of the grammar of focus in English. Doctoral dissertation, MIT.

Bach, E. 1965. On some recurrent types of transformations. In *Sixteenth Annual Round Table Meeting on Linguistics and Language Studies,* Georgetown University Monograph Series on Languages and Linguistics 18, C. W. Kreidler, ed.

_____. 1971. Questions. *Linguistic Inquiry* 2: 153–66.

Baker, C. L. 1970. Notes on the description of English questions: the role of an abstract question morpheme. *Foundations of Language* 6: 197–219.

Bever, T. G. 1970. The cognitive base for linguistic structure. In *Cognition and Language Learning.* J. R. Hayes, ed. New York: Wiley.

Bowers, J. 1969. Some adjectival nominalizations in English. Unpublished paper, MIT.

Bresnan, J. 1970. On complementizers: towards a syntactic theory of complement types. *Foundations of Language* 6: 297–321.

_____. 1971. Sentence stress and syntactic transformations. *Language* 47: 257–281.

_____. 1972. The theory of complementation in English syntax. Doctoral dissertation, MIT.

Chomsky, N. 1964. *Current Issues in Linguistic Theory.* The Hague: Mouton.

_____. 1965. *Aspects of the Theory of Syntax.* Cambridge, Mass.: MIT Press.

_____. 1968. *Language and Mind.* New York: Harcourt Brace Jovanovich.

_____. 1970a. Deep structure, surface structure, and semantic interpretation. In *Studies in General and Oriental Linguistics* (Commemorative Volume for Dr. Shiro Hattori), R. Jakobson and S. Kawamoto, eds. Tokyo: TEC Corporation for Language Research.

_____. 1970b. Remarks on nominalization. In *Readings in English Transformational Grammar.* R. Jacobs and P. Rosenbaum, eds. Waltham, Mass.: Ginn.

_____. 1971. *Problems of Knowledge and Freedom.* New York: Pantheon.

_____. 1972a. Empirical issues in the theory of transformational grammar. In *Goals of Linguistic Theory* (Proceedings of the Linguistics Conference at the University of Texas, Oct. 1969), S. Peters, ed. Englewood Cliffs, New Jersey: Prentice-Hall.

_____. 1972b. *Studies on Semantics in Generative Grammar.* The Hague: Mouton. (This contains Chomsky (1970a; 1970b; 1972a).)

Chomsky, N. and Halle, M. 1968. *Sound Patterns of English.* New York: Harper and Row.

Culicover, P. 1971. Syntactic and semantic investigations. Doctoral dissertation, MIT.

Dean Fodor, J. 1967. Noun phrase complementation in English and German. Unpublished paper, MIT.

Dougherty, R. 1970. A grammar of coordinate conjoined structures: I. *Language* 46: 850–898.

Emonds, J. 1970. Root and structure-preserving transformations. Doctoral dissertation, MIT.

Fauconnier, G. R. 1971. Theoretical implications of some global phenomena in syntax. Doctoral dissertation, University of California, San Diego.

Helke, M. 1971. The grammar of English reflexives. Doctoral dissertation, MIT.

Jackendoff, R. S. 1969. Some rules of semantic interpretation for English. Doctoral dissertation, MIT.

_____. 1972. *Semantic Interpretation in Generative Grammar.* Cambridge, Mass.: MIT.

Katz, J. and Postal, P. 1964. *An Integrated Theory of Linguistic Descriptions.* Cambridge, Mass.: MIT Press.

Kayne, R. 1969. The transformational cycle in French syntax. Doctoral dissertation, MIT.

Kiparsky, P. and Kiparsky, C. 1970. Fact. In *Progress in Linguistics,* M. Bierwisch and K. E. Heidolph, eds. The Hague: Mouton.

Langendoen, D. T. 1970. Generative grammar from a functional perspective. Unpublished paper, CCNY.

Lasnik, H. 1971. A general constraint: some evidence from negation. *Quarterly Progress Report of the Research Laboratory of Electronics, 101,* MIT., 215–17.

McCawley, J. D. 1970. English as a VSO language. *Language* 46: 286–99.

Miller, G. A. and Chomsky, N. 1963. Finitary models of language users. In *Handbook of Mathematical Psychology,* Vol. II. R. Luce, R. Bush, and E. Galanter, eds. New York: Wiley.

Perlmutter, D. 1971. *Deep and Surface Structure Constraints in Syntax.* New York: Holt, Rinehart, and Winston.

Peters, S. and Ritchie, R. W. On the generative power of transformational grammars. *Information Sciences* 6: 49–83.

Postal, P. 1966. A note on "understood transitively". IJAL 32: 90–93.

_____. 1969. Review of A. McIntosh and M. A. K. Halliday, *Papers in General, Descriptive and Applied Linguistics*. In *Foundations of Language* 5: 409–39.

_____. 1971. *Cross-Over Phenomena*. New York: Holt, Rinehart, and Winston.

Ross, J. R. 1967. Constraints on variables in syntax. Doctoral dissertation, MIT.

Selkirk, L. 1970. On the determiner systems of noun phrase and adjective phrase. Unpublished paper, MIT.

Wasow, T. and Roeper, T. 1972. On the subject of Gerunds. *Foundations of language* 8: 44–61.

# Conditions on
# Rules of Grammar

# Conditions on Rules of Grammar*

In this discussion, I will assume without supporting argument a general framework that I have outlined and discussed elsewhere,[1] and will review some recent ideas on grammatical theory, within this framework.

A person who has learned a language has constructed a system of rules and principles—a grammar—determining a sound–meaning relation of some sort over an infinite domain. The linguist's grammar is a theory of this attained competence, under conventional and entirely appropriate idealizations. The general theory of grammar—call it "universal grammar" (UG)—is a system of principles that determines: (1) what counts as a grammar and (2) how grammars function to generate structural descriptions of sentences. Thus within UG we have conditions on the form of grammar and conditions on the function of grammatical rules. Among the conditions on the form of grammar are the specification of possible base structures, grammatical transformations, phonological rules, and so on. Among the conditions on function that have been proposed are, for example, the A-over-A condition and the coordinate structure constraint. We may assume, at this point, that it is in part a matter of expository convenience how we choose to construe some feature of UG, in these terms.

Naturally, we will attempt to make these conditions explicit and as restrictive as possible. We want UG to make as strong a statement as possible about the nature of language and thus to be subject to critical tests and to provide explanations for the phenomena attested in

---

* This paper is based on lectures presented at the Linguistic Institute, University of South Florida, June, 1975. It appeared in *Linguistic Analysis,* Vol. 2, No. 4 (1976). A more detailed and extensive study covering topics discussed here and other related matters is in preparation.

[1] For example, in Chomsky (1965; 1975b). The latter contains a somewhat more detailed discussion of some of the topics taken up here, both topics within the theory of grammar and others relating to the general framework presupposed and the ongoing debate concerning its validity.

descriptive study. We can explain the fact that linguistic competence has the property $P$ insofar as we can show that property $P$ conforms to UG and is, furthermore, the special case of UG determined by experience. In the most interesting cases, the role of experience is limited or even nonexistent so that the property $P$ simply reflects some property of UG and thus gives us direct insight into the nature of UG. We argue that a given language has the property $P$ because UG requires that this be the case. Where it seems that speakers have been exposed to little if any relevant experience, but yet have acquired a language with the property $P$ rather than some alternative, it is reasonable to attribute $P$ to UG itself. The case of structure-dependence of rules is a familiar simple example. If our goal is not only description of linguistic competence but also explanation, we will try to provide as restrictive as possible a theory of UG.

To restate the same commitment (in essence) from a different point of view, I assume that our aim is to assimilate the study of language to the general body of natural science. Linguistics, then, may be regarded as that part of human psychology that is concerned with the nature, function, and origin of a particular "mental organ." We may take UG to be a theory of the language faculty, a common human attribute, genetically determined, one component of the human mind. Through interaction with the environment, this faculty of mind becomes articulated and refined, emerging in the mature person as a system of knowledge of language. To discover the character of this mental faculty, we will try to isolate those properties of attained linguistic competence that hold by necessity rather than as a result of accidental experience, where by "necessity" I of course mean biological rather than logical necessity. We will therefore be particularly interested in properties of attained linguistic competence that are vastly underdetermined by available experience in general, but that nevertheless hold of the linguistic competence attained by any normal speaker of a given language, and in fact by all speakers of all languages (perhaps vacuously in some cases) on the natural assumption of uniformity across the species. The commitment to formulate a restrictive theory of UG is thus nothing other than a commitment to discover the biological endowment that makes language acquisition possible and to determine its particular manifestations. Returning to the matter of "explanatory adequacy," we can explain some property of attained linguistic competence by showing that this property necessarily results from the interplay of the genetically determined language faculty, specified by UG, and the person's (accidental) experience.

Let us assume further that a grammar contains rules that produce derivations, where a derivation $D$ is a sequence of phrase markers $(K_1, \ldots K_n)$, such that each $K_{i+1}$ is derived from $K_i$ by application of some rule. Assume further that the application of these rules is governed by the principle of the (strict) cycle. Among these rules there are syntactic transformations, lexical insertion rules, phonological rules, morphological rules of various sorts, rules that place word boundaries and that determine intonational structures, rules that specify the class of items that are available for lexical insertion, with their intrinsic properties. Of these various types of rules I will now consider only syntactic transformations.

A derivation will be well-formed only if its "initial" and "final" phrase markers ($K_1$ and $K_n$, respectively, in the derivation $(K_1, \ldots, K_n)$) meet certain additional conditions. The initial phrase marker must be a *base structure,* that is, one of an infinite set of structures generated by the *base component* of the grammar. The final phrase marker must also meet a variety of conditions, some of which I will discuss. In a well-formed derivation, the initial phrase marker may be referred to as a *deep structure* and the final phrase marker as a *surface structure.* I should perhaps note that these terms, like other terms of grammar, have been used in varying senses as theory has evolved, a fact that may mislead the unwary reader.

The grammar determines sound–meaning relations. I will assume that the mechanism is a set of rules that associate transformational derivations with representations of sound and representations of meaning. As for the former, I have little to say here. I will assume the framework of *Sound Pattern of English* as modified by Joan Bresnan.[2] Thus surface structures contain phonetic representation, i.e., representation in terms of a universal phonetic system provided by UG.

I will be more concerned here with the relation of a derivation to semantic representation. One may ask, in the first place, whether there is a system of semantic representation analogous to phonetic representation, and if so, what its properties may be. There are various views on this matter. I won't dwell on the issue here, but will, for the moment, put the matter in a rather neutral way. Let us say that the grammar contains a system of rules that associate a derivation with a representation in a system of representation LF (read "logical form," but for the present, without assuming additional properties of this concept). I will understand LF to incorporate

---

[2] Chomsky and Halle (1968); Bresnan (1973).

whatever features of sentence structure (1) enter directly into semantic interpretation of sentences and (2) are strictly determined by properties of (sentence-) grammar. The extension of this concept remains to be determined. Assume further that there is a system of rules that associates logical form and the products of other cognitive faculties with another system of representation SR (read "semantic representation"). Representations in SR, which may involve beliefs, expectations, and so on, in addition to properties of LF determined by grammatical rule, should suffice to determine role in inference, conditions of appropriate use, etc. (some would argue that LF alone should suffice, but I leave that as an open empirical question). Thus the grammar relates LF to phonetic representation through the medium of derivations. I will only be able to touch peripherally on the many questions that arise in this connection. Cf. the references of note 1 and sources cited in these for much additional discussion.

Implicit in this presentation is a certain version of the "thesis of autonomy of syntax" (cf. Chomsky (1975a)). Specifically, I have assumed that the rules of (sentence-) grammar can be subdivided into two categories, the first (call it "formal grammar") sufficing to determine representations on all linguistic levels apart from LF, the second associating such representations with LF. This empirical assumption becomes precise and substantive to the extent that we characterize the properties of the various levels of linguistic representation. It need not be correct, being an empirical assumption (though one of a rather abstract nature). I will continue to assume that it is in fact correct.

What elements of a derivation relate to LF? Several views have coalesced in recent years, in particular, the following two: (1) deep structure determines LF; (2) deep and surface structure jointly determine LF. The first is the viewpoint of the so-called "standard theory." The second is the assumption of the "extended standard theory" (EST) and earlier variants of "generative semantics,"[3] which, I have argued elsewhere, simply amount to a less restrictive variant of EST.[4] I will assume here that EST is generally correct. Thus, LF is determined by properties of both deep and surface

---

[3] For example, Lakoff (1971). Some more recent variants seem to me to eliminate the substantive content of the theory, virtually identifying "generative semantics" with "linguistics," and thus effectively terminating the discussion of the validity of "generative semantics." Cf. Lakoff, in Parret (1974). On the course of generative semantics in recent years, see Dougherty (1975), Katz and Bever (1976), and Brame (1976).

[4] Cf. Chomsky (1972, Chapter 3). Cf. Bresnan (in press) and (1976) for discussion of some of the issues involved.

structure. In particular, "thematic relations" such as agent, instrument, etc., are determined by the interaction of formally defined grammatical relations of deep structure and lexical properties[5] while surface structure determines all other aspects of LF: anaphora, scope of logical operators, the subject-predicate relation, focus and semantic presupposition, and so on. It may be that a suitably enriched version of surface structure suffices to determine LF fully, under a revision of EST along the lines to be discussed (cf. Chomsky (1975b)).

So much for what I will presuppose. Recall the major problem of grammatical theory, as conceived here: to restrict the class of grammars available in principle to the language learner, and thus to progress towards a solution to the most fundamental question that we can raise, namely, the question how people are able to acquire their vast and intricate knowledge of language on the basis of the fragmentary and degenerate evidence available to them.[6]

Within EST, the variety of grammars can be restricted at various points. We might impose conditions on the base, thus restricting the variety of possible systems. We may attempt to limit the expressive power of transformations so that fewer transformations will be available in principle, and we may limit the variety of transformational systems in other ways, say, by imposing general conditions on ordering. Further restriction can be achieved by appropriate conditions on the "interpretive rules" that associate representations in LF with derivations. Furthermore, conditions on rule application that do not in themselves directly restrict the variety of grammars may

---

[5] Chomsky (1972, Chapter, 3). For much more extensive discussion, see Jackendoff (1972), Katz (1972), and more recent papers by these authors.

[6] Just how degenerate is this experience? I know of no reliable evidence, but the problem appears to have been misunderstood, and some incorrect statements have been made about what has been asserted. As for the problem, suppose that a scientist were presented with data, 2 percent of which are wrong (but he doesn't know which 2 percent). Then he faces some serious difficulties, which would be incomparably more serious if the data were simply uncontrolled experience, rather than the result of controlled experiment, devised for its relevance to theoretical hypotheses. The fact that these difficulties do not seem to arise for the language learner, who is, of course, faced with degenerate data of experience, requires explanation. As for false statements, consider, e.g., Labov (1970). He speaks of the "widespread myth that most speech is ungrammatical" and "the current belief of many linguists that most people do not speak in well-formed sentences, and that their actual speech production or 'performance' is ungrammatical." As his sole source, he cites a statement of mine which asserts nothing remotely of the sort. Labov also alleges that "in a number of presentations" I have "asserted that the great majority of the sentences which a child hears are ungrammatical ('95 percent')." He cites no source; there is none. No such statement appears anywhere, to my knowledge, and surely not in my writings. I have discussed the matter "in a number of presentations" but without quantitative estimates (since I know of none) and surely without the estimate that he places within quotes.

contribute to this end in an indirect but significant manner, where they permit a reduction of the expressive power of rules. In each of these categories, there has been recent research that seems to me promising.

On restriction of the base, the most promising line of inquiry, in my opinion, has to do with the "*X*-bar theory," which takes the base to be in its essentials a projection from the lexical features [±Noun], [±Verb], by means of general schemata.[7] I will not pursue this topic here. Rather, I would like to consider the problem of restricting the transformational component of the grammar. Some fairly natural conditions seem to me feasible, at least over an interesting range. It is these conditions that I want to explore.

In all theories of transformations that have been presented even in a semi-explicit way, a transformational rule is defined in terms of a *structural description* (SD) and a *structural change* (SC), where the SD specifies the domain of the transformation and the SC states what effect the transformation has on an arbitrary member of this domain. The domain of a transformation is a set of phrase markers, each the phrase marker of some terminal string. A transformation applies to a phrase marker $K$ of a terminal string $X$ subdivided into the successive *factors* $X_1, \ldots, X_n$ ($X = X_1 \ldots X_n$). The SD specifies the domain of a transformation by placing conditions on such factorization. Let us consider a few simple cases.

Assume given a terminal and nonterminal vocabulary, where the terminal symbols represent grammatical formatives and the nonterminal symbols represent categories (NP, VP, S, etc.).[8] Suppose that we also have the symbol *vbl*, read "variable."[9] We may then construct arbitrary strings in this full vocabulary. Let us assume the following notion:

(1)  E($Y$, $\alpha$, $X$, $K$),

where $Y$ is a substring of the terminal string X, K is a phrase marker of $X$, and $\alpha$ is an arbitrary string in the full vocabulary.

---

[7] In addition to the references cited in Chomsky (1975b, Chapter 3), see now Bresnan (in press) and (1976) and Hornstein (1975).

[8] Thus, categories are nonterminal atomic (prime) elements in the *X*-bar system.

[9] In the earliest work on transformational grammar (e.g., Chomsky, (1955)), the terms of SD were restricted to constants. The effect of variables was achieved by the device of constructing "families of transformations" with a fixed structural change and SD's meeting a fixed condition. The reason had to do with a requirement that transformations be single-valued mappings. This requirement followed, in turn, from the theory of T-markers as a linguistic level. Cf. Chomsky (1955; 1965, Chapter 3); Katz and Postal (1964).

We will read (1) as: $Y$ is a(n) $\alpha$ of $X$ with respect to (wrt) $K$.[10] For example, if $K$ is a phrase marker of the terminal string *the man left*, then E(*the man*, NP, *the man left*, $K$), since *the man* is a noun phrase in the sentence *the man left* wrt $K$.

To explain E, we have to say how it holds under various choices of $\alpha$. Where $\alpha = vbl$, we will say that any string is an $\alpha$; thus E($Y$, *vbl*, $X$, $K$) for any substring $Y$ of $X$. Where $\alpha$ is a terminal string $Z$, then $Y$ is an $\alpha$ of $X$ wrt $K$ just in case $Y = Z$. Where $\alpha$ is a category symbol, then $Y$ is an $\alpha$ of $X$ wrt $K$ just in case $Y$ is assigned to the category $\alpha$ by $K$. To make the latter notion precise, we need to elaborate the notion of "phrase marker." We may assume here any conventional theory, say labeled bracketing. If we take phrase markers to be sets of strings, along the lines of Chomsky (1955), then where $\alpha$ is a terminal string or a category, then E($Y$, $\alpha$, $X$, $K$) when $K$ contains the string formed by replacing $Y$ in $X$ by $\alpha$.

In a very simple case, we may restrict $\alpha$ to a terminal string, a category, or *vbl*, and represent the SD of a transformation as a sequence:

(2)  SD: $(\alpha_1, \ldots, \alpha_n)$.

The transformation defined by SD of (2) applies to the string $X$ with factors $X_1, \ldots, X_n$ and the phrase marker $K$ where for each $i$, E($X_i$, $\alpha_i$, $X$, $K$).

For example, we might formulate the passive transformation in English with the following SD:

(3)  (*vbl*, NP, Aux, V, NP, *by*, #, *vbl*)

In this formulation, the two terms *vbl* are (end-) variables, so that the first and last factors of a string $X$ to which the transformation applies are arbitrary. The second and fifth factors must be NP's (each is an NP), the third an Aux(iliary), the fourth a V, the sixth *by* and the seventh # (*by* and # are terminal symbols; we may think of # as an "abstract" representative of NP). In particular, the passive transformation, so formulated, will apply to the string (4), where – indicates the break between factors:

(4)  yesterday – the boy – PAST – read – the book – by – #

---

[10] For precision, we should distinguish occurrences of $Y$ in $X$. Cf. Chomsky (1955). For a more careful presentation of the notations sketched here, see Chomsky (1961), Chomsky and Miller ((1963). See Peters and Ritchie (1973) for a full formalization of a fairly rich theory of transformations.

Existing transformational grammars do not restrict rules to this simple case. Nevertheless, I want to consider the possibility that only this case is permitted, and in fact, that even this case is "insufficiently simple" in that it permits too rich an expressive power for transformations.

Among the enrichments of the theory of SD's that appear in the literature, theoretical and applied, are the following: disjunctions of sequences of the form (2), meaning that the factors may satisfy any one of the disjuncts[11]; wider possibilities for $\alpha$[12]; SD's defined in terms of Boolean conditions on E for a fixed sequence of factors[13]; conditions expressed in terms of quantifiers[14]; conditions involving grammatical relations[15]; SD's expressing quite arbitrary conditions on phrase markers or even sets of noncontiguous phrase markers of a derivation[16]; SD's expressing conditions not limited to a single derivation[17]; SD's involving extrasyntactic or even extragrammatical factors, e.g., beliefs.[18] These various moves towards enrichment of the theory of transformations are all distinct. Each is unwelcome

---

[11] Consider, for example, a rule of cleft-formation that asserts that NP's or PP's can be clefted; or, the rules of Chomsky (1955) and later work involving the verbal auxiliary. On disjunction, cf. Bresnan (1976; in press).

[12] Thus, it is plausibly argued in Bresnan (1976; in press) that $\alpha$ may be of the form $C+vbl$, where $C$ is a constant terminal (e.g., *wh-*) or category. To achieve the same results within the framework of (2) it might be necessary to assume that *wh-* is a feature of categories, as suggested in Chomsky (1973), and comparable modifications would be required in other cases discussed. This course raises problems that would carry us too far afield here. Bresnan's theory extends to other cases as well.

[13] Bresnan's theory, discussed in note 12, has this property. Or, suppose that (3) is inadequate for the passive, in that we must also require that the string consisting of the sixth plus seventh factors is a PP. Or, consider a rule of extraposition of an S-complement of an NP, which maps a structure [NPN S]VP into N VP S. We might want to say that the transformations applies to three factors, the first an N, the second an S, the third a VP, and the first plus second an NP. For a formalization of a theory of this sort, which is standard in descriptive practice, see Peters and Ritchie (1973). Cf. Kayne (1975) for many examples, in a very careful and extensive study.

[14] For example, we might want to say that a rule applies to an NP only if it is directly dominated by S (i.e., if it is a subject, in the framework of Chomsky (1955)) or if there is no PP dominating it, etc. Similarly, quantifiers would be needed to formulate the A-over-A condition as a property of particular rules.

[15] Cf. Postal (1976) for an argument that the rule of quantifier movement requires reference to the grammatical relation "subject of," and Fiengo and Lasnik (1976) for a counterargument, which I think is correct, showing that the data rule out any such analysis and require rather a simple positional theory of the sort outlined here. For more discussion of the issues mentioned here, see the latter paper.

[16] So-called derivational constraints. Cf. Lakoff (1971) and Postal (1972). On technical difficulties in this proposal, cf. Soames ((1974). On the empirical issues, see Brame (1976) and references cited there.

[17] So-called transderivational constraints.

[18] Cf. Ross (1973; 1975).

(though perhaps necessary, so the facts may show), the more extreme being the more unwelcome for reasons already outlined.[19]

It would take several more articles to discuss these and other related proposals in anything like an adequate way. I will not enter into these fundamental questions here, but will merely remark that I am not convinced by the arguments advanced, particularly, for the more extreme proposals, many of which seem to me to involve nothing more than a failure to distinguish separate and quite distinct components of the full system of language which interact to determine judgments in complex cases.

Let us restrict attention to the simple case mentioned earlier, namely, SD's of the form (2). Let us inquire into the effects of other still more stringent conditions on the expressive power of transformational rules.

The structural change of a transformation with the SD (2) will apply to a string $X$ factored into $n$ successive factors $X_1, \ldots, X_n$, where $E(X_i, \alpha_i, X, K)$, $K$ the phrase marker of $X$. The structural change will in general not affect the form or position of certain factors, while others will be moved, modified, replaced or deleted; briefly, *changed*. A factor changed by the rule, unless arbitrary or a fixed terminal string, must be assigned to a single category, under the assumptions we are now considering. For example, we cannot have a rule that moves a factor $Z$ identified as a $V+NP$ in the SD of the transformation. Rather, if a rule moves such a string, we must assign it to a single category, VP. Considerations of this sort have been regularly adduced in support of one or another assignment of constituent structure since the origins of work in transformational grammar.[20]

We may think of the category symbols that appear in SD's as "type variables." Thus, where NP appears as the $i$th term in (2), it may be "satisfied" by an arbitrary string of the type NP in factoring a string for the transformation. It is argued in Bresnan (1976; in press) that the restriction to type variables in this sense is too narrow and that categorial terms of the SD must be generalized in terms of the $X$-bar system. See Fiengo and Lasnik (1976) for a similar proposal, on different grounds. Suppose that we let $X^n$ stand an arbitrary category with $n$ bars in this system. Then we might permit terms of the form $X^n$ to appear in SD's. Cf. notes 12, 13. Call these "variable categories."

It seems that factors that are truly arbitrary are never changed by

---

[19] Postal argues to the contrary in Postal (1972), but I think he is mistaken for reasons given in my remarks in Parret (1974).

[20] For discussion of the logic of the argument, see Chomsky (1955). In more recent work, the condition was made explicit, perhaps first in Ross (1967).

rules. That is, where $\alpha_i$ in an SD is *vbl*, the *i*th factor will not be changed by the rule but will rather serve as a "context" for whatever changes the rule induces. Let us stipulate, then, that a factor changed by a rule must be either a fixed terminal string or a string of a constant or variable category. An unrestricted variable ($\alpha_i = vbl$) in an SD will be satisfied only by a factor that is not changed by the rule.

A radical restriction in the expressive power of transformations would be achieved if we were to impose a condition that is almost the converse of the condition imposed on factors changed, in the following way. Suppose we were to insist that if a term $\alpha_i$ of SD is a constant or variable category then the factor satisfying $\alpha_i$ must be changed by the rule. That is, categories cannot be used to define the context of the structural change induced by the transformation. Such contexts must either be arbitrary or fixed terminal strings.

Actually, the same result follows in many cases even from weaker conditions on SD's. Suppose that we were to impose a condition of *minimal factorization* that requires that the SD (2) cannot contain two successive categorial terms unless one or the other is satisfied by a factor changed by the rule. This condition in effect extends to the context of the structural change the requirement of analyzability as a single constituent that we have tentatively imposed on the factors changed by the rule. Assuming this condition, which actually is rather well motivated, let us return to the passive transformation.

In Chomsky (1972; 1973) it is suggested that there are really two components to what has been called the "passive transformation," one a rule of NP-postposing that converts the string (4) to (5), and another a rule of NP-preposing that converts (5) to (6):

(5)  yesterday – $t_1$ – PAST – read – the book – by – [the boy]$_1$
(6)  yesterday – [the book]$_2$ – PAST – read – $t_2$ – by – the boy

The symbols $t_1$ and $t_2$ are the "traces" left by movement of the co-indexed phrases. For the moment, we may regard this as a notational proposal, although we will see later that much more is involved.[21] NP-preposing replaces the trace $t_1$ by the NP *the book*.

Under the proposed condition of minimal factorization, we cannot employ (3) in the formulation of the rule of NP-postposing or NP-preposing. In the former case, the constant terms Aux, V, NP and *by* are not changed by the rule; in the case of NP-preposing, the constant

---

[21] Cf. Chomsky (1973; 1975b), Wasow (forthcoming), Fiengo (1974).

terms Aux and V are not changed (we may ignore the factors *by*, *#*) unless we assume that the same rule introduces *be+en*, adjoining it either to Aux or V, an assumption that I would like to reject for reasons discussed elsewhere (cf. Chomsky (1975b, Chapter 3)). Therefore, under the condition of minimal factorization, the rules must be formulated in quite a different way. Assuming now that the passive element *be+en* derives from an independent source, the rule of NP-preposing must be based on the following SD:

(7)  (*vbl*, NP, *vbl*, NP, *vbl*).

Thus the transformation in question will apply to a string factored into five factors, the first, third and fifth arbitrary, and the second and fourth NP's. Terms changed by the rule are specified as constant categories; contexts are arbitrary. The associated structural change will state that the fourth factor moves into the position of the second factor. We might formulate the rule of NP-postposing in the same manner, with a structural change indicating that the second factor moves into the position of the fourth factor.

The difficulties facing such an analysis appear at first—and may prove to be—insurmountable. Whether this is so or not is a question that I would like to explore. Notice that if we can go as far as this, we can take a further step, exploiting Emonds' structure-preserving hypothesis, which entails that NP can move only into an NP position in the phrase marker Emonds (1976). Thus the rules in question reduce to the following formulation:

(8)  Move NP.

This seems a natural consequence of assuming the condition of minimal factorization.

As noted, the condition of minimal factorization extends to the context of a rule the requirement of analyzability as a single constituent imposed on the factors changed by the rule. If this extension seems natural, we are then led to consider the following condition on an SD of the form (2):

(9)  If $\alpha_i$ is satisfied by a factor changed by the rule, then $\alpha_i$ may be terminal or a category; if $\alpha_i$ is satisfied by a factor not changed by the rule, then $\alpha_i$ may be either *vbl* or a terminal string.

The case of terminal strings changed by a rule seems rather marginal.

Perhaps we may consider such rules to be of a special type, what Bach (1965) has called "housekeeping rules". If so, we may say that for the basic rules of the grammar, factors changed by the rule must be analyzed by the SD as categories while contexts (factors not changed) must be either terminal or arbitrary. If terminal contexts can be eliminated in general, we will have rules of the form (8). I think that (9) is probably too strong a condition, but that the weaker condition of minimal factorization may be tenable, despite the fact that its consequences approach (9), as we have seen.

I would now like to consider a few of the problems that arise under such radical restrictions of the expressive power of transformations as those just suggested. Evidently, a grammar limited to such rules as (7) or (8) will overgenerate massively, since intricate constraints cannot be built into specific transformations. Consider the case of NP-preposing; i.e., the leftward movement case of (7). By general conditions on recoverability of deletion (the correct formulation of which is a nontrivial matter; cf. Peters and Ritchie (1973)), the second NP can move only to an NP position that is empty of any lexical material. Assuming that the left NP position, which is to receive the moved NP, is empty, either by virtue of prior NP-postposing or for some other reason, we will have such instances of NP-preposing as the following:

(10) a. John is believed [$t$ is incompetent]
   b. John is believed [$t$ to be incompetent]
   c. John('s) was read [$t$ book]
   d. John seems [$t$ to like Bill]
   e. John seems [Bill to like $t$]
   f. yesterday was lectured $t$
   g. yesterday's lecture $t$

In each case, $t$ is the trace left by movement of the NP (*John, yesterday*). Of these examples, only (b), (d), and (g) are grammatical, although NP-preposing has applied in a comparable way in all cases. Thus the rule overgenerates, specifically, in cases (a), (c), (e), and (f).

There are two general approaches to the problem of overgeneration in such cases as these: we may try to impose (I) conditions on the application of rules or (II) conditions on the output of rules, i.e., on surface structures. The latter may be related to rules of semantic interpretation that determine LF, under the assumptions of EST. As we will see, (I) and (II) may fall together. Both sorts of conditions may be related to perceptual strategies in some way; cf. Chomsky (1973) and references cited there.

In either case (I) or case (II), the conditions in question may be universal or particular; and in the case of (I), if particular, they may be language-particular or rule-particular. In the best case, of course, the conditions will be universal. That is, we try to abstract general properties of transformations that do not have to be built into specific transformations. Thus the set of potentially available grammars is reduced, and we approach the fundamental problem of accounting for the fact that language can be learned.

If we conclude that some condition is language-particular, we must find a way to account for its application in a given case. If the condition is rule-particular, we have to account for the fact that specific rules observe the condition and that speakers have knowledge of this property of the language.

Even if conditions are language- or rule-particular, there are limits to the possible diversity of grammar. Thus, such conditions can be regarded as parameters that have to be fixed (for the language, or for particular rules, in the worst case), in language learning. We would then raise the question how the class of grammars so constituted, with rules that lack expressive power but parameters to be fixed independently, compares with the class of grammars permitted under a theory that permits articulation of conditions on application within the formulation of the rules themselves. It has often been supposed that conditions on application of rules must be quite general, even universal, to be significant, but that need not be the case if establishing a "parametric" condition permits us to reduce substantially the class of possible rules.

We might hope to find that even if some condition C on rule application is language-particular, nevertheless some general principle determines that it applies in languages of some specific type, in which case we will have again reduced the problem, indirectly, to a property of UG. Or, in the case of rule-particular conditions, we might find that they apply to rules of some specific category, say, movement rules. Such a result would be as welcome as a universal condition, in that it limits the choice of grammars in a comparable way. That is, the child would not have to learn anything about the applicability of the condition; a universal principle would determine this. Many proposals of this nature appear in the literature.

I am going to suggest that there are conditions that apply to transformational rules and interpretive rules, and other conditions that apply only to transformational rules. These conditions belong to

175

the theory of (sentence-) grammar. There may be other conditions that apply to the rules that assign semantic representations to LF and elements of other cognitive structures, i.e., to rules that extend beyond sentence-grammar in their scope; for example, to "free anaphora," which may involve properties of discourse, situation, and assumed background belief.

Consider again the examples of overgeneration in (10). In work referred to above, I have suggested that we can account for these examples in terms of certain general conditions on rules. Consider a structure of the form:

(11)  $\ldots X \ldots [_\alpha \ldots Y \ldots] \ldots X \ldots$

Then no rule can involve $X$ and $Y$ in (11) where $\alpha$ is a tensed-S (the *tensed-S condition*)[22] or where $\alpha$ contains a subject distinct from $Y$ and not controlled by $X$ (the *specified subject condition*—henceforth, SSC); (for discussion, cf. Chomsky (1973; 1975b)). I will assume further that transformations, but not interpretive rules, meet the condition of *subjacency,* which restricts their application to a single cyclic node or adjacent cyclic nodes.[23]

The tensed-S condition suffices to explain the difference of status between (10a) and (10b). SSC accounts for the distinction between

---

[22] In the case of a transformational rule, we may understand "$X$ is involved in the rule" to mean that $X$ is changed by the rule or is a constant context for some change (cf. Fiengo and Lasnik (1976) for an interesting case of the latter sort). Thus the terms involved in the rule are the factors that are not arbitrary strings, in accordance with the SD. In an interpretive rule, we may say that $X$ and $Y$ are involved if the rule establishes a relation of anaphora or control relating $X$ and $Y$. Cf. Jackendoff (1972), Wasow (forthcoming). Fiengo (1974). I leave other questions open, pending further investigation. The condition on $\alpha$ raises questions that I will not pursue. For English, tensed sentences and subjunctives fall under $\alpha$. Possibly, the condition may vary within a limited range among languages; thus it might be that the condition holds for $\alpha$ finite only in languages that distinguish finite from infinitive complements. There is some evidence to this effect, but it is too sparse to be convincing.

[23] Among the unsolved problems are some involving so-called "picture-noun reflexivization," which so far resist analysis under any general theory known to me; cf. Jackendoff (1972). It may be, as suggested in Helke (1971), that English reflexivization is a complex of two processes, one a process of bound anaphora restricted by conditions on sentence-grammar, and the other a more general process involving other factors that applies to "reflexives" of very different sorts, for example, in such languages as Korean, where the item that has been called "reflexive" is not bound by principles of sentence-grammar, so it appears, and thus naturally violates grammatical conditions. Note also such examples as *the men expected that pictures of each other would be on sale,* where application of the reciprocal rule violates the tensed-S condition in a nonsubjacent construction, as compared with *\*the men expected (that) each other would win,* observing the tensed-S condition under subjacency. I hope to present a more comprehensive discussion elsewhere.

(10d) and (10e). To exclude (10c), we might appeal to the *A-over-A* condition. Notice that in these cases, at least, we might reformulate the conditions in question as conditions on an enriched surface structure involving traces, instead of conditions on the application of rules.

What about the phrases (10f) and (10g)? Emonds suggests that such examples as these show that NP-preposing cannot be a unitary phenomenon, but must apply differently in sentences and noun phrases. However, we might appeal to a principle of semantic interpretation of surface structures, in part independently motivated, to make the distinction. Consider the next two sentences:

(12) a. beavers build dams
 b. dams are built *t* by beavers
 (where *t* is the trace left by NP-preposing)

Under its most natural interpretation, (b) is false, since some dams are not built by beavers. Thus in (b), under this interpretation, the property *built-by-beavers* is predicated, falsely, of all dams. No such interpretation is possible for (a), which predicates the property *dam-builder* of all beavers (which is not to say, of course, that all beavers build dams; rather, all have the species-property in question). Such examples indicate that the subject-predicate relation is defined on surface structures.

Of course, to understand (b) we must also know that the subject *dams* bears the same "thematic relation" to the verb *build* as it does in (a). Assuming now that traces appear in surface structure, the requisite information appears in (b) under the general convention that the trace *t* is under the control of the phrase *dams* that moved from the position marked by *t*, which we may regard as a bound variable in (b).

Let us return now to the problem of (10f,g), repeated here as (13a,b):

(13) a. yesterday was lectured *t*
 b. yesterday's lecture *t*

Assume that NP-preposing is indeed involved in each case. But the principle of interpretation that assigns the subject-predicate relation will give nonsense when applied to (13a); it makes no sense to predicate *was-lectured* of *yesterday*. We might, then, argue that (13a) is ungrammatical, but by virtue of a violation of a principle of semantic interpretation; i.e., it is "unsemantic" rather than "unsyntactic", if we regard these interpretive rules as part of semantics. In contrast, the principle of subject–predicate interpretation does not apply at all to (13b), which is not a sentence. Rather, the principle of interpretation that applies here is the one that we see exemplified in such structures as "John's kitten," which may be understood to mean the kitten that John has, or that he owns, or that he made out of clay, or that he fathered (or gave birth to, in the case of an oddly named female cat), etc. As we let factual assumptions range, the range of possible interpretations in such cases varies widely, in a manner that has yet to be explained. It seems plausible to suppose that it may comprehend (13b), as a special case.

Thus we might try to account for the distinction between (13a) and (13b) not in terms of an enriched theory of transformations, but in terms of principles of semantic interpretation which are (if this line of reasoning proves correct) independently motivated. This proposal remains a promissory note in the absence of a theory of subject–predicate and possessive interpretation. But such a theory is certainly necessary, and may well accommodate the phenomenon under consideration. It seems to me at least plausible—and perhaps quite reasonable—to adopt the working hypothesis that no enrichment of the theory of transformations is called for in this case.

The discussion of these examples illustrates the possibility of compensating for the overgeneration of a highly restricted theory of transformations in terms of conditions on transformations and on interpretation of surface structures, conditions which may be quite general, perhaps properties of UG itself.

Let us now turn to a somewhat different, though related matter. Consider examples (14) and (15):

(14) a. the men like each other
b. the men like them
c. I like me

(15) a. the men want [John to like each other]
b. the men want [John to like them]
c. I want [John to like me]

Let us assume the following two rules:

(16) Reciprocal interpretation, which assigns an appropriate sense to sentences of the form NP . . . *each other*[24]

---

[24] On the semantics of this construction, see Fiengo and Lasnik (1973), Dougherty (1974).

178

(17) Disjoint reference (DR), which assigns disjoint reference to a pair (NP, pronoun)(and more generally, to two NPs, under somewhat different conditions that extend beyond sentence grammar; cf. note 37)

The reciprocal rule applies to (14a), but cannot apply to (15a) by virtue of SSC. Thus, (14a) is grammatical but (15a) is not. The rule DR applies to (14b), assigning disjoint reference, but is blocked from application in (15b) by SSC. The reference of *them* in (15b) is therefore free; it can, in particular, be understood to refer to the men. In the case of (14c), DR applies, assigning disjoint reference, which is impossible in this case. In the parallel case of (15c), DR cannot apply by virtue of SSC, so that *me* and *I* may be (and must be) coreferential. Hence (14c) is "strange" (whether ungrammatical or not is a matter that need not concern us here; it depends on what status we assign to DR), in a sense in which (15c) is not.

In these examples, as before, SSC functions so as to permit a very simple formulation of rules. Thus such examples as (14) and (15) do not compel us to depart from the simplest possible formulation of the rule of reciprocal interpretation and DR, a formulation which simply asserts that they hold of any NP and an anaphoric element (reciprocal, pronoun).

I suggested before that (10e) is blocked by SSC, but without explaining how. Let us consider two interpretations of this suggestion. We assume now that (10d) derives by NP-preposing from the underlying structure "$X$ seems [John to like Bill]," where $X$ is some terminal "place-holder" for NP, the exact character of which need not detain us now. On one interpretation, SSC prevents the rule from preposing *John* in "$X$ seems [Bill to like John]" to give (10e). Thus, SSC blocks a certain transformational rule. Alternatively, we might construe SSC as a condition on surface structure interpretation but not transformations. Thus, the NP-preposing rule applies freely, giving both (10d) and (10e). But we must surely regard the relation between NP and the trace that it controls as a special case of bound anaphora (cf. Fiengo (1974); Chomsky (1975b): that is, as a relation just like the one that holds between antecedent and reciprocal. Thus, SSC will block the rule of bound anaphora exactly as it blocks reciprocal interpretation and disjoint reference in the cases just described. It is in this sense that we can regard SSC, in such cases, as a condition on surface structures applying quite generally to anaphora (hence to the NP-trace relation), rather than a condition on transformations. In principle, the two interpretations of SSC have distinct empirical consequences, but the issue is complex and it is not easy to sort out the consequences.

Were it not for SSC, the rules as formulated would overgenerate (in the case of (16)) and undergenerate (in the case of (17), since when it applies it rules out certain sentences and interpretations). Thus SSC compensates for certain instances of misgeneration. The same is true of the tensed-S condition. Consider

(18) a. the candidates expected [that each other would win]
     b. the candidates want [each other to win]
     c. the candidates expected [that they would win]
     d. the candidates want [them to win]
     e. I expected [that I would win]
     f. I want [me to win]

The condition blocks the reciprocal rule in (a) but not (b). It blocks DR in (c) but not (d), so that the pronoun may refer to the candidates in (c) but not (d). It blocks DR in (e) but not in (f), which is therefore "strange" or ungrammatical, depending on our conclusion concerning violation of DR.

Now consider examples (19) and (20):

(19) a. the men seem to John [$t$ to like each other]
     b. the men seem to John [$t$ to like them]
     c. I seem to John [$t$ to like me]

(20) a. John seems to the men [$t$ to like each other]
     b. John seems to the men [$t$ to like them]
     c. John seems to me [$t$ to like me]

The examples of (19) are analogous to (14). Thus in (a), *each other* is anaphorically related to *the men*; in (b) the pronoun cannot refer to the men; and (c) is strange or ungrammatical. In short, the rules of reciprocal interpretation and DR apply in (19), as in (14).

Examples (20) are correspondingly analogous to (15). Reciprocal interpretation is blocked in case (a). DR is blocked in case (b), so that the pronoun can refer freely, in particular, to *the men*. And (c) is fine.

These examples are analogous to those discussed earlier, and should fall under the same principle. But SSC does not seem to apply, since there is no subject in the embedded sentences of (20) as there was in (15), to put it into effect.

Examples (19) behave as though there is no specified subject in the embedded sentence; examples (20), in contrast, are treated as though

180

there were a specified subject in the position marked by the trace $t$ left by NP-preposing of the subject of the matrix sentence. In the case of (20), a "mentally present" subject blocks application of the rules by SSC, just as the physically present subject *John* in (15) blocks the same rules. In the case of (19), the mentally present subject does not block application of the rules.

To extend SSC to all of these cases, it is necessary to define "specified subject" as above. Although not logically necessary, this is entirely natural. It amounts to regarding the trace as a bound variable, with all of the (relevant) properties of its "controller," the noun phrase to which it is bound. Let us now stipulate explicitly what we have been tacitly assuming: movement of a phrase by a transformation leaves behind a trace controlled by the moved phrase; the trace will be interpreted as a bound variable, along lines to which we will return. The trace is a zero morpheme—phonetically null but morphologically on a par with any other terminal symbol of the level of phrase structure. Just as the lexical string *John* serves as a specified subject in (15), blocking any rule that relates $Y$ of (11) to $X$, so the trace $t$ serves as a specified subject in (20), blocking any rule that relates $Y$ of (11) to $X$ unless $t$ is bound by $X$. In all cases, then, the rules apply as though the noun phrase binding the trace $t$ were actually present in the position of $t$. The trace theory thus permits otherwise valid conditions to apply, again overcoming cases of misapplication of rules: overgeneration in the case of the reciprocal rule, undergeneration in the case of disjoint reference.

Observe that there is no plausible semantic reason for the inapplicability of the rules in (20). Consider the reciprocal rule. The pair (*each of the men, the other(s)*) is similar in meaning to the pair (*the men, each other*). Thus corresponding to (14a), (15a), (19a), and (20a), repeated here as (21a–d), we have (22a–d), respectively:

(21) a. the men like each other
　　 b. the men want [John to like each other]
　　 c. the men seem to John [$t$ to like each other]
　　 d. John seems to the men [$t$ to like each other]

(22) a. each of the men likes the other(s)
　　 b. each of the men wants [John to like the other(s)]
　　 c. each of the men seems to John [$t$ to like the other(s)]
　　 d. John seems to each of the men [$t$ to like the other(s)]

The sentences of (22) are all fully grammatical. (22a) is similar if not identical in meaning to (21a), and there seems to be no independent semantic principle that explains why (21b–d) should not be correspondingly related in meaning to (22b–d). The effect of SSC in (21) cannot be explained in terms of semantic incoherence or complexity of processing or the like, because any such consideration should apply as well to the corresponding examples of (22). Or to put it differently, suppose that a language were like English except that SSC did not apply. In this language, (21b–d) would be near synonyms of (22b–d) just as (21a) is a near synonym of (22a). The language would be none the worse for that on any general "functional" grounds of comprehensibility, interpretability, and so on. The same would be true of a hypothetical language just like English except that SSC applied only when the specified subject is physically present, so that (21b) would be excluded but (21c,d) quite grammatical, with (roughly) the meanings (22c,d). It seems to be an empirical fact that SSC applies to physically present subjects and mentally present ones (trace). But there is no a priori reason why this should be so. It is a principle of English grammar—and, it is fair to postulate, of UG, since it is difficult to imagine that each person capable of these discriminations has been given explicit evidence or training that bears on them.

There is, in fact, an appearance of paradox here. Thus, we might ask why SSC blocks the reciprocal rule and DR, but not the rule that relates *each of the men* to *the others* in (22b–d). It seems that we are compelled to formulate SSC as a rule-particular principle, this giving the unwanted (though not intolerable) theoretical consequence discussed before. In fact, this consequence is forced on us unless we can find a principled difference between the two cases. Is there such a difference?

The answer is obvious. Reciprocal interpretation and DR are rules of sentence-grammar; the rule interpreting *the others* is not. Thus compare the next two paired cases:

(23) a.  Some of the men left today. The others will leave later.
 a'. Some of the men left today. Each other will leave later.

  b.  Some of the articles are incomprehensible, but we each expected John to understand the others.
  b'. Some of the articles are incomprehensible, but we expected John to understand each other.

The examples (a') and (b') are ungrammatical. The rule of reciprocal interpretation, being a rule of sentence-grammar, is inapplicable in case (a′) and is blocked by SSC in (b′). The rule assigning an interpretation to *the others*, however, is not a rule of sentence-grammar at all, as (a) indicates. Thus it is not subject to the conditions of sentence-grammar, so that (23a,b) are as grammatical as (22b–d).

Note that it is strictly incorrect to imply, as I did, that (22a) is virtually synonymous with (21a). In the case of (22a), we are not required to understand the phrase *the other(s)* as referring to a set related through reciprocal interpretation to the set of *the men*. Thus consider the following context:

(24)   Each of the women likes some of the books; each of the men likes the others.

Namely, the other books. In contrast, replacement of (*each of the men, the others*) by (*the men, each other*) in (24) forces quite a different interpretation.

Returning to the basic theory outlined earlier, the rules of reciprocal interpretation and DR relate derivations (in fact, surface structures, enriched to include traces) to LF, while the rule assigning an interpretation to *the other(s)* belongs to an entirely different component of the system of cognitive structures relating LF and other factors to a full semantic representation. It might be quite appropriate to assign this rule to a theory of performance (pragmatics) rather than to the theory of grammar.

In Chomsky (1973) I pointed out that the rules of anaphora associating *he* with *John* in such sentences as (25) appear to violate otherwise valid conditions, a problem for the theory presented there:

(25)   a. John thought that he would win.
       b. John thought that Bill liked him.

Others have reiterated this point, arguing that it undermines the theory outlined. But my observation was simply an error. The rule of anaphora involved in the (normal but not obligatory) interpretation of (25) should in principle be exempt from the conditions on sentence-grammar, since it is no rule of sentence-grammar at all. Cf. Lasnik (1976).

Consider again the operation of SSC. The context of application in the cases we are considering is (26):

(26)   . . . NP . . . [NP$_s$ . . . $Y$ . . .] . . .

where the rule is prevented from applying to the pair (NP, Y) by virtue of the specified subject $NP_s$. Several cases can be distinguished:

(27) a. $NP_s$ has lexical content and is therefore not controlled by NP.
 b. $NP_s$ is a trace not controlled (bound) by NP.
 c. $NP_s$ is the interpreted subject of a complement—suppose it to be the element PRO—not controlled by NP.

Corresponding to these three cases, we have such examples as (28a–c), respectively, where the reciprocal rule is unable to relate the italicized phrases by virtue of SSC:

(28) a. *The men* wanted [John to like *each other*]
 b. John seemed to *the men* [*t* to like *each other*]
 c. John promised *the men* [PRO to like *each other*]

In each case, NP = *the men*; $NP_s$ is either *John* (as in (a)) or a zero morpheme controlled by *John* (trace in (b) and PRO in (c)). Thus in each case, the rule blocks by SSC. Notice that it is a lexical property of *promise* (as distinct, say, from *persuade*) that the subject of the matrix sentence, rather than the object, controls the subject of the embedded sentence.[25]

Suppose that the subject of an embedded sentence is actually deleted, rather than assigned an interpretation as in the case (28c). Matters become rather delicate at this point. We would expect that rules should apply over the deleted subject. There are, I think, good reasons to believe that many cases of so-called EQUI—e.g., in the complement of *want*-type verbs—involve deletion of an embedded subject. Assuming this to be true, for the moment, we would then conclude that in the case of (29), a rule relating *the book* to a phrase outside of the brackets should apply freely, there being no specified subject. But in the case of (30) and (31), the phrase *the book* should be subject to a rule relating it to a phrase outside of the brackets only if this phrase is *John*, the controller of PRO:

(29) John wants [to read the book]
(30) John promised Bill [PRO to read the book]
(31) Bill persuaded John [PRO to read the book]

---

[25] On this matter, see Jackendoff (1972; 1976) and references cited therein, and for an analysis of a number of cases in terms of a theory of the sort under discussion here, see Chomsky (1973).

Thus in principle we should be able to find three kinds of cases in which there is a phonetically null subject of an embedded sentence: cases (b) and (c) of (27) and a case like (29), where the embedded subject is deleted. To summarize, we should have the following cases, where $NP_s$ is, again, the embedded subject and NP is the outside phrase involved in the rule:

(32)  a.  $NP_s$ is a trace not bound by NP   (= (27b))
      b.  $NP_s$ is PRO not controlled by NP   (= (27c))
      c.  $NP_s$ is deleted by a transformation   (= (29))

In cases (32a) and (32b), the phonetically null subject should block application of rules, but in case (32c) it should not.

To find actual examples bearing on, let alone verifying such predictions as these is no small task. Not only might the data be rather exotic and the subject's judgments, one might expect, difficult to evaluate, but furthermore, it is necessary to accept quite a few assumptions in assigning an analysis along the lines of (32) to given examples. In the present state of linguistic theory and its application, there are just too many unsolved problems and too many alternative approaches that cannot be conclusively rejected for particular proposals of such intricacy to a carry a high degree of conviction. Nevertheless, I would like to try to pursue the line of argument.

We have already seen good reason to suppose that cases (32a) and (32b) operate as expected. Unfortunately, I have found no relevant examples in English to test (32c). However, some recent work of Carlos Quicoli on clitic movement in Portuguese is highly suggestive.[26] The rule of clitic movement assigns a clitic from an embedded sentence to the verb of the matrix sentence. The rule observes the tensed-S condition; thus, only infinitival complements are subject to clitic movement to the matrix verb.

Consider now the case of SSC. We have such examples as the following one:

(33)   Paulo us saw [$t$ examine the girl]
       Paulo nos viu examinar a garota
       'Paulo saw us examine the girl'

Here, the subject of the embedded sentence cliticizes to the matrix

---

[26] Quicoli's study extends to clitic and quantifier movement in other languages as well. I am indebted to him for the examples that follow, which only touch the surface of the very interesting material he is developing. Cf. Kayne (1975) for presentation of some of the basic ideas and analyses, regarding SSC.

verb. On the other hand, we cannot have (34), in which the object of the embedded sentence cliticizes to the matrix verb, violating SSC:

(34)  Paulo us saw [the specialist examine $t$]
       Paulo nos viu o especialista examinar
       'Paulo saw the specialist examine us'

Thus lexical subjects behave as expected.

Suppose that *wh*-movement has applied, giving such structures as follow:

(35)  a.  The man [who$_1$ Maria saw [us examine $t_1$]] disappeared
       b.  The man [who$_1$ Maria saw [$t_1$ examine us]] disappeared

Suppose we now apply clitic movement. We derive the next sentence:

(36)  'The man who Maria us saw examine disappeared'
       O homem que Maria nos viu examinar sumiu

In fact, (36) has the meaning of (35a) but not (35b). Expressing the fact in terms of trace theory, we have the surface structure (37a) but not (37b) for (36):

(37)  a.  The man [who$_1$ Maria us$_2$ saw [$t_2$ examine $t_1$]] disappeared
       b.  The man [who$_1$ Maria us$_2$ saw [$t_1$ examine $t_2$]] disappeared

We can explain these facts in terms of SSC. The trace will block clitic movement applied to (35b) but not (35a).

Thus lexical subjects and traces behaved as expected.

Consider now the case of an interpreted subject (i.e., case (32b)). As predicted, we do not find (38):

(38)  a.  The doctor us promised [PRO to examine $t$]
       b.  Paulo us convinced the doctor [PRO to examine $t$]

where $t$ is the trace left by clitic movement. That is, the zero element PRO, just like trace, acts as a specified subject, as in English, blocking clitic movement.

Thus lexical subjects, traces and PRO behave as expected.

As noted earlier, there is in principle another case of a phonetically null subject, the case of a deleted subject, namely, (32c). Thus in principle we might expect to find a matrix verb V with a complement sentence in which the subject is deleted as we have assumed to be true in the case of English *want*; and in such a case, we should expect clitic movement to be possible. In fact, taking V to be *querer* 'want', we find just these facts. Thus, we have (39), although the superficially comparable (38a) is excluded:

(39)  The doctor us wants [to examine *t*]
      O medico nos quer examinar

To summarize, lexical subjects serve to bring SSC into operation, blocking clitic movement where the clitic is distinct from the embedded lexical subject. Where the embedded subject is phonetically null, we have the three cases of (32): trace, PRO, and deleted subject. Trace and PRO block the rule, as expected. But there is a null subject that does not block the rule, namely, after *querer*. This example fills the gap in the paradigm; assuming that the subject is deleted in this case, SSC will not apply to block clitic movement.

If this analysis withstands further investigation, we will have the striking conclusion that the three kinds of mentally present, physically missing subjects permitted in principle all are exemplified, with the predicted behavior. Putting it differently, assuming SSC, we have an experimental probe to choose among proposed analyses that postulate various choices among the various kinds of phonetically null subjects permitted in principle.

There are many questions that can be raised about these analyses. This is, however, the kind of inquiry that might be expected to give considerable insight into the formal properties of grammars and the general properties of the human language faculty that make language acquisition possible.

Before we leave this topic, a few additional observations may be relevant. I mentioned that there are some reasons for believing that in English EQUI constructions with the verb *want* actually involve deletion of the subject of the embedded sentence. A few observations may indicate why this is a plausible hypothesis. In the first place, there are phonological arguments for this conclusion. As is well known, the verb *want* followed by *to* undergoes elision, giving the form *wanna* from *want to*: thus:

(40) a. You wanna see Bill.
     b. Who do you wanna see?

But as has been noted,[27] (40b) is possible only when the *wh*-word is understood to be the object, not the subject, of the embedded sentence. Thus (40b) can be derived from (41) but not (42):

(41)  You want [X to see who]
(42)  You want [who to see]

Correspondingly, (43), deriving from (44), is impossible:

(43)  Who do you wanna see Bill
(44)  You want [who to see Bill]

In our terms, we have the surface structures (45)–(47) (overlooking subject–auxiliary inversion, which is irrelevant in this particular case):

(45)  Who [you want [X to see t]]      (underlying (41))
(46)  Who [you want [t to see]]      (underlying (42))
(47)  Who [you want [t to see Bill]]      (from (44))

Of the structures (45)–(47), only (45) undergoes elision. Assume that elision involves a rule adjoining the morpheme *to* to *want*, with the form *want + to* then subject to elision by later phonological rules. But the adjunction rule will be blocked by any intervening morphological material, e.g., *John* in (48) or the zero morpheme *t* in (46) and (47):

(48)  You want [John to see Bill]

A zero morpheme is indistinguishable within syntax and morphology from other formatives. It is simply a terminal element that happens to be assigned a null phonetic representation by later rules. Thus, elision is impossible in (46) and (47), as in (48). Correspondingly, (43) is impossible and (40b) can have only the meaning corresponding to (41).

But for this explanation to carry through, we must assume that X in (45) is null on the morphological as well as the phonetic level, that is, that it is not a zero morpheme but has been literally deleted. Thus we

---

[27] See discussion in Bresnan (1971). For more on the matter, see Baker and Brame (1972), Selkirk (1972), Lightfoot (1975b). Various approaches have been developed to account for the facts. It is difficult to compare these directly, since they involve somewhat different assumptions with regard to underlying theory and particular analyses.

have an indirect argument on phonological grounds for assuming that the embedded subject is deleted after *want*, while the trace remains at the morphological level, though it is phonetically null.

There is corroborating evidence of a syntactic and semantic nature, although it is more complex. To sketch some relevant points briefly, it has been noted by Howard Lasnik and Joan Bresnan that there are two general types of verbs with complements, with some intersection between the types: *want*-type verbs (*want, prefer, hope* . . .) and "epistemic" *believe*-type verbs (*believe, consider, imagine* . . .). Verbs of the *want*-type take the complementizer *for* in the complement sentence, as in (49), a fact sometimes obscured on the surface since *for* deletes immediately after the verb, obligatorily for some (*want*) and optionally for others (*prefer*); thus (50) and (51):

(49)  I want very much for Bill to win.
(50)  I want Bill to win.
(51)  I prefer (for) Bill to win.

Let us assume that epistemic verbs take a zero complementizer.

With regard to reflexivization and EQUI, verbs of these types are in close to complementary distribution. Thus epistemic verbs undergo reflexivization but not EQUI (cf. (52)) while *want*-type verbs undergo EQUI but not reflexivization, though some speakers find reflexivization possible in some cases (cf. (53)):

(52) a. John believed [himself to be incompetent]
     b. John believed [to be incompetent]     [*]   (EQUI)

(53) a. John wanted [himself to be a contender]     [*,?]
     b. John much preferred [for himself to be the candidate]     [*,?]
     c. John wanted [to be a contender]     (EQUI)

Both types of verbs undergo the rules of reciprocal interpretation (16) and disjoint reference (17):

(54) a. They believed [each other to be incompetent]
     b. John believed [him to be incompetent]     (John ≠ him)

(55) a. They wanted [each other to win]
     b. John wanted [him to win]     (John ≠ him)

The two categories are also in complementary distribution with regard to NP-movement; thus we have (56) but not (57):

(56)   John was believed [*t* to be incompetent]
(57)   John was wanted (preferred) [*t* to win][28]

The inapplicability of NP-movement to the subject of the complement of *want*-type verbs can be explained in terms of properties of the complementizer; I believe that it follows from a general surface constraint that excludes *for–to* constructions, although the issue need not concern us here.[29]

The behavior of the two types of verbs with regard to reflexivization and EQUI can be easily explained on the assumption that reflexivization is free throughout, while there is a rule (58) that is optional or obligatory, depending in part on style and perhaps dialect:

(58)   *for X-self* $\longrightarrow$ null / — VP

When (58) applies, we have EQUI. The major facts follow directly from this rule, which can be formulated as a deletion transformation.[30]

The arguments against assuming EQUI to be a rule deleting a full NP seem to me compelling. The facts just reviewed suggest that a deletion rule nevertheless explains more than an interpretation rule of the sort that has sometimes been proposed. This analysis meshes easily with Helke's analysis of base-generated reflexives (1971), which I think is correct in its essentials. For independent arguments in support of a similar conclusion, see Fodor (1975).

Thus in addition to the phonological arguments, there are a range of other considerations in support of the conclusion that the subject of the complement sentence to *want*-type verbs is actually deleted, rather than just interpreted. We might go on to consider a general principle that NP's may be realized either as PRO or with lexical

---

[28] Note that *want* is partially defective in this respect even as a pure transitive verb: e.g., *the book was wanted* [?], *a man who is wanted by the police——was here, any books wanted for this course——can be obtained at the college bookstore* [?]. Other verbs of this category, e.g., *prefer*, are subject to NP-preposing as pure transitives (e.g., *this solution is preferred by most people, the solution preferred by most people——is this one*), though examples such as (57) are impossible. The fact is easily explained on the assumption that there is no rule of raising to object position, an assumption that I will continue to adopt here (cf. Chomsky (1973; 1976)). For a review of this question that seems to me generally convincing, cf. Lightfoot (1975a).

[29] Bresnan, whose analysis I generally follow here, postulates instead a condition on rules involving the complementizer, but I think that there are difficulties that suggest rather that a surface filter is involved. Cf. Bresnan (1972). Bresnan also assumes no complementizer instead of a zero complementizer for epistemic verbs.

[30] I suspect that rule (59) actually results from the interaction of *X-self* deletion and rules preventing *for–to* constructions.

material, but not in both ways. We might think of PRO as an optional feature on the category NP; NP can be expanded by rules of the base only when it is [−PRO]. This assumption would compel us to take the embedded subject to be PRO in (30) and (31) but to be an arbitrary lexically specified NP (one case being the base-generated reflexive) after *want*-type verbs, with *for X-self* deleted in the latter case to give (29). The principle might be modified to permit interpretive analysis of "gapping" and other phenomena as discussed, e.g., in Wasow (forthcoming) Fiengo (1974) but I will not pursue this question here.

Before we leave this topic, consider again the examples (35)–(37), which I repeat here as (59)–(61):

(59) a. The man [$_\alpha$who$_1$ Maria saw [us examine $t_1$]] disappeared
     b. The man [$_\alpha$who$_1$ Maria saw [$t_1$ examine us]] disappeared

(60)    The man who Maria us saw examine disappeared.

(61) a. The man [$_\alpha$who$_1$ Maria us$_2$ saw [$t_2$ examine $t_1$]] disappeared
     b. The man [$_\alpha$who$_1$ Maria us$_2$ saw [$t_1$ examine $t_2$]] disappeared

Recall that (60) means (59a) but not (59b); that is, the surface structure (61a) is acceptable (giving (60)) but not (61b). We explained this, following Quicoli, by assuming that *wh*-movement first applies, leaving a trace $t_1$, which blocks clitic movement by SSC. On the assumption that *wh*-movement is cyclic, we need not assume that *wh*-movement on the cycle $\alpha$ precedes clitic placement, since $t_1$ will in any event be placed by *wh*-movement in the internal cycle. Or, if we were to assume that *wh*-movement applies only on the cycle $\alpha$, following clitic placement, the latter rule would in any event be blocked by SSC with *who* in the position of $t_1$ in (61b). In this case we would have an instance of (27a).

In fact, we might once again choose to reinterpret SSC as a condition on surface structure interpretation rather than a condition on rules, along the lines discussed earlier. Then independently of any considerations involving ordering, the surface structure (61b) is blocked by SSC.

We might also investigate the possibility of relating this interpretation of SSC to some general prohibition against anaphoric structures of the form (62) rather than the permissible (63), where items with the same subscript are anaphorically related.

(62)    . . . $x_1$ . . . $x_2$ . . . $y_1$ . . . $y_2$ . . .
(63)    . . . $x_1$ . . . $x_2$ . . . $y_2$ . . . $y_1$

It is not clear whether such a condition is tenable in general. Consider such examples as (64):

(64) a. [what books]$_1$ have [those men]$_2$ written $t_1$ about [each other]$_2$
    b. I told them$_1$ [what books]$_2$ PRO$_1$ to read $t_2$
    c. I$_1$ asked them [what books]$_2$ PRO$_1$ to read $t_2$
    d. [to whom]$_1$ did John$_2$ seem $t_1$ [$t_2$ to be referring]
    e. whom$_1$ did you$_2$ ask $t_1$ [what$_3$ PRO$_2$ to read $t_3$]
    f. Dnes me$_1$ ji$_2$ Jana ukázala $t_1$ $t_2$
       today to-him her Jana showed[31]
       'Jana showed her to him today.'

But there are many unexplored possibilities, and it may be that some broader principle may be involved. For some discussion of related ideas, cf. Bordelois (1974). For the moment, however, it seems to me reasonable to postulate SSC as a surface condition.[32]

Let us now turn to another class of cases, related to some of the examples in (64). Consider the next two examples:

(65)   You told Bill who to visit–you told Bill$_1$
       [who$_2$ PRO$_1$ to visit $t_2$]
(66)   Who did you tell Bill to visit–who$_1$ you told Bill$_2$
       [($t_1$) PRO$_2$ to visit $t_1$]

The parenthesized trace in (66) is present under the analysis of *wh*-movement in Chomsky (1973); for ease of exposition, let us assume that it is not present, although nothing hinges on this in the present context.

The appropriate "logical form" for (65) and (66) should be essentially (67) and (68), respectively, assuming that an appropriate sense is given to the "quantifier" *for which person x*:[33]

(67)   You told Bill for which person $x$, Bill to visit $x$
(68)   For which person $x$, you told Bill, Bill to visit $x$

We can obtain the logical forms (67) and (68) from the sentences (65)

---

[31] This Czech example is from Toman (1975).

[32] Examples such as those of (65), (66) do not violate SSC for reasons discussed in Chomsky (1973). The question whether SSC must also govern transformational rules is complex. Cf. Fiengo and Lasnik (1973) for an example suggesting that it must.

[33] Alternatively, for (67): "for $y = Bill$, you told $y$ for which person $x$, $y$ to visit $x$." And for (68): "for $y = Bill$, for which person $x$, you told $y$, $y$ to visit $x$." Cf. (71), below.

and (66), respectively, by the following rules:

(69) i.  Find the place from which *who* moved.
     ii. Mark this position by $x$.
     iii. Interpret *who* as "for which person $x$", controlling the free variable $x$.
     iv. Determine control of the subject of the embedded verb (namely, as the object of the matrix sentence).

Let us disregard step (iv), assuming this to be determined by mechanisms discussed in Jackendoff (1972). As for (i–iii), if we consider the surface structures to be as represented in (65) and (66) to the right of –, in accordance with the trace theory, then steps (i) and (ii) of (69) have already been accomplished, in effect. Thus, to interpret these surface structures it suffices to carry out step (iii) of (69), namely, to replace *who* by its meaning, *for which person x*. Hence interpretation of the enriched surface structures is direct. Thus in these cases surface structures can be directly mapped into LF merely by replacement of "quantifier words" by their meanings, with obvious notational conventions.

We might proceed in the same way in the case of simple NP-raising, as follows:

(70) John seems to be a nice fellow – John seems [$t$ to be a nice fellow]

The surface structure of (70) can be associated directly with the LF representation (71):

(71) For $x$ = John, $x$ seems [$x$ to be a nice fellow]

We might then try to devise general rules of inference, truth conditions, etc., for such representations as (67), (68), and (71).

Recall again the discussion of (12), repeated as (72):

(72) a. Beavers build dams.
     b. Dams are built by beavers.

In the standard and extended standard theories, such examples were used to illustrate the fact that "thematic relations" are determined by deep structure configurations; thus to understand (72b) we must know that *dams* is the object of *build*, as in (72a), just as in (70) we must know that *John* is subject of *be a nice fellow*. But under the trace theory, such examples as (70) and (72b) do not choose between the theory of deep structure interpretation and surface structure interpretation, since the appropriate grammatical relations are also represented in the (enriched) surface structures. Since there is good evidence that some properties of LF are based on properties of surface structure (e.g., the subject–predicate relation in (72)—see above; or the logical form of (65) and (66), both of which we may take as derived, essentially, from the deep structure *you told Bill [COMP PRO to visit who]*) we might try to unify the theory of semantic interpretation by revising EST in accordance with the following principle:

(73)  Surface structure determines LF.

Let us look further into *wh*-movement and its semantic interpretation, turning to some cases discussed by Postal and reanalyzed by Wasow (forthcoming), whose analysis I adapt and somewhat modify here. Consider these sentences:

(74) a.  Who said Mary kissed him?
     b.  Who did he say Mary kissed?
     c.  Who said he kissed Mary?

In (74a) and (74c), the pronoun *he, him* can function as an anaphoric pronoun, referring to the person whose name answers the question: *who?* But in (74b), the pronoun functions essentially as a name, referring to someone whose identity is established elsewhere, as it may also under another interpretation of (a) and (c). If we replace the pronoun by *John* in (74), cases (a) and (c) keep the latter interpretation, but lose the first, while case (b) keeps its single interpretation. Thus under this replacement, we simply refer to that third person in a different way, by the name *John* instead of the pronoun *he*. To put it in a conventional but highly misleading way, in (a) and (c) there is a relation of "anaphora" between *who* and *he–him,* while in (b) there is not.

Consider the surface structures of (74) under the trace theory. They are, respectively, (75a–c), ignoring auxiliary inversion:

(75) a.  who [*t* said Mary kissed him]
     b.  who [he said Mary kissed *t*]
     c.  who [*t* said he kissed Mary]

194

Applying again the principles of interpretation for *wh*-structures already outlined (cf. (69)), we replace *who* by its meaning, deriving:

(76) a. for which person $x$, $x$ said Mary kissed him
    b. for which person $x$, he said Mary kissed $x$
    c. for which person $x$, $x$ said he kissed Mary

There are familiar general principles of anaphora, the exact character of which need not concern us, which dictate that the pronoun can be anaphoric to *John* in (77) and (79), but not (78):

(77)    John said Mary kissed him.
(78)    He said Mary kissed John.
(79)    John said he kissed Mary.

Taking the bound variable $x$ in (76) to function essentially as a name, the same principles of anaphora that govern (77)–(79) require that no relation of anaphora can hold of *he* and $x$ in (76b), although such a relation may hold in (76a), (76c). Thus we can account for the full range of interpretations in (74) by appeal to independently motivated principles of anaphora, again on the assumption (72) that surface structure determines LF with the natural additional assumption that bound variables function (to first approximation) as names. We need not speak of a relation of "anaphora" between *who* and *he*–*him*, which would be strictly meaningless, since *who* is not a referring expression but a kind of quanitifer; nor need we invoke any principle beyond established principles of anaphora that apply in (77)–(79).

Our revised EST now has roughly this general structure:

(80)  $\xrightarrow{B}$  base structures  $\xrightarrow{T}$  surface structures  $\xrightarrow{SI-1}$  LF

           (LF, other cognitive representations)
                  $\xrightarrow{SI-2}$  semantic representation

A more precise version of (80) would replace "surface structure" by another notion, abstracting away from "stylistic rules" (e.g., scrambling) which may apply to give the actual surface form of sentences. I ignore this matter here.

That is, the base rules B generate base structures which are converted by the transformational component T to surface structures enriched with trace. The latter are interpreted by rules of semantic interpretation SI-1, giving the representations LF. These along with other cognitive representations are associated with fuller representations of meaning by rules SI-2. The rules SI-1 are rules of sentence-grammar, while the rules of SI-2 are in general not. The distinction has already been discussed in connection with examples (21)–(24).

We have now discussed several rules belonging to SI-1:

(81) i.   reciprocal interpretation
ii.  disjoint reference (DR)
iii. replacement of *who* by its meaning
iv.  conventions on control and variable binding
v.   conditions on anaphora

The rules (v), involved in (77)–(79) and (76), are rules of sentence-grammar, which apply to such strictly sentence-internal structures as reciprocals and reflexives (but see fn. 23). The rules (v) apply to structures formed by rules (iii) and (iv), that is, to partially formed representations in LF. Thus we already have a degree of internal structure within SI-1.

There are other reasons for supposing that the rules of anaphora apply to (partially formed) representations in LF, rather than surface structures. Consider the discourses (82) and (83):

(82)   Every soldier has his orders.

(83) a.  Every soldier is armed, but will he shoot?
b.  Every soldier is armed. I don't think he'll shoot, though.
c.  If every soldier is armed, then he'll shoot.

Sentence (82) can and normally would be construed with the pronoun as anaphoric (bound), but in the examples of (83) the pronoun *he* must literally be construed (contrary to the obviously intended sense) as referring to someone whose identity is established elsewhere.[34] In our

---

[34] The literal meaning is contrary to the obviously intended sense; hence, the latter may actually be assigned in discourse, as in the case of other deviant structures. But I think that the correct interpretation is as presented here. Suppose *every* is replaced by *each* in (83). Then the construal of the structures in the intended sense is perhaps somewhat easier, at least in (a) and (c). The quantifier *each* permits us to dissociate the individuals under consideration for the purposes of anaphora outside the scope of the quantifier, at least more readily than its near-synonym *every*. Replacement of *every* by *all* makes the structures still more deviant in the intended sense. Further complications arise as we consider other connectives. Compare *as soon as every student finishes his exam, he is to hand it in* (*he* not anaphoric); *as soon as each student finishes his exam, he is to hand it in* (possible, with anaphoric *he*, and of course a completely different interpretation of the quantifier than in *as soon as every student finishes his exam, the lights will be put out*). In all of these cases, *his*, being within the scope of the quantifier, can be (and normally would be) anaphoric. Further complications are many but do not, I think, affect the central point under discussion here. Cf. Kroch (1974) for more discussion.

terms, the fact is easily explained. Quantification is generally clause-bound. Thus the rules SI-1 involving quantifiers and variables give the structures (84) for (82) and (85) for (83):

(84)   [for all $x$, $x$ a soldier, $x$ has his orders]

(85)   a. [for all $x$, $x$ a soldier, $x$ is armed], but will he shoot
       b. For all $x$, $x$ a soldier, $x$ is armed. I don't think he'll shoot, though
       c. If [for all $x$, $x$ a soldier, $x$ is armed], then he'll shoot

As has often been observed, there is one quantifier, namely *any*, that includes within its scope a logical operator dominating it in surface structure. The role for *any*-interpretation, which is rather complex and not fully understood (cf. fn. 39), thus gives (87) as the representation for (86):

(86)   If any soldier is armed, then he'll shoot.
(87)   [for all $x$, $x$ a soldier, if $x$ is armed then he'll shoot]

In the partial logical forms (85) and (87), brackets bound the phrase within the scope of the universal quantifier.

The rules of anaphora do not permit a pronoun that is outside the scope of a quantifier to be assigned an anaphoric relation to a bound variable within this scope (but see fn. 34). Thus (82) and (86) have (88) and (89), respectively, as permissible interpretations:

(88)   for all $x$, $x$ a soldier, $x$ has $x$'s orders
(89)   for all $x$, $x$ a soldier, if $x$ is armed then $x$ will shoot

But in the examples of (85), such interpretations are excluded, as the corresponding interpretations were excluded in the case of (78) and (74b)(=(76b)).

The analysis requires that the scope of quantification be determined prior to application of the principle of anaphora. In other words, here too the principle of anaphora (=(81v)) applies to partially determined logical forms, with quantifier scope and variable binding determined.

This analysis is pretty much along the lines of standard logical analysis of the sentences of natural language. A rather different approach has recently been suggested within the framework of Montague grammar.[35] With the motivation of relating surface struc-

---

[35] For a clear and simple exposition, see Lewis (1972), and for much more detail, Partee (1975).

ture and semantic representation more closely, it is suggested that the sentences (90), all with the surface structure NP–VP, have essentially the same logical representation (at some level):

(90) a. John is here.
    b. Every soldier is here.
    c. Some soldier is here.

This result is achieved by associating each individual with the set of its properties (its *character*). Then we may interpret (90) as stating that the property of being here is a member of the character of John (90a), a member of the intersection of the characters of all soldiers (90b), a member of the union of characters of all soldiers (90c). In contrast, a standard logical analysis might assign to (90) the analyses (91), or—taking a noun phrase to specify a type variable—(92):

(91) a. Here (John)
    b. for all $x$, if soldier $(x)$ then here $(x)$
    c. for some $x$, soldier $(x)$ and here $(x)$

(92) a. Here (John)
    b. for all $x$, $x$ a soldier, here $(x)$
    c. for some $x$, $x$ a soldier, here $(x)$

(I am ignoring here the question of specificity of indefinites.) We have essentially been assuming (92), so far. Under the interpretations (91) or (92), the sentence (90a) is given a very different analysis from (90b,c).

It is difficult to find an empirical test for these varying logical analyses, but if we take them literally, it seems that Montague grammar and the standard analysis should make a different prediction for the case where the sentences of (90) appear in such contexts as (83), say (93):

(93) a. John is here. Will he shoot?
    b. Every soldier is here. Will he shoot?
    c. Some soldier is here. Will he shoot?

Since *John, every soldier,* and *some soldier* are understood to have the same logical status in Montague grammar, the prediction should be that they function in a parallel way in (93). But this is false. In (93a), *he* may be anaphoric, while in (93b) it may not. And in (93c), while there is, arguably, a relation of "anaphora," it is quite different and considerably more complex than the relation observed in earlier examples; thus, *he* does not have the semantic function of "some soldier," but rather refers to that soldier, whoever he may be, who is identified as here in the first sentence.[36]

In the "classical" theories as extended earlier (i.e., with the anaphora rule applying to partially specified LF and quantification clause-bound in the case of *every* and *some*), the discourse (93a) has an entirely different status from (93b) and (93c). In (93a) the pronoun *he* simply refers to John, and under one central interpretation can be replaced by *John* without change of meaning.[37] In the other two cases, such an anaphora relation cannot hold, because *he* is outside the scope of the quantifier. It is strictly meaningless, in the classical approach, for *he* to have an anaphoric relation to *every soldier* or *some soldier* (nonspecific). This conclusion seems to me correct so far as it goes (it does not yet account for (93c) or the examples of notes 34 and 36). Thus there would seem to be empirical confirmation for the classical analysis over Montague grammar in the rather small area where they have different predictions, if taken to have empirical content. The behavior of anaphoric pronouns indicates that the logical structure of (90a) is quite different from (90b,c), and also that the principles of anaphora apply to a partially developed logical form, not to surface structures.

Returning now to the main theme, let us consider some of the more complex examples of *wh*-movement and anaphora discussed by Postal and Wasow. Consider the sentence (94):

(94)  Who did the woman he loved betray?

By the principles so far proposed, this should be assigned the

---

[36] Complications mount rapidly as we move to sentences with two quantifiers or to plurals. Thus consider: *Some soldiers have guns. Will they shoot them?* We might want to say that *they* is anaphoric to *some soldiers* and *them* to *guns*, but the question asks whether each soldier who has a gun will shoot the gun that he has, not whether some soldiers will shoot guns.

[37] The same conclusion holds in multiclause sentences, although the substitution of *John* for *he* is less natural or impossible: *John is here, but will he shoot?*; *If John is here, then he will shoot*. In the latter case, and perhaps the former as well, substitution of *John* for *he* seems to me to impose disjoint reference. It seems that the rule applying here is not a rule of sentence-grammar, but is rather a rule assigning a higher degree of preference to disjoint interpretation the closer the grammatical connection. Thus, substitution of *John* for *he* is difficult in (93a). Disjoint reference is preferred, but it would be strange to use the same name, *John*, in simple successive sentences with difference of reference. In contrast, substitution of *every soldier* for *he* in (93b) and *some soldier* for *he* in (93c) changes the interpretation radically.

representation (95) which can be converted to the LF (96):

(95)  for which person $x$, the woman he loved betrayed $x$
(96)  for which person $x$, the woman $x$ loved betrayed $x$

Conversion of (95) to (96) does not appear to violate the conditions (81v) on anaphora; compare (97), where *he* may be anaphoric to *John*.

(97)  The woman he loved betrayed John.

But (96) is not a possible interpretation of (94). Why not?

Wasow notes that while the general "precede-and-command" conditions of anaphora do not require that the pronoun be nonanaphoric in (97), nevertheless some constraint prevents an "anaphoric" relation from holding between the italicized phrases of (98):

(98)  The woman *he* loved betrayed *someone*

Suppose that we establish a subsidiary principle of anaphora that prevents a phrase $X$ from serving as antecedent to a pronoun to its left when this phrase is "indeterminate," where *someone* is indeterminate. Then it will follow that an anaphoric relation cannot hold in (98), though it can in the following example:

(99)  Someone was betrayed by the woman he loved.

Returning to (94), it has often been noted that there are striking similarities between *wh*-questions and indefinites. Pursuing this analogy, Wasow suggests that the trace left by *wh*-movement should share with indefinites the property of indeterminateness. Then, it will follow that (95) cannot have the interpretation of (96), as required.

There are some problems with this suggestion. As in the case of (74), it is misleading to speak of an "anaphoric relation" between *someone* and *he* in (98) since *someone*, like *who*, is not referential. Furthermore, the property of determinateness is not an easy one to characterize, as Wasow points out. The cases to be covered are fairly clear—indefinites (apart from specific and generic), the trace left by *wh*-movement in questions and relatives—but it is not clear just what semantic property these cases might have in common. Thus, in the case of relatives, the analogy between *wh*-structures and indefinites breaks down and the *wh*-element even seems to have something of the character of a definite noun phrase—see Kuroda (1968). But the trace behaves as in questions. Cf. (100), which cannot have the interpretation (101), just as (94) cannot have the interpretation (96):

(100)    The man *who* the woman *he* loved betrayed – is despondent
(101)    the man *x* such that the woman *x* loved betrayed *x* – is despondent

Wasow does give some reason to believe that in restrictive relatives the head is indeterminate, but the matter is quite unclear, as is the question how this property, whatever it may be exactly, inheres in the trace.

We can overcome all of these difficulties by revising Wasow's theory along the lines of our earlier discussion. Again, let us assume that the rules (81i–iv) of SI-1 apply to the surface structures of (94) and (100) to give (102) and (103), respectively.[38] Assume also that (98) is analyzed by a familiar rule, to give (104):

(102)    for which person *x*, [the woman he loved betrayed *x*]
(103)    the man *x* such that [the woman he loved betrayed *x*] is despondent
(104)    for some *x*, [the woman he loved betrayed *x*]

Whatever the rules of anaphora may be, they should treat the bracketed phrases in (102)–(104) in the same way, since they are identical. Thus, (94), (100), and (98) should have parallel interpretations, as in fact they do. It remains only to determine the subsidiary principle of anaphora that is involved in all of these cases. Assume it to be (105):

(105)    A variable cannot be the antecedent of a pronoun to its left.

Suppose that *someone* in (98) is replaced by *anyone*. The sentence as it stands is not well-formed. It becomes well-formed in the context (106):

(106)    If the woman he loved betrayed anyone, he will be despondent.

---

[38] On rules for relativization, see Chomsky (1975a), and for a detailed analysis along these lines, Vergnaud (1974).

By the *any*-rule mentioned earlier, the scope of *any* includes *if*, so the "first-stage" logical form should be (107)[39]:

(107)  for every person $x$, [if the woman he loved betrayed $x$, then he will be despondent]

If principle (105) is correct, then the leftmost occurrence of *he* cannot have $x$ as antecedent, though the rightmost may. Thus, apart from the reading in which neither occurrence of *he* in (106) is anaphoric, the only interpretation of (106) should be (108), where $x$ is not the antecedent of *he*; that is, an interpretation analogous to (109):

(108)  for every person $x$, if the woman he loved betrayed $x$, then $x$ will be despondent
(109)  for every person $x$, if the woman John loved betrayed $x$, then $x$ will be despondent

I think I can convince myself that this is correct, but without much faith in the conclusion.

We may think of the principle (105) as part of a rule replacing a pronoun by a variable, at some level of the derivation that will ultimately specify LF. We have given insufficient evidence to determine the rule in detail. Let us take it to assert that a pronoun $P$ within the scope of a quantifier may be rewritten as the variable bound by this quantifier unless $P$ is to the left of an occurrence of a variable already bound by this quantifier. This rule will be one part of a more comprehensive convention specifying anaphora relations in partially developed logical forms. For ease of reference, let us call the rule in question $A$ (anaphora). The rule $A$ applied to (110), underlying (112), will give (111) (optionally):

(110)  for some $x$, $x$ was betrayed by the woman he loved
(111)  for some $x$, $x$ was betrayed by the woman $x$ loved
(112)  someone was betrayed by the woman he loved

---

[39] On the rule of interpretation for *any*, see Hintikka (1975). A somewhat similar proposal is mentioned in Lasnik (1972). Hintikka argues that violations of compositionality, as illustrated in (87) and (107), constitute counterexamples to Fregean theories of meaning, and to theories of the sort suggested by Davidson and Montague. He also points out that *any*-sentences provide counterexamples to the criterion of material adequacy for a truth definition of the Tarski type. Under his formulation of the *any*-rule, it also follows, as he shows, that the class of well-formed sentences is not recursive or even recursively enumerable, but I think that there are other formulations that cover the clear facts as well that do not lead to this conclusion, although there are, perhaps, other and simpler examples that lead to conclusions similar to his with regard to the set of sentences well-formed by some plausible criterion.

But *A* cannot apply to the pronoun *he* in the structures (113):

(113) a. for which *x*, the woman he loved betrayed *x*    (underlying (94))
    b. for some *x*, the woman he loved betrayed *x*    (underlying (98))
    c. the man *x* such that the woman he loved betrayed *x* – is despondent    (underlying (100))

The reason is that *A* obeys condition (105).

Notice that the rule *A* is oblivious to the source of the variable in (113) that prevents it from applying. In the case of (113a) and (113c), the variable is introduced by a syntactic movement rule, under the trace theory. In (113b), the variable is introduced by a rule of semantic interpretation belonging to SI-1. The sentences for which these are the underlying structures are quite different in form and in surface structure, but alike in semantic representation at the stage following the rule that assigns to *someone* its meaning. It is at this stage, it appears, that *A* applies. Thus *A* is "local," like other rules of grammar, in that it applies to the last step of the derivation so far constructed, paying no heed to the original source of the elements that determine how the rule applies.

We noted earlier that a bound variable, as in (113), behaves quite differently from a name in the same position, as in (114) (=(97)):

(114) The woman he loved betrayed John

Thus in (114), the rules of anaphora *A* can associate *he* and *John*. But a qualification is necessary. In (114), the rule *A* can associate *he* and *John* only if the main stress is on *betray*. If the main stress is on *John*, then the word cannot serve as the antecedent of *he*. Thus stress on *John* gives the word essentially the status of a bound variable. What is the explanation for this fact?

A possible explanation is this. Consider the rule of SI-1 that determines the focus of a sentence. Consider the simplest cases, e.g., (115) and (116), where capitalization indicates main stress:

(115) Bill likes JOHN.
(116) BILL likes John.

Let us say that a rule FOCUS assigns to (115) the representation (117) and to (116) the representation (118):

(117)   the $x$ such that Bill likes $x$ – is John
(118)   the $x$ such that $x$ likes John – is Bill

We may take (117) and (118) to be partially developed logical forms, informally presented. As such, they seem to give an accurate representation of an important aspect of semantic representation in a natural way.

The rule FOCUS applied to (114) with main stress on *John* gives:

(119)   the $x$ such that the woman he loved betrayed $x$ – is John

But observe that the rule $A$ that replaces *he* by $x$ cannot apply to (119); it is blocked by the principle (105), exactly as in the examples of (113). In contrast, the rule would not have been blocked had main stress been on *betray* rather than *John* in (114). Thus we find still another instance of (105): it applies in the case of the trace of a movement rule (e.g., (113a,c)), the variable introduced by interpretation of existential and universal quantifiers (e.g., (113b)), and the variable introduced by the rule FOCUS (e.g., (119)). Thus, a number of disparate phenomena fall together, giving an interesting range of empirical evidence bearing on the nature of LF.

Notice that it makes quite a difference what notation we choose for representing phenomena in LF, just as it matters what phenomena we take to belong to LF. These are by no means questions of convention to be resolved by fiat or convenience for one or another purpose, so it appears. Rather, they can—and should—be interpreted as empirical questions that can be subjected to test, I believe.

The examples just reviewed give independent support for the general conclusions proposed earlier. The rules of SI-1 apply to an enriched surface structure, including trace, giving an analysis in terms of quantifiers and bound variables. Further rules of SI-1 (those of anaphora) assign these representations a specific range of more explicit representations within LF.[40] These examples enhance the

---

[40] These considerations again seem to me to support the classical logical analysis over the revision suggested by Montague, if we take these as theories with empirical import. With regard to anaphora, a good indication of referential function, the noun phrases *someone* and *everyone* behave very differently from names or definite descriptions, as the classical theory, taken literally, predicts. And furthermore the rules of anaphora apply to a logical form that contains quantifiers and variables rather than to a surface structure.

general plausibility of the conception sketched in (80), and in particular, the trace theory of movement rules, which we have motivated quite independently in earlier discussion. I cannot review here other evidence bearing on these assumptions.[41]

The preceding discussion illustrates some of the ways in which we might hope to overcome the difficulties that immediately face a theory of transformations that is radically limited in expressive power. We may try to discover narrower conditions on base structures, conditions on application of rules, and conditions on surface structure. Under EST, principles of semantic interpretation, at least those of SI-1, would be expected to relate very closely, in many cases, to conditions on base and surface structures; particularly, surface structures, if the revision of EST suggested here proves to be essentially correct. It may be that conditions on transformations can be assimilated to conditions on surface structures and (in the best case) to independently motivated rules of semantic interpretation, under the trace theory.

I do not mean to suggest that the problems that lie in the way of developing a theory with restricted expressive power, along the lines sketched at the outset, have been overcome. But I think that there has been encouraging progress. I am inclined to think that the program outlined is feasible and that the general approach I have been reviewing may prove to be well founded.

If we pursue this approach further, we find, I believe, that the rules of (sentence-)grammar fall into several distinct types. At the core of syntax we have the two rules of (120), each of considerably broader scope than has hitherto been imagined:

(120) i. NP-movement
      ii. *wh*-movement

The rule of NP-movement appears superficially to violate subjacency (cf. e.g., *John seems to be likely to win*) while it observes SSC, the tensed-S condition, and other constraints. The explanation is that the rule is cyclic and bounded (observes subjacency).

The rule of *wh*-movement, which may involve several subtypes, seems superficially to violate subjacency, SSC, and the tensed-S condition while observing the complex noun phrase constraint and other island conditions. The explanation is that the rule is cyclic and

---

[41] For discussion, see Chomsky (1975b) and references cited there, particularly, Fiengo (1974). Also, van Riemsdijk (1973), Jackendoff ((1975), Quicoli ((1975; 1976), Lightfoot (1975b).

bounded, while movement is permitted from complementizer position in a tensed-S (depending on the nature of the matrix verb). From these assumptions, it follows that (120ii) has its familiar properties. Cf. Chomsky (1973; 1975b). Included in this category, I believe, are the rules involved in formation of direct and indirect *wh*-questions, relatives, topicalization, cleft, comparatives, and a variety of infinitival complement constructions. But this proposal remains to be explained and justified.

Interpretive rules may violate subjacency, but otherwise generally observe SSC and tensed-S condition, although there are some problems (cf. fn. 23).

Other movement rules, such as clitic movement, prepositional phrase movement and quantifier movement, seem to observe subjacency and other constraints, cf. Akmajian (1975), Fiengo and Lasnik (1973), Kayne (1975), Quicoli (1975; 1976).

Root transformations and minor movement rules are as described in Emonds (1976).

There are also "housekeeping rules" such as, for example, those that govern deletion of complementizers.

Other rules have quite different properties, e.g., agreement rules (which have something of the character of phonological rules of matching of feature matrices), scrambling and other stylistic rules, which are not readily formulable as transformations at all, and others.

This is not intended as a comprehensive or precise analysis, needless to say. I think that (120) may constitute, in a certain sense, the core of cyclic grammar, determining an enriched surface structure that is close, in interesting respects, to logical form.

It may be possible to devise an alternative to transformational grammar in which rules of the type (120) are regarded as interpretive,[42] but meeting conditions quite different from those observed by the rules here called "interpretive." Thus, we would have three types of rules for interpreting base-generated structures including traces: rules with the properties of (120i) and (120ii), with their cyclic interactions and the properties just outlined, and rules of anaphora, etc., that have the properties sketched in the foregoing analysis. If this speculation is correct, we should be able to move to a more abstract characterization of linguistic systems, adopting a point of view from which much of the core of transformational grammar will be seen to be simply one concrete realization of a set of abstract conditions that characterize the human language faculty.

---

[42] Cf. Chomsky (1973) for a brief comment.

The pure study of language, based solely on evidence of the sort reviewed here, can carry us only to the understanding of abstract conditions on grammatical systems. No particular realization of these conditions has any privileged status. From a more abstract point of view, if it can be attained, we may see in retrospect that we moved towards the understanding of the abstract general conditions on linguistic structures by the detailed investigation of one or another "concrete" realization: for example, transformational grammar, a particular instance of a system with these general properties. The abstract conditions may relate to transformational grammar rather in the way that modern algebra relates to the number system.

We should be concerned to abstract from successful grammars and successful theories those more general properties that account for their success, and to develop UG as a theory of these abstract properties, which might be realized in a variety of different ways. To choose among such realizations, it will be necessary to move to a much broader domain of evidence. What linguistics should try to provide is an abstract characterization of particular and universal grammar that will serve as a guide and framework for this more general inquiry. This is not to say that the study of highly specific mechanisms (e.g., phonological rules, conditions on transformations, etc.) should be abandoned. On the contrary, it is only through the detailed investigation of these particular systems that we have any hope of advancing towards a grasp of the abstract structures, conditions and properties that should, some day, constitute the subject matter of general linguistic theory. The goal may be remote, but it is well to keep it in mind as we develop intricate specific theories and try to refine and sharpen them in detailed empirical inquiry.

## REFERENCES

Akmajian, A. 1975. More evidence for an NP cycle. *Linguistic Inquiry* 6: 115–30.

Bach, E. 1965. On some recurrent types of transformations. In *Sixteenth Annual Round Table Meeting on Linguistics and Language Studies*, Georgetown University Monograph Series on Languages and Linguistics 18, C. W. Kreidler, ed.

Baker, C. L. and Brame, M. K. 1972. "Global rules": a rejoinder. *Language* 48: 51–75.

Bordelois, I. 1974. The grammar of Spanish causative complements. Doctoral dissertation, MIT.

Brame, M. K. 1976. *Conjectures and Refutations in Syntax and Semantics.* New York: Elsevier North-Holland.

Bresnan, J. 1971. Contraction and the transformational cycle in English. Mimeograph, MIT.

―――. 1972. Theory of complementation in English syntax. Doctoral dissertation, MIT.

―――. 1973. Sentence stress and syntactic transformations. In *Approaches to Natural Language* K. J. J. Hintikka, J. M. E. Moravcsik, and P. Suppes, eds. Dordrecht, Holland: Reidel.

―――. in press. Transformations and categories in syntax. In *Proceedings of the Fifth International Congress on Logic, Methodology, and Philosophy of Science,* University of Western Ontario, London, Ontario, 1975, R. Butts and J. Hintikka, eds.

―――. 1976. On the form and functioning of transformations. *Linguistic Inquiry* 7: 3–40.

Chomsky, N. 1955. The logical structure of linguistic theory. Mimeograph; published in large part in 1975 as *The Logical Structure of Linguistic Theory.* New York: Plenum.

―――. 1961. On the notion "rule of grammar," In *Structure of Language and Its Mathematical Aspects,* Proceedings of the Symposia in Applied Mathematics, vol. XII, American Mathematical Society, Providence, R. I.

―――. 1965. *Aspects of the Theory of Syntax,* Cambridge, Mass.: MIT Press.

―――. 1972. *Studies on Semantics in Generative Grammar.* The Hague: Mouton.

―――. 1973. Conditions on transformations. In *A Festschrift for Morris Halle,* S. R. Anderson and P. Kiparsky, eds. New York: Holt, Rinehart and Winston. Essay 3, above.

―――. 1975a. Questions of form and interpretation. *Linguistic Analysis* 1: 75–107. Essay 1, above.

―――. 1975b. *Reflections on Language.* New York: Pantheon.

Chomsky, N. and Halle, M. 1968. *Sound Pattern of English.* New York: Harper & Row.

Chomsky, N. and Miller, G. A. 1963. Introduction to the formal analysis of natural languages. In *Handbook of Mathematical Psychology,* vol. II, R. D. Luce, R. R. Bush, and E. Galanter, eds. New York: John Wiley. pp. 419–91.

Dougherty, R. C. 1974. The syntax and semantics of *each other* constructions. *Foundations of Language* 12: 1–48.

―――. 1975. Reflections on the Bloomfieldian counterrevolution. *International Journal of Dravidian Linguistics* III, no. 2: 255–86.

Emonds, J. E. 1976. *A Transformational Approach to Syntax: Root and Structure-Preserving Transformations.* New York: Academic Press.

208

Fiengo, R. 1974. Semantic conditions on surface structure. Doctoral dissertation, MIT.

Fiengo, R. and Lasnik, H. 1973. The logical structure of reciprocal sentences in English. *Foundations of Language* 9: 447–68.

———. 1976. Some issues in the theory of transformations. *Linguistic Inquiry* 7: 182–191.

Fodor, J. A. 1975. *The Language of Thought.* New York: Crowell.

Helke, M. 1971. The grammar of English reflexives. Doctoral dissertation, MIT.

Hintikka, J. 1975. On the limitations of generative grammar. Mimeograph, Stanford.

Hornstein, N. 1975. S and the X̄ convention, *Montreal Working Papers in Linguistics* 4: 35–71.

Jackendoff, R. S. 1972. *Semantic Interpretation in Generative Grammar.* Cambridge, Mass.: MIT Press.

———. 1975. *Tough* and the trace theory of movement rules. *Linguistic Inquiry* 6: 437–446.

———. 1976. Toward an explanatory semantic representation. *Linguistic Inquiry* 7: 89–150.

Katz, J. J. 1972. *Semantic Theory* New York: Harper & Row.

———. forthcoming. *Propositional Structure: A Study of the Contribution of Sentence Meaning to Speech Acts.* New York: Crowell.

Katz, J. J. and Bever, T. G. 1976. The fall and rise of empiricism. In *Integrated Theory of Linguistic Knowledge,* T. G. Bever, J. J. Katz, and D. T. Langendoen, eds. New York: Crowell.

Katz, J. J. and Postal, P. M. 1964. *An Integrated Theory of Linguistic Descriptions,* Cambridge, Mass.: MIT Press.

Kayne, R. S. 1975. *French Syntax: The Transformational Cycle.* Cambridge, Mass.: MIT Press.

Kroch, A. 1974. The semantics of scope in English. Doctoral dissertation, MIT.

Kuroda, S.-Y. 1968. English relativization and certain related problems. *Language* 44: 244–66.

———. 1973. Where epistemology, style, and grammar meet: a case study from Japanese. In *A Festschrift for Morris Halle,* S. R. Anderson and P. Kiparsky, eds. New York: Holt, Rinehart and Winston. pp. 377–91.

Labov, W. 1970. The logic of nonstandard English. In *The Politics of Literature,* Louis Kampf and Paul Lauter, eds. New York: Pantheon.

Lakoff, G. 1971. On generative semantics. In *Semantics: an Interdisciplinary Reader,* D. Steinberg and L. Jacobovits, eds. New York: Cambridge University Press.

Lasnik, H. 1972. Analyses of negation in English. Doctoral dissertation, MIT.

———. 1976. Remarks on coreference. *Linguistic Analysis* 2: 1–22.

Lewis, D. 1972. General semantics. In *Semantics of Natural Language,* G. Harman and D. Davidson, eds. Dordrecht, Holland: Reidel. pp. 169–218.

Lightfoot, D. 1975a. The theoretical implications of subject raising. *Foundations of Language* 13: 115–43.

———. 1975b. Traces and doubly moved NPs. Mimeograph.

Parret, H., ed. 1974. *Discussing Language.* The Hague: Mouton.

Partee, B. 1975. Montague grammar and transformational grammar. *Linguistic Inquiry* 6: 203–300.

Peters, P. S. and Ritchie, R. W. 1973. On the generative power of transformational grammars. *Information Sciences* 6: 49–83.

Postal, P. M. 1972. The best theory. In *Goals of Linguistic Theory,* P. S. Peters, ed. Englewood Cliffs, N. J.: Prentice-Hall.

———. 1976. Avoiding reference to subject. *Linguistic Inquiry* 7: 151–181.

Quicoli, A. C. 1975. Conditions on quantifier movement in French. Mimeograph, MIT.

———. 1976. Clitic movement in Portuguese. *Linguistic Analysis* 2: 199–223.

Ross, J. R. 1967. Constraints on variables in syntax. Doctoral dissertation, MIT.

———. 1973. Nouniness. In *Three Dimensions of Linguistic Theory,* O. Fujimura, ed. Tokyo: TEC Company.

———. 1975. Where to do things with words. In *Syntax and Semantics,* vol. 3, P. Cole and J. Morgan, eds. New York: Academic Press.

Selkirk, E. O. 1972. The phrase phonology of English and French. Doctoral dissertation, MIT.

Soames, S. 1974. Rule orderings, obligatory transformations, and derivational constraints. *Theoretical Linguistics* 1: 116–38.

Toman, J. 1975. Pronominal clitics in Czech. Mimeograph, MIT.

van Riemsdijk, H. 1973. A case for a trace: preposition stranding in Züritüütsch. Mimeograph, Amsterdam.

Vergnaud, J.-R. 1974. French relative clauses. Doctoral dissertation, MIT.

Wasow, T. forthcoming. *Anaphora in Generative Grammar.*

# Index

211

Construal, rules of, 6, 19, 20
Control, rules of, 11–14
    for *persuade* and for *promise*, 13–14,
        114–116, 119, 184
    *see also* PRO, control of
Core grammar, 6, 19
Coreference Assignment, 89
Crossover Principle, 130
Culicover, P., 87
Cycle
    and subjacency, 55, 97, 103–104, 106, 176
    Strict, 6, 97, 100, 102, 165
    transformational, 5–6, 10, 97–99, 103–105,
        119, 133–144 *passim*, 176, 205–206
Cyclicity
    principle of bounded, 70–71
    of rules, 6, 20, 55, 115, 205–206


Deep structure, 5, 57, 58, 144, 165, 166, 167
    and interpretation, 193–194
Definite noun phrases, 29, 47–52, 92, 200
Derivation, 165
    constraints on, 136, 170
    extended to logical form, 9–10, 17, 83, 166
Dictionary, 36, 42, 43, 57, 58
Disjoint reference, 179, 180, 182, 183, 189,
    199
Dougherty, R., 86, 90, 91, 115, 122, 123, 140,
    166


*each*-Insertion, 90–91
*each*-Movement, 91, 103, 106, 108, 109–110,
    111, 114, 115, 122, 123, 124, 130, 132,
    134, 135
Emonds, J. E., 6, 8, 83, 87, 135, 138, 142,
    143, 173, 177, 206
Empirical issues, 16, 34
    *see also* Adequacy, empirical; Linguistic
        theory, the goal of
Equi-NP Deletion, 120, 157, 184, 187–190
Evaluation measure, 45, 84, 85
Existential quantification, 39, 51
Extended Standard Theory, 5, 18, 58–59, 91,
    166, 193, 205
    revised, 167, 194, 195, 205–206
Extraction rules, 87, 89, 137, 139
    conditions on, 104, 107, 108, 112, 127

*see also* Subjacency Condition
Extraposition, 138, 142, 170


Fauconnier, G. R., 116
Fact and belief. *See* Belief and knowledge
    systems.
Factives, 104
Factorization, 82–83, 141, 168–174
    condition of minimal, 172–174
Features
    categorical, 170
    contextual, 103
    distinctive, 64, 82
    lexical, 168
    percolation of, 140
    rule, 57
    selectional, 56
    syntactic, 143
Fiengo, R., 10, 59, 75, 170, 171, 172, 176,
    179, 191, 192, 205, 206
Fillmore, C., 6
Filter, surface. *See* Surface Exclusion Filter.
Focus, 203–204
Fodor, J. A., 56, 190
*for*-Placement, 110
*for-to* constructions, 87, 92–94, 126–127,
    189–190
Form-meaning correlation, 40–50, 52, 56
    *see also* Autonomy thesis; Sound-meaning
        relationship; Syntax and semantics
Formal expression, 26, 27
Free expression, 26, 32


Gabbay, D. M., 29
Gapping, 191
Generics. *See* Indefinite generics.
Generative semantics. *See* Syntax and
        semantics
    *see also names of generative semanticists*
Grammar
    formal, 10, 18, 26, 27, 41, 42, 52, 56–57,
        163, 166, 175–176, 182–183, 196, 199,
        205
    particular, 3, 40, 43
    *see also* Extended Standard Theory;
        Universal grammar
Grammatical relations, 91, 170, 194
Grammaticality, 3, 33, 34, 40, 144

212

216